Understanding Drug Misuse

Understanding Drug Misuse

Models of Care and Control

Jan Keene

palgrave
macmillan

First published 2010 by
PALGRAVE MACMILLAN

Palgrave Macmillan in the UK is an imprint of Macmillan Publishers Limited,
registered in England, company number 785998, of Houndmills, Basingstoke,
Hampshire RG21 6XS.

Palgrave Macmillan in the US is a division of St Martin's Press LLC,
175 Fifth Avenue, New York, NY 10010.

Palgrave Macmillan is the global academic imprint of the above companies
and has companies and representatives throughout the world.

Palgrave® and Macmillan® are registered trademarks in the United States,
the United Kingdom, Europe and other countries.

ISBN 978–0–230–20243–6

This book is printed on paper suitable for recycling and made from fully
managed and sustained forest sources. Logging, pulping and manufacturing
processes are expected to conform to the environmental regulations of the
country of origin.

A catalogue record for this book is available from the British Library.

A catalog record for this book is available from the Library of Congress.

10   9   8   7   6   5   4   3   2   1
19   18   17   16   15   14   13   12   11   10

Printed in China

Contents

List of Figures and Tables

Acknowledgements

I would like to thank the drug users, professionals and researchers who have contributed equally to this book.

Preface

This book provides an overview of drug misuse problems and explains how each theoretical model contributes different types of solution, whether treatment, harm minimization or social intervention. It then gives practical guidelines for the care and control of drug users within this overall framework.

Chapter 1 provides an introduction and perhaps for the first time, a clear overall framework for understanding different types of problems, whether dependency, health related risk or social harm. It gives an understanding of the complexity of drug use and a comprehensive view of the field as a whole, enabling each separate area to be understood in its wider context. This framework also reflects the structure of the book itself and provides an introduction and background to each separate section.

The book then outlines the range of professional models of care and control in each of three areas; dependency treatment, harm minimization and social interventions. Each section initially explores the beliefs of drug users themselves, to give a direct understanding of the physical, psychological and social effects of drug use, before moving on to examine the theories and research literature that inform professional work with drug users.

Qualitative methodology and methods are used to interview users and analyse their beliefs without recourse to any one theoretical approach. An outline of this methodology and method is included at the start of Chapter 2.

Dependency: treatment and recovery

Chapter 2 explores user views of drug use and dependency. This is followed by Chapter 3, which provides an overview of different theories of dependency and the research evidence for the effectiveness of different therapeutic solutions.

Health risks: harm minimization and public health

Chapter 4 explores user views of the health risks and health-related harm associated with drug use and Chapter 5 examines the harm minimization solutions for individuals and the public health solutions for communities.

Social harm: social inclusion and crime reduction

Chapter 6 explore users' views of the social harm associated with drug use. Chapter 7 then examines the theories, evidence and potential solutions for both individuals and communities, focusing on the problems of social exclusion for individuals and the problems of public order and crime for communities.

Working with users: treatment, harm minimization and social inclusion

The final section of the book brings together the views of users with research and professional experience in order to demonstrate the practical implications for working with drug users.

Chapter 8 provides practical guidelines for motivation, maintenance and recovery. It gives a detailed description of the sequence of steps necessary in the helping process, from initial provision of safety information, to motivation and on to maintenance and treatment interventions.

Chapter 9 then provides practical guidelines for aftercare. It gives an overview of methods for developing individual skills and examines relapse prevention techniques. Finally, it examines methods of social inclusion and social interventions aimed at the development of new relationships and new social support networks.

Chapter 1

Care and Control: Drug Dependency, Health Risks and Social Harm

Drug use causes three different types of problem, for which there are different solutions. In addition, drugs not only cause different types of problems for individual drug users but also for the communities they live in. Drug dependence itself can involve physiological and psychological dependence and neurological compulsion. Health-related harm can include individual health problems such as overdose and public health problems such as transmission of blood-borne diseases. Social harm can include individual problems such as social exclusion and community problems such as crime.

It is therefore difficult for any one intervention to be successful in dealing with all aspects of dependency and health and social harm to individuals and communities at the same time. For this reason it is necessary to clarify and distinguish different types of problems associated with drug use, before attempting to provide solutions in terms of care and control.

There are many different interpretations and theories of drug dependency and the health or social problems associated with drug use. These different theories result in different understandings of problems, different solutions and different definitions of success or failure. Unfortunately, each separate theory or approach can also limit the type of help offered, the length of time it is offered for and the people it is offered to.

Different types of solution for different types of problems

This book is designed to examine each type of problem, whether dependency, health related risk or social harm, and the respective solutions in terms of both care for individuals and control for communities.

1

Table 1.1 Categorization of drug problems and their solutions

Different problems associated with drug use

Type of problem	Harm to individual drug user	Harm to wider population
Dependence	Bio-psycho-social harm	Socio-economic harm
Health-related harm	Short and long term risks to individual health	Transmission of blood-borne diseases (HIV, hepatitis)
Social harm	Social exclusion, unemployment homelessness	Crime, risks to community order

Different solutions

Type of solution	Care: Reducing harm to individual drug users	Control: Reducing harm in wider populations
Dependence	Voluntary treatment: maintenance or abstinence	Compulsory treatment: maintenance or abstinence
Health-related harm	Harm minimization: reducing health risk	Public health: Prevention and education
Social harm	Social inclusion	Crime reduction

Table 1.1 provides a rough categorization of different types of drug problems and their respective solutions.

The table illustrates the range of different problems and solutions associated with drug use, though it should be noted that some problems and solutions do not fit neatly into one of these categories. The wide range of potential solutions has led to a series of controversies, not only because one solution can be used for different problems, but also because some interventions that provide a solution to one type of problem can make another type of problem worse.

Understanding the complexity: the example of prescribed drugs

A brief example will be used to illustrate the complexity of drug problems. This will be followed by an overview of different types of care and control, before returning to the example in order to illustrate how different models are implemented in practice. It should be noted that the concepts of care and control are not as clear cut as they initially appear here and can sometimes overlap or become confused.

Maintenance prescribing of heroin substitutes such as Methadone will be used as an example because this can be seen as the solution to different types of problems:

- *Dependence*
  Voluntary maintenance treatment for drug dependence (care)
  Coercive maintenance treatment for drug dependence (control)

- *Health-related harm*
  Reducing health-related harm to individuals (care)
  Reducing the spread of blood-borne diseases such as HIV, hepatitis B or C (control)

- *Social harm*
  Reducing social exclusion (care)
  Reducing crime (control)

Long-term Methadone prescribing can therefore be seen as a solution to a range of different problems, including dependency. However, it is controversial whether prescribing should be aimed at abstinence and recovery from dependency, or at reducing public health or social problems. Whilst maintenance prescribing is often described as 'treatment' it does not reduce dependency itself, in contrast it may exacerbate physiological dependency, psychological dependency and neuro-chemical compulsion, as an individual's drug use becomes more entrenched. Long-term maintenance prescribing of substitute opiates, such as Methadone can be seen as a clinical solution to dependency, but is perhaps more often seen either as a means of reducing individual drug-related harm, a public health measure to reduce wider harm such as HIV in populations, or a controlling measure to reduce crime.

It will be apparent that the situation is complex and confusing. This example is used because it perhaps best illustrates how complicated the drugs field is for professionals trying to care for drug users and control drug use at the same time. It can be seen that an intervention aimed at controlling crime and reducing harm through long-term prescription of maintenance drugs might conflict with the need to treat physiological addiction. Harm minimization interventions can decrease the likelihood of future recovery and abstinence because substitute prescribing can contribute to increasingly entrenched, compulsive drug use and long-term addiction. Whereas, abstinence-orientated interventions can undermine harm minimization objectives because they may increase the risk of future relapse and associated harm. Perhaps for this reason the controversy between these two approaches remains as fierce and unre-solved as it was a century ago and the rationale for prescribing drugs may sometimes be unclear.

It is hoped that this example has raised a series of concerns and questions. These will be returned to at the end of this section. However in order to gain a clear overview of the complexity that underlies these controversies, it is first necessary to go back in time to get a broader overall perspective of responses to drug use over the years. In this way it will be possible to understand how drug problems became under-stood in terms of dependency and/or health and social harm and how solutions were developed for each type of problem.

The wider picture: policy and practice in perspective

Drug dependency is a disputed concept and its treatment controversial. By the same token, drug-related health and social harm encompasses both harm to the drug user and harm to the wider society. Perhaps because this is such a complex area, fashions in theory, policy and practice change rapidly, often distorted by contemporary political con-text. It will therefore be useful to give an overview of the range of dif-ferent understandings and responses over the past hundred or so years, in order to provide a foundation for the contemporary approaches dis-cussed in later chapters.

Overall, drug use literature has focused on physiological and psycho-logical aspects of drug use, that is, what can be reliably assessed and measured. This has led to lack of focus on less accessible aspects of drug use such as loss of control, compulsion and craving and social factors such as relationships, social exclusion and offending. In order to gain a broad understanding it is therefore necessary to go back before medical and psychological models took precedence and envisage drug use in a more general way. The following section will give an account of beliefs and theories in the past hundred years and compare this with contemporary beliefs and theories. From this dis-tance it will be possible to get a clear view of the overall problem, to see how little has changed and how much any one theory or policy may narrow and distort our understanding and our interventions at any one time.

Controversies in the drug field today reflect those of the late nine-teenth century. A hundred or so years ago drug problems were under-stood largely in terms of the harm that an individual's drug use caused others (families or the wider community) and occasionally themselves, through compulsive use. Solutions were seen largely in terms of control of supply. However, towards the end of the nineteenth and early twentieth centuries 'physiological addiction' itself became the focus of attention, rather than harm caused to others, and solutions were seen largely in terms of clinical treatment. In the late twentieth century the health-related harm caused to drug users and others, through transmission of HIV and hepatitis, became the focus of public health interventions and solutions were again seen largely in terms of public health and health-care interventions. In the early twenty-first century the harm caused to others (through drug-related crime) has once again become the main focus and solutions are seen in terms of control of supply and control of individuals.

Contemporary research literature in the drug-use field has reflected these changes in attitudes, moving from treatment models of addiction and dependency towards models of harm minimization and crime prevention based on public health and social understandings of drug use respectively.

Drug use has always been controversial and has often become a political issue. There has seldom been agreement about what constitutes a drug problem or what constitutes an effective solution. Consequently there have been continuing conflicts between drug users themselves, academic theorists, treatment providers and politicians. The various theoretical models have included a moral model; a spiritual disease model; a medical disease model; a cognitive/behavioural model; a social deprivation model; a public health model and a neuroscience model. Different types of theory or model are associated with different policy and practice at various points in history. However, all these approaches remain active today though they may be seen as mutually exclusive rather than as describing different phenomena associated with drug use.

It is possible that the effects of drug use on the human physiology and psyche reflect or accentuate normal individual or social processes. If this were so, it would be sensible to see drug use in the context of human nature as a whole, rather than as a separate and distinct problem. Beliefs about drug use through the ages have been, to some extent, a reflection of wider beliefs about human nature held by particular groups, whether religious, moral, academic or professional. So for example, the moral and religious models of the nineteenth century were based within the context of beliefs about human nature and the soul: these were followed in the twentieth century by medical and clinical models, based on newly developing professional beliefs about human nature and the psyche. It is possible that future models for the twenty-first century may reflect new advances in neuroscience and potential models of human nature based on the significance of brain chemistry.

It is clear that medical and psychological models have had limited success. Despite the fact that medical and disease models of physiological addiction were developed more than a hundred years ago, it has proved very difficult to demonstrate that drug treatment is effective or that any one type of treatment is more effective than another. As a consequence these treatment models have come increasing under scrutiny and the approaches adopted in pre-clinical times considered again today. For example, as neuroscience develops it is likely that a sophisticated understanding of the chemistry of the brain will shed new light on how drugs affect social (and perhaps moral) functioning and why some drug use becomes compulsive and intractable for some individuals without necessarily being physiologically addictive (Moos, 2007, 2008; Morganstern and McKay, 2007; Marlatt, 1996).

In order to shed light on the complexity of contemporary models and solutions, a series of historical models will be briefly outlined in terms of their aims and objectives. These will be set out in chronological order, examining how nineteenth century theories of the social causes and consequences of drug use, and ideas about spiritual and moral degeneration, were replaced by medical and psychological models of the twentieth century only to be revived again in the twenty-first century.

Historical models of care and control of opiates

Theories of physiological addiction were not developed in Britain until doctors began to become interested in these phenomena, in association with opiate use, at the turn of the nineteenth century. Prior to this, for example, little medical interest had been taken in opium use. Instead it was often understood as useful for individual health if used safely in moderation and as a social or moral problem if used compulsively or excessively.

The following section will briefly outline each of these traditional approaches to opiate use in chronological order and show how each contributes to contemporary practice alongside the newer disciplines of psychology and neuroscience. It will become apparent that social problems were the first to be identified, followed by health-related harm, with notions of dependency and treatment only developing in the past hundred or so years. These problems are dealt with in reverse order later in the book in order to reflect the contemporary emphasis on dependency, not because dependency is necessarily more important.

- *Problems and solutions to social harm*
  Reducing social harm to individual users
  Reducing social or moral harm to populations

- *Problems and solutions to health-related harm*
  Reducing health-related harm to individual users
  Reducing public health-related harm to populations

- *Problems and solutions to dependency*
  Dependency and treatment

Reducing social harm to individuals: the social model

Berridge and Stanton (1999), Berridge and Edwards (1981) and Harding (1988) give the most detailed accounts of the extent of opiate use in the nineteenth century. They conclude that in the early part of the nineteenth century 'working-class opium eating' was commonplace, stating that the equivalent of 600mg per head was consumed each year in 1827 and that this increased to three-and-a-half times as much in 1859. This opium was used for many minor ailments as well as more serious illnesses and was sold widely by chemists, shop-keepers and travelling salesmen (Anderson and Berridge, 2000). It is interesting that whilst alcohol was often seen as a cause of social evils, excessive opiate use was often seen as a consequence. Harding (1988) states that opium eating was 'regarded at worst as a minor vice or a bad habit' continuing, 'the use of opium imported into Britain continued along with an essentially relaxed attitude to its consumption for much of the early 19th Century'. At this time 'working class consumption was attributed to poor housing conditions and fever epidemics' (quoted by Harding from parliamentary paper, Report to the Commissioners for Inquiring into the State of Large Towns and Populous Districts: XVlll, 1844.) 'While its consumption by the middle classes was held to result from their experience of pressure from severe mental distress.' (quoted by Harding from 'Medicus, Teetotalism and Opium Taking', *Lancet*, 1851: 694). These beliefs underpinned the thinking of a large section of the population, known as opium apologists and are not dissimilar to some social theorists today (see Chapter 7).

Reducing social harm in populations: the moral model

Despite the political tolerance of opiate use, the first attempts to control the use of opiates by the Society for the Suppression of the Opium Trade (founded in 1874) influenced the control of drug use over the following decades. In contrast to the opium apologists who utilized a social model of drug use, these organizations proposed that drug use was the cause rather than the consequence of social evil. They (and the newly formed Temperance groups) believed that any drug use changed natural human functioning for the worse and as a consequence they opposed the idea of the free trade in drugs and drink respectively (Berridge, 1999).

The Society for the Suppression of the Opium Trade (SSOT, was founded by the Quakers and the ideas are therefore based on Quaker religious and moral beliefs, not merely about the nature of drug use, but also of the nature of man and morality. Essentially the SSOT believed opium use to have 'the property of impairing the habitual user, not just physically, but also morally... opium dependence was seen as a "vice" caused by a pathologically debilitated will and pathologically impaired moral faculty' (Harding 1988). The beliefs of the Quakers and SSOT corresponded closely to those held by the early religious groups attempting to deal with alcoholism (for example, The Oxford Group) and with those held by the founders of Alcoholics Anonymous in America. They also correspond with the beliefs held by many laymen and professionals who have contact with the Narcotics Anonymous Fellowship in Britain today, and are still well integrated into the contemporary American approach to drug policy and treatment. These beliefs about impaired moral and social functioning may also be reflected in the findings of modern neuroscience concerning the effects of drugs on decision making and impulse control (see Chapter 3).

Reducing health-related harm to individuals: the harm reduction model

The Poisons and Pharmacy Act of 1868 was the first to attempt to regulate opium use in the general population. The problem facing the Government at this time was not complicated by notions of addictive disease or moral deterioration, it was simply an issue of how to regulate the sale of opiates in order to reduce 'poisonings', that is, to reduce accidental deaths by overdose and suicide. This new area became a monopoly of professional pharmacists in the early twentieth century and was an important factor in the establishment of the pharmaceutical profession. 'Even the minimal safeguard of labelling each opiate dispensed as a poison was sufficient to produce a 26 per cent decline in the mortality rate at the start of the twentieth century. The more substantial regulation of opiates after 1908 brought about a further decline of 20 per cent (Parssinen, 1983: 75). This is reflected in the contemporary society where UK pharmacists can dispense opiates in a controlled way with increasing powers to prescribe independently of doctors: similarly in France a partial opiate agonist/antagonist (Subutex) can be sold over the counter in pharmacies (see Chapter 5).

Reducing health-related harm in populations: public health model

Early public health legislators lobbying for general health and safety measures were concerned with developing laws to control the widespread use of opium in the population as a whole. This group were often in conflict with doctors and it was this group, rather than medical practitioners, that was responsible for its eventual decline in the late nineteenth and early twentieth centuries (Anderson and Berridge, 2000). This situation again reflects a contemporary conflict between public health professionals who advocate harm minimization and clinicians who advocate treatment and abstinence. The public health model of this time is perhaps most clearly correlated with the public health and harm minimization approaches of today where reducing health-related harm is the main objective and information and education are the main methods (Berridge, 1999) (see Chapter 5).

Reducing addiction, dependency and compulsion: the medical and disease models

The early twentieth century models of addiction incorporated three distinct phenomena; physiological addiction, psychological dependence and compulsion. In contrast with the public health campaigners and pharmacists, the medical profession was less concerned with the general consumption of opiates but specifically with the therapeutic morphia addicts. That is, with physiological addiction itself rather than simply entrenched use, risky use or compulsive behaviour.

The earliest medical theory was formulated by Levinstein in *Morbid Craving for Morphia* (1878) where he describes this new disease, 'the uncontrollable desire of a person to use morphia as a stimulant and a tonic, and the diseased state of the system caused by the injudicious use of the said remedy' (quoted in Parssinen, 1983: 86). It can be seen that this initial approach identified two phenomena, distinguishing between compulsion and its physiological consequences. This was followed by work by Dr Kerr, who proposed a third phenomenon associated with addiction, psychological dependence. In an early text of this time *Inebriety or Narcomania: Its Etiology, Pathology, Treatment and Jurisprudence*, Kerr (1894) modified Levinstein's conception of the disease of addiction by stressing that it had a psychological aetiology and by emphasizing the difficulty of reversing a patient's opium habit once it was fully established. These three themes became prominent in the twentieth century literature on dependence and addiction (see Chapter 3).

The concept of entrenched use existed separately and prior to the notion of physical addiction. It is significant that medical interest in opiate use and physiological addiction only developed when morphia began to be prescribed in an injectable form soon after the hypodermic syringe was invented in the second half of the nineteenth century. Morphia was used in much greater concentrations than the opium commonly sold prior to that time and physiological dependency and withdrawal symptoms were therefore more likely to be identified. Morphia was initially available as a medical treatment for pain and various illnesses, but there was no restriction on its sale until the 1920s. Patients received the type of repeat prescriptions that remained their property and could be refilled continually, allowing the user to continue use after its 'medical use' for as long as they wished. Doctors focused on the minority of therapeutic morphia addicts after the Rolleston Committee of 1924 (which was largely composed of doctors) reinforced the notion of drug use as a disease and therefore clearly within the remit of doctors. The problem was seen as a purely medical concern defined in terms of physical disease rather than in terms of morality and social control, though with little understanding of its cause, as no organic source of addiction had been discovered (Harding, 1988). In this way the medical model of physiological addiction was born, defining addiction in terms only of its effects on the functioning of the body, with little interest in its effects on the social, psychological or moral functioning of individuals. Nevertheless, opiates could now be prescribed, under certain conditions determined by the doctor, on a maintenance basis. The Rolleston Report laid the guidelines for drug policy in Britain for much of the twentieth century, and it can be seen as defining what came to be known as 'the British system' of substitute prescribing for addicted patients.

Contemporary models of care and control

Current controversies reflect those of the previous centuries. Those advocating treatment argue about whether the problem is best understood as addiction, dependency or compulsion and whether the solutions should be abstinence or maintenance. Those advocating social or public-health approaches argue about whether the problem is best understood as a consequence of deprivation or a moral decline and whether the solution should be to help individuals to cope or to attempt to control their behaviour.

Contemporary authors such as Ashton (2008), McKeganey (2007), Stimson (2007), Simpson (2004), Warner-Smith *et al.* (2001), Preble and Casey (1998), Granfield and Cloud (1996), argue either for an abstinence-orientated or maintenance treatment approach in the same way as those through the past hundred years. Advocates of both camps have evidence that their approach can have advantages, and the alternative approach, disadvantages. This is because each approach can be successful in achieving its own ends, but in doing so undermines the objectives of the other. There is no doubt that maintenance can reduce drug related harm (Stimson, 2007; O'Brien and McLellan, 1996) but this approach reduces the chances of eventual abstinence as it increases entrenched use and addiction (Best *et al.*, 2008; McKeganey, 2007). Alternatively, a treatment approach can achieve abstinence and recovery but only at increased risk of relapse and overdose (Warner-Smith *et al.*, 2001). Perhaps the best illustration of the continuing nature of these controversies is that a recent paper by O'Brien and McLellan in the *Lancet* in 1996, 'Myths about the treatment of addiction', directly reflects the views expressed in early *Lancet* articles of the nineteenth century (for example, *Lancet*, 1851: 694).

The following chapters will examine both user views and professional solutions for each type of problem in turn, and illustrate how present theory and practice reflect that of our predecessors.

- **Chapters 2 and 3**
  Dependency and treatment (medical, psychological and disease models of treatment)

- **Chapters 4 and 5**
  Reducing health-related harm to individual users (harm minimization)

  Reducing heath-related harm to populations (public health interventions)

- **Chapters 6 and 7**
  Reducing social harm to individual users (social inclusion)

  Reducing social and 'moral' harm to populations (crime prevention)

It should be noted, that whilst our understanding of physical, psychological and social processes has developed in the past century, the twenty-first century may also bring a new approach to understanding drug use. The recent study of neuroscience may contribute to understanding the short- and long-term effects of drug use partly because it enables the measurement of phenomena that were previously not measurable, such as craving, compulsion, impaired decision making and poor impulse control. At present we have little knowledge about the neurochemical processes that drugs influence and therefore little is known about the impact of drug use on these processes. Similarly, we have limited understanding of the effects of therapeutic drugs on brain chemistry and researchers have, in effect, had to guess at the neurochemical processes that underlie the outcomes of clinical trial. At present it appears as if neuroscience research will broaden clinical conceptions by focusing on a continuum of increasingly compulsive forms of drug use and craving in the context of models of normal brain functioning (Carter and Hall, 2007; Curren *et al.*, 2001; Lyvers and Yakimoff, 2003) (see Chapter 3).

Understanding the complexity: returning to the example of prescribed drugs

At the start of this chapter, the complexity of drug problems and their solutions were illustrated with the example of Methadone maintenance. It is hoped that this historical overview will now enable a clearer understanding of the different contemporary reasons for prescribing Methadone and the different type of solutions it provides in terms of both care and control of drug users.

* *Prescribing substitute drugs to treat dependency and addiction (care and control)*
  Long term substitute prescribing can be seen as a treatment for a chronic relapsing illness.
  Contemporary policy and practice developed from early medical treatment at the end of the nineteenth century. This practice was again based on the early clinical premise that illicit drug use was a medical problem and prescribed drug use was the medical solution, a foundation on which many national policies and practices are based. The extensive long-term prescribing of opiates to opiate users increased significantly in the 1960s with a return to the theories of earlier medical prescribers. Drs Dole and Nyswander (1968) revived earlier notions of addiction as a metabolic disorder or physiological dependency (identified by a withdrawal syndrome), which could be effectively treated like any other chronic illness with opiate substitute medication (Methadone maintenance).

- *Prescribing substitute drugs to reduce health-related harm to individual drug users (care)*
  Harm minimization, or prescribing drugs in order to reduce the risks to individual health has been established practice for several decades. It has been shown to reduce the risk of overdose and the risks associated with injecting drugs.

- *Prescribing substitute drugs to reduce blood-borne diseases in populations (control)*
  This practice developed towards the end of the twentieth century, largely to combat the spread of HIV. It is also used to reduce the risk of hepatitis B and C.

- *Prescribing substitute drugs to reduce social harm to individual drug users (care)*
  This practice developed in order to provide a regular source of legal drugs to reduce the need for an illicit supply. It increases the likelihood of the social inclusion of users and the enhancement of social life chances, such as training, employment, leisure and housing.

- *Prescribing substitute drugs to reduce crime (control)*
  This practice developed in order to reduce the need for offenders to commit crime in order to obtain drugs. It also provided the authorities with greater control in terms of monitoring and surveillance of potential offenders.

Complex conceptual issues can lead to confusion and controversy in policy and practice if guidelines are too simplistic

It can be seen that the rationale for prescribing for treatment is different from that for public health or harm minimization objectives. The rationale for prescribing and the indicators of successful outcome become even more complicated when drug treatment is used as a crime reduction measure (DoH, 2004; Home Office, 2004). When the aims of public health and public safety are combined there is a further confusion about whether public health models of health protection or disease prevention in populations can be utilized for crime prevention (that is, whether that disease prevention and crime prevention can be understood in the same way).

It is not therefore surprising that the theoretical and ethical issues arising from prescribing practice have caused controversy amongst clinicians and consequently professional engagement in prescribing regimes can be problematic. For example Leason (2002) found that professionals were concerned about substitute prescribing maintenance services for those who might otherwise achieve abstinence anyway. Sondi *et al.* (2002) found that defence solicitors would not recommend that their clients accept drug treatment option at the point of arrest and charge. Edmunds *et al.* (1999) found that inter-professional part-nerships working with drug users could fail because of organizational culture clashes, role conflicts and differences in values between criminal justice and treatment agencies.

Advantages and disadvantages of prescribed opiates

There are clear-cut advantages to prescribing opiates for drug users. This book will outline a wide range of research evidence demonstrat-ing the advantages in terms of reducing suffering, saving lives, prevent-ing the spread of disease and controlling criminal behaviour.

Opiate prescription can be useful for withdrawal when a client is already physiologically dependent on heroin or for harm minimization when there is a significant risk of health related harm (Bloor *et al.*, 2008; Strang and Gossop, 1994; Gossop *et al.*, 2000a; Keene, 1997b, 1997a). Long-term opiate prescription has been shown to be particu-larly effective within the context of a comprehensive range of other health and social care service provision with long-term, treatment with-drawal opportunities (NTA, 2002), though it is unclear how much of this success is due to the provision of health and social care services rather than opiates *per se*. The relationship of successful treatment and/ or harm minimization to reduced crime has been more difficult to establish conclusively for the offending population as a whole (Keene, 1997a; Simpson, 2004), though there is much evidence that this is the case for a small group of heavy heroin users who are also repeat offenders (Gossop, 1996, 1998, Home Office, 2004).

In contrast, long-term opiate prescriptions might be less than useful when a client is not addicted initially or there is no significant health risk to the client or others. In these cases, it is possible that clients may become physiologically dependent on opiates, become more 'entrenched' in their physiological dependence, increase their addiction to larger doses, lose personal control over their drug use and/or become more dependent on services. It is unusual for clients to successfully give up Methadone scripts in a short time (McKeganey *et al.*, 2006; Bloor *et al.*, 2008). If the treatment conditions are not adhered to, the client may be discharged and prescription drugs terminated. This can then leave the individual client worse off as, if they have acquired a worse physiological dependency and lost previous social and market contacts, they will be faced with physiological withdrawals, unsafe illicit drugs and unsafe illicit markets. In addition, inter-professional working and shared information might bring increased police surveillance and likelihood of future arrest.

One of the main problems in the drug use field is non-compliance with prescribed drug regimes. It is therefore important to understand both the professional rationale for prescribing and the user perspective. This is particularly relevant where patients are ambivalent about prescribed regimes of opiate drugs, because the rationale for prescribing these drugs is less clear than that for generic health prescriptions and the risks may be greater for the patient in terms of loss of control, physiological dependence and stigma. Because of the varied and complicated reasons for prescribing drugs to illicit drug users, it is important to examine reasons for poor compliance through the understandings of participants themselves, rather than assume that non-compliance is a perverse or even pathological reaction to treatment.

As McKeganey *et al.* (2006) point out, one of the most significant developments in the field in the past decade has been the growth of the consumer perspective. Users' views and beliefs may be as complicated and contradictory as those of professionals and academics. Nevertheless, studies indicate that user views can be as important as those of professionals in determining the success of interventions (Keene, 1997a; McKeganey *et al.*, 2004). It is partly for this reason that each section examines these views, before moving to the professional theories and models.

Conclusion

There is no doubt that fashions in theory and practice are constantly changing. As Griffith Edwards asked, 'In the past the received wisdom was exactly the opposite of what we accept today.....How is the ebb and flow to be explained?' (Edwards, 1989a).

Medical theories such as the Dependence Syndrome (Edwards, 1986) focus on the physiological and psychological effects of drug use, including increasing levels of physical tolerance and craving, physical withdrawal symptoms on stopping and the rapid re-instatement of physical levels of tolerance when re-starting. Psychological theories focus on the cognitive and behaviour changes that occur through the stopping period and after. However the theoretical limitations of each approach restrict our understanding. So the physical model of addiction has led us to ignore obsessive/compulsive behaviour without a clear physiological withdrawal syndrome, whereas the psychological model has led us to ignore the physical aspects of drug use. More importantly both the medical and psychological clinical approaches may have excluded neurological or social aspects of drug use by focusing too narrowly on the physical and behavioural aspects of the 'treatment period' respectively. It is possible that the neurochemistry of brain changes at each stage of drug use may contribute greater understanding of these processes, particularly subjective experiences of craving and compulsion. For example, it has been shown that the decrease in dopaminergic activity caused by drug use can create disruption in limbic and prefrontal regions. This disruption can decrease drug users' ability to control compulsive urges to use drugs (Volkow and Fowler 2000; Volkow *et al.* 2003), reduce self control generally (Volkow and Li, 2005) and impair decision making (Bechara *et al.*, 1998; Yucel and Luban, 2007). In addition, these changes can make individuals more sensitive to the effects of drugs and less sensitive to the rewarding effects of natural reinforcers such as food, work and relationships. These neuro-adaptions can persist for months, maybe years after abstinence, (Volkow and Li, 2004).

It is possible that the twenty-first century will again lead to greater emphasis on the importance of physiological and neurological symptoms as researchers utilize the scientific methodologies from newly developing areas of neuroscience to identify and measure chemical changes in the brains of drug users. However, it is equally possible that social science will enable greater understanding of the social processes that contribute to entrenched drug use, increasing social exclusion and relapse (Moos, 2008, 2007).

Despite the development of new theories and practice over time, the three different approaches to dependence and health and social harm have remained in place over the past two centuries. Social/moral models have been developed further, moral models are still apparent in the criminal justice approach to drug use and moral religious models are still active in the Twelve Step 'spiritual disease' model of addiction. Early nineteenth century public-health approaches to health-related harm have been revived in the late twentieth century, and the medical and psychological professions continue to differ over whether dependency is a physiological or psychological problem. As might be expected, the major controversies also exist today, as they did a hundred years ago. It could be argued that the history of theories of drug use has not been progressive, but circular, with present understandings being closer to those of the nineteenth century rather than the twentieth century and current policy reflecting that of the Victorians with a focus on public health and control of drug use, rather than the treatment and cure of the twentieth century (Berridge, 1998).

Differences between contemporary professional groups also reflect those of a hundred years ago, each professional group utilizing their own particular framework and theory to interpret and explain the phenomenon of drug use within the context of their professional function and remit. Professionals from psychiatry, psychology, social policy and social work provide different theoretical understandings of the process of dependence and addiction and its treatment. The controversies between social reformers, opium apologists and politicians in the nineteenth century are not dissimilar to those of public health campaigners, clinicians and politicians today (Berridge, 1998). Many contemporary arguments concerning the development of drugs policies also bear a strong resemblance to those of different professionals and interested parties at the turn of the nineteenth century. For example, arguments concerning free will and personal responsibility have been revived again in criminal justice programmes that offer 'tough choices' to offenders when they are arrested and charged with drug related offences (Keene *et al.*, 2007). While this philosophical problem is complicated by the medical profession with notions of the pathology of dependency, and side-stepped by behavioural psychologists and neuroscientists with notions of a value-free science, the moral and philosophical implications regarding the nature of man and social order remain. Perhaps the continuing importance of notions of justice and retribution best illustrate the strength of the moral response to drug use. Each of these models or theories contributes to our understanding of drug use, although the variety of different ways of understanding and responding to problems can cause confusion. For this reason each of the following chapters provides a comprehensive overall framework for understanding each distinct type of drug problem and its solution.

Chapter 2

Drug Users' Perspectives on Drug Use and Dependence

Introduction

This chapter is concerned with respondent beliefs about why they use drugs and their descriptions and interpretations of the effects. It will first examine experiences of starting to use drugs, then experiences of ongoing use and dependency, together with accounts of loss of control, compulsion, craving. Finally it will explore descriptions of stopping drug use, treatment, relapse and experiences of drug services.

Methodology for exploring user views

Before moving on to examine user views, it is important to clarify the methodology and methods used to explore user beliefs. Methodology and methods were chosen in order not to impose any pre-determined theory, but to identify and categorize the theories and beliefs of drug users themselves.

The material employed in chapters concerned with user perspectives is taken from a series of research studies using qualitative methods and analysis. The essence of this approach is that the categories used, the concepts deployed and the theories constructed arise from the data themselves rather than being created as abstract theoretical entities which are then applied to the material to see if it fits (Glaser and Strauss, 1970, 1992). This methodology and analysis therefore allow an understanding of drug users' views in terms of their own concepts and beliefs (Lofland, 1971). As Spencer and Dale (1979: 697) observe, such methods provide 'many opportunities for developing and refining concepts rather than relying on the assumption that we know the relevant properties and categories in advance'.

The methodology used is based on a phenomenological perspective. Phenomena are seen as socially embedded events which take place as a

18

consequence of the reflective capacity of people to create meaning through subjective interpretations of the processes and interactions between them. That is, the users themselves are seen as making sense of their own drug use together. A Grounded Theory approach was used to analyse the data systematically (Glaser and Strauss, 1970, 1992) by examining emerging themes and patterns. Themes were identified and refined through open coding and analysis using a strict process of validation against the data, through examination, comparison and categorization. Data were analysed until the categories were well defined and saturated. Emerging themes are identified by section headings and quotes recorded in the text are those most illustrative of each theme as a whole.

The methods used include semi-structured interviews and questionnaires with drug users and non-participant observation in informal settings (Spradely, 1980). The interviews were conducted in drug agencies, drug users' own homes, clubs and cafes, police stations and prisons. This informal approach used with respondents who have no experience of research made it all the more important that their independence and privacy were respected and so ethical guidelines to ensure confidentiality and anonymity were closely adhered to. Information about questionnaires and interview protocols was available to all respondents, who were informed that participation was entirely voluntary and that they could withdraw or withhold their own interview tapes or transcripts.

There are, of course, many weaknesses in the qualitative approach; its inability to produce testable hypotheses, develop replicable experiments or control variables has to be recognized. It is therefore not usually considered possible to generalize from small groups to larger populations. The intention here is to use the qualitative approach to give an in-depth understanding of the phenomenon of drug use through an analysis of drug users' own beliefs. That is, to understand the subjective views of drug users, not the objective impact of drug use.

In conclusion, it is worthy of note that qualitative data, although not scientific, are of particular relevance to clinicians. Clinical knowledge and professional experience are themselves based on deep understanding gained from listening to the subjective experience of individual clients. The case studies of psychiatry and clinical psychotherapy are in essence products of subjective interpretation. Diagnosis and treatment are often based as much on individual casework and experience as research findings and many clinicians see their activities as a professional art rather than the unthinking application of scientific procedures. The chapters outlining user views may go some way to explaining why professionals may find understanding of individual experience as useful as the more scientific evidence outlined in the following chapters. So this chapter will now examine user understandings of the effects of drugs and growing dependency. This is followed by Chapter 3, which examines professional theories and research evidence.

User views of drug use and dependency

This chapter will include descriptions of a range of physiological, neurological, psychological and social effects of drugs. It will be seen that experiences of drug use varied depending on the stage users were at, experiences when first starting to use drugs are described differently to experiences of dependency. Whilst there are clear differences between the descriptions of the effects of different drugs, particularly between stimulants and depressants, drugs are often used interchangeably or in conjunction with each other and the general effects of drugs are often described together.

STARTING TO USE DRUGS

The positive effects of starting to use drugs

Most drug users described initial drug use in terms of positive feelings 'rushes' or 'buzzes' and as a means to relax and become more social.

> "The rush!

> "Gives you a good head, you become very happy and relaxed.

> "You become more friendly.

> "Buzz, confidence, feeling that I'm the best person here!!

The negative effects of starting to use drugs

Users were clear about the short term after-effects when starting to use drugs. The main problems were seen in terms of the comedowns after using drugs, unpleasant side-effects and the health issues associated with unknown quality.

> "Paranoia, lack of sleep.

> "Comedowns, feeling knackered, irritable; snappy.

> "Physical exhaustion, which is very easy when using class A stimulants.

CONTINUING TO USE DRUGS

As drug use becomes more entrenched, the picture becomes much more complex and descriptions of experiences become more detailed and complicated. Users distinguish between different types of drugs and describe the interactive effects of stimulants and depressants. However, the physiological, neurological and psychological effects can be confused by many who have difficulty in identifying the effects, side-effects and interactive effects of different drugs, identifying instead a range of experiences which they often find it difficult to describe or explain.

Experiences of different drugs

Many respondents used a range of drugs and the majority also used cannabis, this was so much taken for granted that it was often not even mentioned initially. Most respondents had tried most drugs, some had decided that stimulants (crack and cocaine) or depressants (heroin) were not their choice.

> 66What tends to happen is when you take heroin or drugs like that you have got no feeling, it blocks out the real world and the everyday things where sometimes people feel down or on a natural high – that takes it all away, you don't have them natural feelings – love, everything, it takes it all away and you are like pretty numb as a person.

> 66It [heroin] numbs me brain. It saves me from all the bad things. It keeps all the demons away... nothing matters, no pain.

> 66There's a big difference. When you are on heroin it mellows and 'mongs' you out, but then when you are on cocaine there is more of a rush, more of a high.

> 66Yeah, I've got mental health problems (from using crack) but they are the same as anyone else really. I get paranoid and think people are after me.

Experiences of the interactive effects of drugs
(concurrently or consecutively)

Many respondents used different types of drugs in order to accentuate or ameliorate the effects of each other (either using stimulants and depressants in combination or sequentially).

> 66What it is, with the cocaine, with that and drinking it stops the effects of the drink so much, you know, so you don't end up getting drunk. So if you are going out, a couple of lines of that seems to help us.

❝With me, I can't smoke crack without brown [heroin] because I start getting all paranoid and things like that, so I need a come down so I use the brown as a come down. So if I know I can't use brown – the heroin – I won't have crack, because I know I will have a come down and I'll be feeling all funny and that.

❝A lot of people get this problem where they get a script but keep using crack – then want to come down off the crack with heroin.

THE MEANING OF DEPENDENCY AND ADDICTION

Some respondents had a clear idea of 'addiction' as a serious, permanent state, different to more temporary or habitual behaviours or psychological needs, which they described as 'dependencies'. Others described their drug use as either dependency or addiction, or used the terms interchangeably; as a consequence it is not possible to be certain about the meaning of the term for each respondent.

Some respondents were very confused about what was wrong with them and could not make any sense of their condition or what was happening to them. This confusion contributed to their suffering. Respondents might have started using for one reason, but eventually the drugs got less and less effective and they said they were no longer using for the initial reasons [for example, hedonistic or coping]. Yet they could not stop for a mixture of physiological and psychological reasons. It is interesting that while some professionals understand drug use as a learned behaviour, the dependent drug users here appear to have a quite different understanding of it as something much more than a psychological dependency or habitual behaviour, rather a stronger, more complex and more permanent phenomenon.

It should be noted that many respondents also say that they use in order to cope or to self-medicate for a specific psychological problem. General coping and specific self-medication are split into two distinct categories, but in effect there seems to be a continuum from needing drugs to cope generally with life to specifically self-medicating for a psychological disorder such as depression.

Experiences of craving and compulsion

Respondents found it difficult to describe the experience of craving or compulsive urges and behaviours. There seemed a lack of language or concepts for talking about these aspects of drug use, perhaps because this aspect of drug use is the least understood in terms of theory or clinical models. Craving was also associated with dependency (though as with loss of control, it is also believed to exist independently.) It was seen as just as powerful and as difficult to deal with as the physical side of dependency.

> ❝Crack is like a mental sort of drug, you can sit there and think about it and then you want it. I used to sit and think about it and get a belly ache and want it more and I would have to go out and get money to get it.

> ❝It's social. I get myself into situations where the drug is there. I can sit down and watch you use for half an hour and not ask, but then all of a sudden it's like 'I need it – sort me a bit out', you know?

> ❝Its difficult to describe, I got in the car [with another user] and that was that I got the urge for some.

Uncontrollability

Respondents associated dependency with breakdown in self control, and saw this loss of control as leading to chaotic use. However not all uncontrollability was associated with dependency, some long-term users recognized the slow development of problematic feelings and behaviours, as their drug use became more entrenched (even if they did not increase dose or frequency), but it was difficult for them to find the words to describe these effects.

> ❝I think there is a potential for all of us to become addicted. I used too much until it became uncontrollable.

> ❝When you think you are cured, it gets dangerous. Because you think you can handle it but you can't.

> ❝I don't understand myself. I'm quite puzzled at the moment. I never used to be like this – it's only been the past six months that I started to get myself in a bit of trouble and say to myself 'I want that'. I've got to try and work out why I want it – it's stupid. It's not for my habit. There has been times when it's been for my habit (physical dependency) but not all the time.

The phenomenon of dependency

Whilst some respondents identified craving and/or loss of control as problems when they were not dependent, almost all respondents also associated these phenomena with dependence itself. To many respondents, the notion of dependency or addiction as something very powerful or overpowering, had come to dominate their behaviour and their lives. They often saw it as usually a permanent state and as providing an all-encompassing explanation for almost everything that occurred.

> 66If you are addicted you need it for daily life. You will organize your life around it. It becomes more important than water and food.

> 66I don't know where to start with things without my drugs. I was trying to build a shed the other day and I just didn't know where to start. I think I am physically dependent as well because I need energy because of my illness and the paranoia at bed times. I also suffer from with-drawal, for example, sweating, vomiting, stomach cramps.

> 66So yes, I am getting fed up with it, in a way I haven't even started my life yet because I am still young and it is already going downhill. As time has gone by, it has become normal to pick up my script but I do agree, it is not normal. For me, it is just like drinking a cup of tea. I see it as, like, a normal thing to me. I do it every day, it has become a normal everyday thing, but it is wrong.

Lack of will power: moral explanations

It was not uncommon for drug users to see their behaviour in terms of character defects. In comparing themselves with others, they ascribed their taking of drugs to a lack of moral strength or weakness of will. Respondents believed that dependency can include loss of will power, loss of control and craving. It should be emphasized that these factors are not necessarily part of dependence and were also reported by those who are not physically dependent on drugs. However, whilst dependent users tended to see these elements as an integral part of their depend-ency, they were often confused about the nature of the relationship between these things.

> 66I feel it is a moral issue. I will have to change my lifestyle and attitudes.

> 66My behaviour has gradually become childish, petulant and inexplicable. I have been shocked and frightened by my behaviour.

> 66I thought I had the will-power but didn't use it, then I suddenly realised the will-power was non-existent.

Disease of the whole person

A group of respondents believed in the basic premises of the Twelve Step (Alcoholics Anonymous) model, that is, that addiction itself is a physical and spiritual disease. Those who has contact with Twelve Step and believed this approach saw themselves as 'born addicts' or having 'addictive personalities', however much of what they said about the effects of drugs corresponded closely with other users.

> 66I think that I have had an illness which I am trying to recover from.

❝I'm a born addict, anything I do, I do to extremes.

❝I have come to believe that it is in-built, something to do with my make-up.

It can be seen that respondents believed that a range of factors were involved in dependency, however there was much confusion about what caused the drug use and what causes the problems. Most respondents believed that drugs solve some problems, despite causing others.

REASONS FOR BECOMING DEPENDENT

Coping and self-medication

A common explanation for drug dependence was that it is a form of self-medication for a variety of problems, drug use was seen as rational and often necessary means to an end. It is also possible that some respondents were in effect 'self-medicating' for the side-effects of drugs or for withdrawal symptoms without realizing it.

❝Some people manage to settle [drug free], but some become mentally disorientated and confused, they don't know how to keep a relationship going. There are problems if you haven't been taught to cope with life, then there is a weakness which you cover with drugs or drink. These are my problems.

❝I can't cope with nightmares and depression if I don't take them. I've had bad experiences in my life and drugs help me forget.

❝I was depressed, but now I don't know if the drugs came first or not. I don't know.

THE RISKS AND CONSEQUENCES OF DEPENDENT DRUG USE

Respondents recognized that there were many ill-effects of drug use but when discussing its consequences, many respondents were confused between causes and consequences of drug use and were also unable to distinguish clearly between the effects of drug use and the effects of withdrawing from drugs, as both were an integral part of their pattern of drug use.

General risks

When asked about risks, those associated with injecting, such as hepatitis and HIV, were most commonly mentioned, but a larger number of respondents mentioned the dangers of overdose, together with risks to long-term physical and mental health. Risks to social life and relationships were also common; respondents referred to the ill-effects of their dependency on their family and friends and many people mentioned destroying relationships, losing jobs and accommodation and, more generally, being rejected by the conventional social world.

> 66 I see tremendous risks associated with becoming dependent, feelings of no self-worth, it damages the health, family problems, relationship problems. There is also a risk with sharing needles, risks of unknown dealers, overdoses because you don't really know the percentage of the street drugs and injecting causes clots. I have taken a lot of risks, I have shared needles and I have used the same needle on myself up to seven times. I tried to manage the risks by sticking to my script and staying away from street drugs. I also stick to one dealer but I never used to. You can also cut down the risks by not letting someone else hit (inject) you because you just don't know what's in it.

HIV and hepatitis

Most respondents were aware of the risks of HIV and hepatitis C.

> 66 One day, I had to share a needle because I had no money and the needle exchange was shut. I was sharing with a friend and I caught hepatitis B off him. I collapsed and was put in hospital for two months, then I went through 'cold turkey'.

> 66 We were washing them [syringes] in between. Used to share needles but not any more. I keep needles clean, make sure of that.

EXPERIENCES OF CONTROLLING, REDUCING OR STOPPING DRUG USE

Clinical knowledge of the effects of stopping drug use is much more extensive than knowledge of the effects of starting or continuing use, therefore respondents also found this easier to describe.

> 66 If you are using heroin, it's either you go through that 10 days of … well it's bad – not many people can go through it. I've gone through like a day and a half and I just can't go through it. Then having that thought of about 10 days!

> 66 Do you know when you stop using heroin your emotions are like a roller coaster.

> 66 When I was coming off the first time I didn't know what was happening to me, I thought I was going mad. 'Cause there was no one there to explain to me 'you are going to feel like this, because this is reality' because I didn't even know what reality was.

EXPERIENCES OF RELAPSE

Descriptions of relapse were again difficult for some respondents who were less clear about this process, often using similar terms as those used to describe compulsion or entrenched use, where the effects of drugs are not clearly understood.

> ❝Do you know what for me it's the buzz, that's why I relapse. For me it's the buzz, I like the buzz from heroin, I just don't like what follows with it – the withdrawal symptoms and having to use it everyday and things like that, but the buzz I love.

> ❝Yes. I find that personally I need a structured day because boredom leads me into taking drugs again – it leads me into a depressive state and eventually I will use, especially if I start to surround myself with people that use.

> ❝[I've] been taking heroin for five years but then was clean for five years after finding out I was schizophrenic. Now I take medication but it feels like I have half a brain. Smoking makes me feel normal again [crack or heroin] in a way that the medication for schizophrenia can't do. This is why I sometimes relapse, when tempted to feel normal.

What do you need and what is your experience of services?

All the respondents were asked what their needs were and what kind of help they wanted. They identified a wide range of different needs arising from the previously identified problems and gave some idea of the kind of services they found useful. Not all needs were directly related to dependence, nor were all services requested concerned with overcoming this problem. Some respondents felt that the answer to dependence was a regular script for substitute drugs, most agreed that solving related problems would help them deal with dependence itself.

In previous studies where the views of consumers are sought in health, mental health and social care services, studies indicate that clients often see their own needs differently to professionals, identifying a wider range and interacting difficulties and problems, and therefore a need for appropriate services, [Baldock, 1997; Ungerson, 1994]. Difficulties in the working relationships between clients and professionals may be understood partly in terms of these conflicting perspectives, [Mayer and Timms, 1970; Sainsbury *et al.*, 1982].

WHAT HELP DO YOU NEED FROM SERVICES?

Clients identified needs for joined up, accessible services. They wanted stability and familiar staff.

66Ah well, if I was coming to this the first time again, I'd be confused. I think the first thing that you need when you go to ask for help, the first thing you need is stability, you need familiar surroundings, familiar faces. This is not what you get at all.

66The staff are constrained. They can only provide certain services. All these different departments, all these different agencies, are all separate, they don't seem to act as one, they only communicate on a part-time basis. There doesn't seem to be any central information. I can only speak from my point of view but I'm reasonably intelligent, right, I really do wonder what happens to people who aren't or who don't [persevere.]

Clients' views of professionals

Clients were able to distinguish between different types of professional, many wanted both the professional knowledge and resources of the clinician and the informal friendly support of the non-statutory worker. However many respondents had difficulty understanding professionals or their rationale for practice.

66I don't think he really knows, the only thing he knows about me is whatever is down on paper, which is an awful lot by now, I'm sure, but he doesn't know me as a person at all. He was looking at me purely as what clinical signs I was showing I suppose, where I was at that precise moment when I saw him.

66I trusted him [non-statutory worker] straight away for some reason as well. I felt he understood me. When I said, like I could talk normally to him, I didn't have to think medically, I could talk normally to him.

66I've come away from there, furious sometimes. I've actually sat in the room and I have ended up actually arguing with him and then the next week I'll go back and he'll say something, like 'I touched on a nerve there' or something and I don't know whether he's doing it deliberate to get me to argue with him or not, but like I say I respect him. I trust him to know what he's doing, but I don't actually know what it is he's trying to do, so it's a bit of a strange relationship.

66I felt I had to present myself in a particular way because that is what would count. It was like I was performing for them, and I was incapable of performing. I didn't know what I had to present like, even so I didn't know what it was I was trying to do.

66Unless I feel comfortable somewhere, I'm quite likely to change how I am to suit how they want me to be. I don't do it on purpose, I don't think, it's something that just happens. It's not until I think about it, that

I think that now I am just saying that because that's what they want to hear. Bit sort of manipulative, really I suppose.

SPECIFIC SERVICES

Help with withdrawal

The difficulties of withdrawal were commonly mentioned as an important. Respondents emphasized the need for better inpatient detoxification services and aftercare.

❝You should give a quicker reduction at first [e.g. from 50 mls of Methadone down to 15 mls within two to three months], then a much slower reduction while you sort things out ... and prescribed sleeping tablets are essential as script reduces and afterwards.

❝De-tox should be in general hospitals, not in mental hospitals.

❝I think the best thing is residential rehabilitation. Relaxed and responsible, long-term [one to twelve months].

Need for a maintenance prescription

Many respondents felt that they needed a maintenance prescription for drugs (at least temporarily) however some were confused about why they needed it.

❝If I am provided with a Methadone supply, I find I have no problems except possibly money.

❝I think Methadone is the only way for me, I had a script for five years and I was all right then.

❝I now maintain my script use because of withdrawal, for example, vomiting, sweating, cramps and because I am paranoid at bed time. I think that scripted drugs are clean drugs but street drugs make me feel dirty, as if I have got the plague.

The need for counselling

Whilst some respondents found counselling useful, particularly the one-one relationship, many could not see the point of therapy itself.

❝She sits there and listens to me. That's the good thing about her. She doesn't butt in, she doesn't preach, she just seems to know what to say to me. She says 'Why do you feel like that?' ... . I don't know where I'd be without her – the bottom of the river I expect. If it wasn't for this place, I think I'd be in prison or homeless or broke. She helps me to keep a cool head – to keep a lid on it. She gives me advice but by the time I'm out the door it's forgotten. It just feels better talking to her.

❝You share things you don't share with your partner or family. You get feedback from the group or just listen. They help you along, they help you to cope and find solutions you can't find yourself. You talk out of the problem.

❝Don't have groups, it is easy to make contacts in them.

Cognitive behavioural techniques for relaxation, anger and anxiety management and self-control

The rationale for cognitive behavioural interventions was better understood.

❝It's a role-play of situations you're going to find yourself in – working through different options. It helped me to see there's more to life than just drugs. It's made me say no. It's made me avoid them situations. It's made me paranoid as well!

❝Before I would do things, make snap decisions. If someone is saying something now, I think about what's going to happen. Combined with the tablets, it's making me feel slower.

AFTERCARE

Almost all respondents felt that aftercare was very important, as the problems of dependency did not end after withdrawal.

❝Follow-up support should continue for a long time after treatment and staff should consider and plan this carefully before treatment is ended. I think that relationships are the most important thing, then health, then security ... you need all this if you are going to stay off.

❝Anybody can stop, the problem is to do with starting again, because things happen and people come round and offer you things ... and you think, well, why not really. I can stay off for quite a long time ... something bad happens and I go back to it. You don't get any help afterwards, you finish and they say 'Right, off you go' ...

❝Need help to sort out what to do with my life in the future. It is a long-term thing. You need something to do and you need money, a job or something.

Discussion

The quotations here have shown how different understandings of dependence can influence the client's self-image and so also their beliefs about their own problems and capacity for change. This in turn influences what they feel they need and has important implications for the kind of support that professionals provide.

It will have become clear from the way in which dependent users talk about themselves that the meanings they give to their behaviour and circumstances are complex, change through time, and are not easily categorized. For example, although dependency is perceived to be accompanied by loss of will power, loss of control and craving, it will become clear in following chapters that these phenomena are also seen to exist independently of physical dependency. Similarly, although some dependent users see taking risks as a consequence of physical dependency, risk taking also occurs independently of physical dependency. The boundary between risky and dependent use is not clear and absolute.

It is apparent that some respondents do not see dependence as the worst of their problems and some do not see it as a problem at all, but rather a less than perfect solution to many other difficulties. Many respondents felt that their more serious worries would be resolved by having a long-term prescription for the drug on which they were dependent, though others believed that Methadone prescriptions either created or contributed to their dependency on opiates. Users often believed that factors associated with illicit drug dependence were more problematic than the dependence itself, particularly health and legal risks and general elements of the lifestyle, although dependence was seen as aggravating these problems as the need for a continuing large supply of drug increased.

Whilst dependence is not necessarily associated with high-risk drug use, much dependence was correlated with high-risk use at some time. It is also important to note that drug use varies from month to month and year to year. Most respondents had periods of heavy, uncontrolled dependent use, interspersed with periods when they used less and had their use under control. Some felt that help was only necessary in these more difficult periods, which could be avoided altogether if legal prescribed drugs were available.

Clients emphasized the need for understanding of what they saw as often complex and interacting problems. They emphasized the need for greater understanding of the nature of their problems and the consequent importance of long-term support and easy access to services particularly in emergencies.

Finally, respondents asked for clarification concerning the profes-sional/client relationship as some could not make sense of the proce-dures and protocols used to determine their access to help nor the rationales for the help itself. The client's ideal solution was a profes-sional who knew them well, but also had respect and influence among other professional groups and so could obtain services. Respondents thought however that these two things did not often coincide in the same practitioner but could be found in different people; the ongoing maintenance, support and friendship of non-statutory workers and the expertise, contacts and resources of statutory professionals.

It should be noted that many respondents in this section were clients of drug agencies and although the aim in the research was to interview as many as possible prior to contact with staff, it is clear that many of their responses may have been influenced by the agency context. As might be expected, those respondents who had attended agencies for some time tended to understand their problems in the way the staff of that agency did. So clients attending a Twelve Step, abstinence-orientated agency would see themselves as addicted, whereas those attending a harm minimization service or psychologically orientated agency would be more likely to see it as a behavioural problem over which they could exert control. There was also a lot of ambivalence within individuals, who could believe contradictory things about their drug use, sometimes seeing it as pathological and sometimes as simply recreational or medicinal.

Lack of understanding and the limitations of simplistic notions of dependency

Perhaps the most striking finding from these data is that drug users have very little understanding of what is happening to them when they use drugs or become dependent. It can be seen that respondents often found the effects of drugs at different stages confusing and a bit of a mystery. They had difficulty finding the words to describe some exper-iences, particularly those of compulsion and the gradual process of drug use becoming more entrenched.

Respondents often relied on drug agency models to help then under-stand their experiences, however these models seemed less useful for explaining the wide range of interacting phenomena which were associ-ated with the process of developing dependency [or existed independ-ently of dependency itself]. For example, whilst clinical models of dependency tend to focus on physical withdrawals or cognitive behav-ioural effects of the 'stopping' period, users themselves describe a far more wide-ranging and complex experiences of drug use, identifying the following stages of a continuing process:

- Starting period when the most important part of drug use are the positive effects of intoxication and the unpleasant physical side effects or coming down after a period of intoxication.
- A period of ongoing pleasure but increasing compulsion and craving as the drug use becomes more entrenched.
- Stopping period, involving a range of symptoms or effects of stopping, from immediate mild effects to full blown physical withdrawal syndromes and a range of short-term and longer-term after-effects.
- Relapse and reinstatement of drug using habits.

This chapter has examined how drug users themselves try to make sense of their experiences at different stages in drug use. Whilst physical dependency or addiction is important, it is clearly not the most significant aspect of drug use for many users who have much difficulty understanding their experiences simply in terms of physical or cognitive behavioural models. The difficulty users have in understanding the effects of their longer-term drug use raises many more questions than answers, perhaps illustrating our own lack of knowledge as well as theirs.

For example we know little about the following stages in the process of long-term drug use:

- Induction phase or starting period when the process begins.

We know very little about the physical, psychological and neurochemical changes that may take place in the initial period of use of any drug. These may involve risks for beginners, such as mood swings, loss of control of thoughts and feelings such as paranoia.

- Period of ongoing pleasure but increasing compulsion and craving, involving oscillation between varying levels of sensitivity and tolerance.

On-going use, even if not regular or escalating, may lead to increasing levels of compulsion with, or without, physiological dependency. We know little about how users attempt to increase sensitivity and reduce tolerance by varying levels of use over periods of time, or how they might use some drugs to ameliorate the side effects of others. Users themselves find it difficult to describe these processes in detail. It is possible, for example, that some drug use patterns may accentuate the craving and contribute to an ongoing process of increasing compulsion, whilst others may not.

• Stopping period, involving a range of effects or symptoms on stopping. This can vary from mild effects to full blown physical withdrawal syndromes.

The stopping period may be significant even if there are no serious physical effects or withdrawal syndrome. This period might for example involve similar effects to those on starting such as depression or mood swings.

• Short-term and long-term after-effects in the months after stopping.

Short-term after-effects may be important in inducing lapse and relapse particularly in the first few months after stopping. Long-term after-effects may change the brain chemistry for long periods, if not permanently. It is possible that this process normally recurs several times or more and the 'starting period' may be shorter with each new iteration. We know little about the wider effects of the rapid reinstating of this compulsive process.

It can be seen that drug users themselves can make sense of some of their experiences, but that they are unsure of the short and long-term effects of drug use. Chapters 4 and 6 will examine in more detail their beliefs about drug problems that are not related to dependency itself, such as health risks and social harm.

Chapter 3

Reducing Dependence: Approaches to Treatment

Introduction

This chapter will build on the issues identified in the previous chapter by examining research evidence and theories of dependency in order to clarify the professional knowledge base and show how this informs service provision for dependent drug users. However the views and beliefs of drug users themselves should be kept in mind throughout this chapter, as these not only shed light on why services are effective when they are, but also why they might be less useful in some circumstances.

The chapter is divided into four sections. The first, an introduction, examines problems of definition of dependence; the second analyses the three major treatment perspectives; the third considers research issues and implications for practice; the fourth focuses on the importance of treatment process and aftercare. Finally a post-script examines co-morbidity with dependence, particularly with mental health problems.

Treatment: what is it and what is it for?

Although, in practice, treatment of drug dependence and harm minimization are not necessarily clear-cut categories, for the purposes of clarity, 'treatment' here will be used to refer to the professional response to physical and/or psychological dependence.

The chapter is therefore concerned with treatment of drug dependence and related drug problems, rather than the wide range of problems that are associated in some way with drug use. Treatment generally involves therapeutic strategies for changing the drug user and/or their drug-use behaviour, whether this takes the form of stopping, reducing or controlling drug dependence. Many drug workers feel strongly that harm minimization methods should always be used alongside treatment, but this does not necessarily mean that treatment methods should be used alongside harm minimization.

Having distinguished harm minimization from treatment, it is then necessary to clarify what exactly it is that is being treated. Much of the confusion in the field of dependency and addiction stems from both researchers and practitioners behaving as if there were general agreement about the concept of 'dependence', whereas this is not the case. Many researchers erroneously presuppose there is consensus and that the phenomenon they call addiction or dependence can be easily defined and isolated, all peripheral variables controlled and experimental comparisons made. There is also a further presupposition that data inaccessible to this approach (such as subjective interpretations and the treatment process itself) are superfluous. This would, of course, be entirely valid if there were a general consensus about what addiction or dependence are and how to measure it, but there is not.

Understanding the problem

Dependence: physiological addiction, behavioural disorder or spiritual disease?

It is important to recognize that the experts do not agree about what dependence is, why it develops or what to do about it. Professionals cannot even agree about what to call it, some dismissing the word 'addiction' altogether. In deference to this latter camp the phenomenon will be referred to as 'dependence', but the term will be used to embrace a range of different conceptions of drug use based on three perspectives – the physiological, the cognitive/behavioural and the 'disease' models.

The physiological perspective focuses on the physical aspects of dependence and is concerned with increasing tolerance to a drug, physiological withdrawals and craving. The psychological perspective is based on a cognitive/behavioural approach involving the control of drug-using behaviour, as in 'controlled drinking' regimes. The abstinence-orientated perspective of Narcotics Anonymous understands drug dependence as a 'disease of the whole person' and recovery in terms of abstinence. This use of the word 'disease' can obviously lead to confusion since it may be an essential part of any medical model. For the purposes of this chapter, the term will be used to characterize the Alcoholics Anonymous/Narcotics Anonymous perspective.

Current controversies about drug dependence bear a strong resemblance to those at the turn of the century. Opinion is divided between those who believe that drug use is a matter of personal choice and habitual behaviour (the cognitive/behavioural approach), those who regard it as a form of physiological dependence (the medical approach) and those who see the problem in terms of loss of self-control and personal pathology (Narcotics Anonymous, NA). It will become apparent that there is little common ground between the models or communication between the practitioners of each. Differences between doctors, psychiatrists and psychologists are focused on the relative importance of physical and behavioural factors. The medical approach emphasizes the over-riding importance of physiological factors particularly physiological tolerance and the withdrawal syndrome. The psychological approach emphasizes the importance of the cognitive and behavioural aspects of dependence, even to the extent of suggesting as Stockwell (1994) does, that physiological dependence and withdrawal are '... an adaption to heavy drinking of no practical significance'. Both the psychological and medical approaches stand in contrast to the disease model of NA which has very different underlying theoretical premises concerning the nature of addiction and recovery and a knowledge base derived from experience rather than research.

Drug treatment within the statutory professions in Britain, Western Europe and Australia is based largely on physiological and psychological perspectives and consequently takes less account of social (or spiritual) factors. This is in direct contrast to North America and many East European countries where the Narcotics Anonymous is more widespread and there is general agreement among laymen and professionals alike that dependence is a disease which influences all aspects of a person's social and spiritual lifestyle. As a consequence, the approach of Narcotics Anonymous and the Minnesota Method is usually limited to voluntary and private residential services in Britain, whereas it is far more widespread in other countries, particularly in North America.

There are lessons to be learned from both the North American and the British approaches to treatment. For example, the British psychological approach offers simple practical cognitive behavioural interventions that have been shown to be cheap and effective for a majority of people with substance-use problems. The American approach offers important lessons about treatment process and the relevance of social factors. Perhaps more importantly in the light of relapse rates, the Americans have much to teach the British about the importance of long-term after-care. In Britain, after-care has not been seen as a significant and separate aspect of treatment and the importance of social and life skills is often ignored in the research literature, if not in the everyday practice of professionals.

It is also important to examine literature that does not fit conveniently into any one of the three camps, concerning motivation, treatment process, after-care, social factors and relapse prevention. It should be emphasized that the author does not advocate any one perspective or approach: instead, the benefits of each will be outlined in order to allow a greater understanding of all methods available. This chapter will outline the basic positions within different professions and examine theoretical controversies in the literature.

The continuum of dependence: a biopsychosocial model?

Much of the discussion about models of dependency and addiction is couched in terms of alcohol, particularly the seminal work of Griffith Edwards. Overall it is doubtful whether the three perspectives can be reconciled into an encompassing theory whichever drug is discussed. As will become apparent, they contain essentially contradictory and irreconcilable components. However, several early attempts were made to amalgamate them into a 'biopsychosocial' model. Orford (1985) and Galizio and Maisto (1985) give comprehensive accounts of such models. There were problems with these over-generalized understandings in that they were limited in their clinical usefulness and difficult to test within the framework of a behavioural science (Schwartz, 1982). Edwards *et al.* (1997, 2000) and Orford (2008) revisited these issues more recently highlighting the disappointingly negative results of methodologically rigorous controlled trials of psychological treatments within the biopsychosocial model and the need to consider all aspects independently.

However, the working definition given at the beginning of this section is taken from the most practically useful and comprehensive integrated approach which has been developed internationally; this is the concept of a 'continuum of dependence' which is now used for both clinical and screening purposes. In this approach, dependence is understood as a biopsychosocial continuum along which anybody can travel under certain circumstances. This is the model created by Griffith Edwards to guide clinicians and practitioners (Edwards and Gross, 1976).

Although the World Health Organization (WHO) initially supported a disease model of drug dependence (Jellinek, 1960), it does not now support either the disease or cognitive behavioural approach, stating that the syndrome defined a 'cluster' of physiological, behavioural and social phenomena. For alcohol and the drug dependence syndrome, this is specified as: narrowing of drinking repertoire, salience of drink-seeking behaviour, tolerance, withdrawals and craving, relief drinking and the rapid reinstatement of the syndrome after abstinence (McKellar *et al.*, 2006; Edwards and Grant, 1976, 1977).

The syndrome includes characteristics from physiological, behavioural and disease models – physiological characteristics such as tolerance and withdrawal, behavioural characteristics such as narrowing of the drinking repertoire (Edwards and Davies, 1994; Edwards and Taylor, 1994b), together with characteristics identified by the Anonymous Fellowship, such as particularly the salience of drinking and reinstatement of the syndrome (which the WHO refers to as 'remission'). The syndrome therefore can be seen as incorporating aspects of all three models (Edwards *et al.*, 1997, 2000). However, recently the controversy about terminology has been revived and both the medical and psychological components questioned (Morgenstern and McKay, 2007; Moos, 2007). It is argued that the terminology has remained largely medical and as such is seen (by those who are not doctors) as too closely related to the medical model, being criticized by both NA advocates and cognitive behavioural psychologists. The former state that dependence is a disease and not a medical problem (Timko and Debenedetti, 2007; Moos, 2007; Lefevre, n.d.) and the latter assert that it is based on a physiological perspective and is therefore an ineffectual attempt to support the medical perspective in the face of the evidence of behavioural research (Morgenstern, and McKay, 2007; Orford, 2008; Heather and Robertson, 1981).

The three perspectives

The physiological perspective

Introduction

For heuristic purposes, this perspective (and the two that follow) are treated as 'ideal types'; that is, their characteristics are isolated, accentuated and expressed as abstract depictions which are not intended to represent reality. They are ideal in the logical sense. This method of analysis allows us to see the essential character of each approach. In this first case, it is most unlikely that any clinician faced with a drug user would concentrate entirely on physical symptoms to the exclusion of all other considerations. Indeed, the standard texts for general practitioners in Britain cover psychological and social issues as well as narrowly clinical ones. Nevertheless, clinicians can be expected to give priority to clinical matters and to deal with physical evidence (such as physiological tolerance and withdrawal symptoms) in the way that their training has taught them to do.

The physiology of dependence and compulsion

From the medical perspective, one of the problems inherent in the notion of psychological theories is that drugs have both short- and long-term physiological effects (Grunberg, 1994). In addition, it can be demonstrated that physiological factors influence the significance of psychological expectancy factors for those dependent on alcohol.

Research with subjects who are physically dependent on alcohol demonstrates that they respond to the alcoholic content in drinks, whereas the response of less dependent subjects is determined mainly by their beliefs and expectancies about drinking. (Edwards, and Taylor, 1994a) The effect of an initial drink on a severely dependent subject's craving to drink further is not merely the result of cues, beliefs and rationalization; it occurs without the drinker being aware that they have consumed alcohol. It has been demonstrated that there is a statistically significant increase in craving three hours after a 'primary dose' (Hodgson and Stockwell, 1977; Bodin and Romelsjo, 2006). The authors state that this can be explained using the behavioural perspective, but only if it is possible to find out what pattern of reinforcement history differentiates the severely dependent from the less dependent drinker. They suggest that this altered physiological state is a component of craving but only for seriously dependent alcoholics for whom it has become a discriminative stimulus. For less serious alcoholics this physiological state is seen only as a component of craving when the alcoholic believes they have consumed alcohol. Marlatt, Demming and Reid (1997) carried out an experiment in order to test whether people addicted to alcohol lose control of their drinking (a premise integral to the disease concept and opposed to the cognitive behavioural approach). They found no difference between 'alcoholics' and social drinkers in alcohol consumption based on actual primer drinks (physiological stimuli), but found increases based on expectation. These results have been replicated since (Edwards *et al.*, 2000, 1997; Orford, 2008; Orford *et al.*, 2009) but with less certainty and greater perception of the limits of present models of understanding. In essence there is still no agreement about the significance of physiological addiction in initiating craving and compulsive drug use.

There is also much less research or understanding of compulsion and dependence in other drugs. Whilst heroin has been shown to produce more severe physiological withdrawal symptoms than either cocaine or amphetamine (Gossop, 1992), it is unclear whether stimulants produce a greater feeling of compulsion or craving. Gossop demonstrated that severity of dependence was also influenced by route of administration, amounts used and length of time using.

There is therefore conflicting evidence regarding the interaction of physiological or behavioural factors and subjective expectations and cognitions. It is impossible to research these interactions 'scientifically' because subjective interpretation is not observable. Much research is based on apparently positivist methodology examining observed behavioural and physiological changes but also involves the notion of craving. Yet craving is not as yet defined in physiological or behavioural terms; instead, it is often based on vague cognitive and emotional concepts far removed from any scientific approach, however, the concept remains a dominant one in the field due to its clinical usefulness.

The importance of withdrawal symptoms

Much of the literature on the physiology of dependence has focused on the negative effects of withdrawal, rather then the physical effects of starting to use, using over a long period of time, or the post abstinence effects (Grunberg, 1994). Physiological dependence is seen as causing adaptive changes in physiology which cause unpleasant effects when withdrawing. It is therefore suggested that it is the need to stop these physiological withdrawals that motivates people to keep on using the drug.

Traditionally the depressants, especially the opiates, were seen as the only seriously 'addictive' drugs (the exception being nicotine), though a withdrawal or abstinence syndrome for cocaine was first recognized in 1976 (Caldwell, 1976). There is less certainty today, however depression is a common feature of withdrawal; it is suggested that this is related to the physiological effects of both amphetamines and cocaine blocking the uptake in the brain of the neurotransmitters noradrenaline and dopamine (together with changes in the beta-adrenergic and dopaminergic receptors: Banks and Waller, 1988). As a consequence, tricyclic antidepressants have been shown to be useful in the treatment of cocaine dependence (Gawin and Kleber, 1984).

This will come as no surprise to practitioners who may have heard stimulant users complaining of depression or at least an inability to feel good after giving up their stimulants. Those who work with opiate users will know that they complain of the same thing for several months after giving up. Dackis and Marks (1983) have demonstrated that depression in opiate users more than doubles in the weeks following withdrawal. It is also possible that depression occurs after benzodiazepine withdrawal (Petursson and Lader, 1984).

Substitute drugs

Substitute drugs will be discussed in detail in the following chapter on harm minimization, however these prescribed drugs are also used as a form of drug treatment for withdrawal. The main substitute drug for opiates is Methadone which is a direct substitute opiate and has a similar effect to heroin. As such, it is valued by heroin users although it has less hedonistic effect. It induces physiological dependence in the same way as heroin. Methadone prescribing in the UK and the US has increased in last few decades. In the UK, government policy has supported flexible prescribing, as harm minimization and crime prevention influence the need to attract and retain heroin users in treatment (see also Chapter 7). Similarly, in the US it is perhaps the increase of drug-related criminal activity that had kept prescribing policies active.

Research demonstrates that Methadone prescribing can reduce health-related harm as it is associated with a reduction in the amount of injecting and sharing of needles and syringes. A prescription for drugs can also reduce criminal activity as it removes the need to buy drugs (Hammersley *et al.*, 1990; Jarvis and Parker, 1989; Bean and Wilkinson, 1988). Following UK government guidelines, there was a doubling of opiate treatment in the period 1995–2005 (Strang *et al.*, 2007).

The effectiveness of Methadone in maintenance and withdrawal is less clear. Strang and Stimson (1990), Caplehorn *et al.* (1993), Strain *et al.* (1993), Novick *et al.* (1993) and others give some indication of the positive effects of Methadone prescribing. Caplehorn and his colleagues have shown that the greater the Methadone script, the less chance that the patient would use heroin. Maremmani *et al.* (1994) have also demonstrated a positive correlation between Methadone dose and treatment compliance. They conclude that Methadone can have a rehabilitative effect and prevent relapse, if high enough doses are prescribed.

Strain *et al.* (1993) have demonstrated that patients prescribed Methadone show improvements over time on scales of psychological and psychosocial functioning. The Amsterdam Methadone Maintenance programme results in clients who take better care of themselves, use less heroin or Methadone post-treatment and, perhaps more significantly, are more likely to develop new social networks with non-drug users (Reijneveld and Plomp, 1993). A difficulty of prescribing Methadone is that a prescription may involve the professional in a controlling role. This is distasteful for some professionals, particularly those concerned with psychodynamic aspects of treatment. Summerhill (1990) highlights some of these difficulties.

The use of Methadone is however controversial mainly because it is in effect keeping the client physically dependent on opiates and indeed may increase that dependency as it provides a consistent supply over long periods of time. Other prescribed drugs include the partial antagonist Subutext, and Buprenorphine which relieves withdrawal symptoms and helps prevent the hedonistic effects of any heroin used afterwards.

This is also the case for Naltrexone, which effectively stops heroin users deriving pleasure from the drug. It should also be noted that one of the problems with all antagonists is that in effect they block the body's natural pain control and pleasure receptors and consequently may cause unnecessary pain and detract from ordinary everyday life. There are at present no similar 'blockers' or antagonists for cocaine and amphetamine.

The psychological perspective

Generic psychological theories have been appropriated to explain drug use and the methods derived from these generic theories have then been applied to those with drug problems. Cognitive and behavioural change methods derive from social learning theory and cognitive psychology. These methods can be very effective for certain conditions ranging from depression to phobias and, more significantly, for obsessive/compulsive behaviours (Bandura, 1977; Ellis, 1987; Beck, 1989). Similar methods based on social learning theory can also be used to control drug dependence. These methods have also been demonstrated to be effective in helping people control their drinking and drug use when reducing substance-related harm (see Chapter 5).

Social learning theory is a general theory offering an explanation of behaviour formation and maintenance. It assumes that behaviour can be either positively or negatively reinforced and that the sooner the reinforcement occurs, the more effective it will be. (Therefore short-term positive reinforcement could be seen to outweigh long-term negative reinforcement.) The development of behavioural habits can also be influenced by 'modelling' and other social factors such as the need to conform (Bergin and Garfield, 1978; Bandura, 1977; Bolles, 1979; Catania and Hamad, 1988). The social context of drug use is discussed in Chapter 7.

The advantage of placing the phenomenon of dependency disorders within the context of social learning theory and behavioural methods is that these methods are empirically testable. Thus if the maladaptive behaviour is not changed after 'treatment' in a controlled setting, then the chosen method can be shown to be of no use in dealing with the phenomenon in question. A great deal of research has now been completed in this area which sheds some light not only on the effectiveness of behavioural techniques in dealing with behavioural disorders, but also on the usefulness of defining dependence in behavioural terms. Cognitive and behavioural techniques of dependency treatment have been gradually refined in outcome studies with clients with diverse characteristics (Sanchez-Craig, 1990). These techniques are based on the notion that dependent drinkers and drug users can control their use, that clients are capable of self-control and of taking responsibility for much of their treatment. Raistrick and Davidson (1985) give a useful account of the application of psychological techniques to alcoholism and drug dependence.

Theories of drug-dependent behaviour have also been integrated with a cognitive approach to encompass the phenomenon of dependence as a cognitive/behavioural phenomenon in its own right. The influence of cognitive psychology is demonstrated in the work of Orford (2008), Orford *et al.* (2009a), Heather *et al.* (2002), Stockwell (2006), Witkiewitz and Marlatt (2006), Babor *et al.* (1999) and Morgenstern and McKay (2007). This work on the psychological interpretation dependence has to a greater or lesser extent adapted cognitive psychology to the particular problems of dependence generally. This approach is also particularly useful for after-care and relapse prevention.

The behavioural approach can be criticized because of the limitations of its theoretical base and cognitive psychology can be criticized for its lack of scientific testing but there seems little doubt from the accumulated evidence that psychology has a good deal to offer in the field of dependence. The most severe criticism is that while psychological theories and methods of treatment are useful in dealing with psychological dependencies, they have not yet been shown to be effective in serious cases of physiological dependence.

Behavioural interventions

Behavioural interventions are concerned with the accurate description of behavioural problems and change in the specific behaviours identified. The approach usually involves close monitoring of concrete changes in behaviour.

Initial assessment: Drug use behaviour is likely to have been strongly reinforced over long periods of time. It is necessary in any assessment to identify which variables are important in continuing this reinforcement for each individual.

Positive and negative reinforcement: The aim is then to change the reinforcing properties of drug use behaviour, either by offering positive reinforcement for non-drug-using behaviours or negative reinforcement for drug use. For example, it is possible to use prescribed drugs (e.g. Naltrexone) to block the physiologically reinforcing effects of opiates (although there is little evidence for effective long term, post-treatment results).

Cue exposure or extinction: The typical cues for drug use are pro-
duced without the reinforcing antecedents. The client is gradually and
then repeatedly exposed to drugs or drug use situations which elicit
craving, without actually using the drugs or without feeling positively
reinforcing effects. Over time the craving induced by such cues is
reduced.

Self-monitoring and self-control training: In effect, the terms 'self-
monitoring' and 'self-control' refer to the basic behavioural techniques
of identifying the antecedents and consequences of any problem behaviour and learning to alter behaviour by changing either or both. So the
client is taught to identify those situations and cues that are likely to
stimulate drug-using behaviour and to respond by avoiding the situation, refusing drugs and/or developing alternative coping strategies.

Cognitive interventions

Most contemporary behavioural psychologists also include a cognitive
element in both their theory and practice. The way people define or
interpret their experience is considered to have a strong influence on
their behaviour (Ellis, 1962; Orford, 1977; Beck, 1989). Cognitive
processes are considered influential in both loss of control and relapse
(Brown, Goldman and Christiansen, 1985). Cognitive findings are also
reviewed by Marlatt (1985) who demonstrates that the influence of
expectation and social cues can be significant in loss of control and
relapse.

As with behavioural interventions, cognitive interventions are concerned with the accurate description of cognition and beliefs, followed
by identification of maladaptive beliefs and consequent changes to
more constructive alternative beliefs. Accurate initial descriptions of
relevant beliefs about drugs and drug use are therefore essential in initial assessment, followed by continuing assessment, self-monitoring
and feedback. The first step in the helping process is to examine the
beliefs, thinking processes and patterns of behaviour which lead to and
maintain drug use.

This is followed first, by demonstration of inaccuracies in beliefs and
second, by identification of inconsistencies in personal belief and value
systems. Information about the effects of withdrawal and tolerance are
very useful here. For example, a client attempting to withdraw from
benzodiazepines may believe that they are inherently depressive or anxious, without realizing that these are the withdrawal effects of these
drugs. Similarly, clients unaware of the decreased tolerance following a
period of abstinence may misinterpret their increased vulnerability to

the drug as a sign of complete lack of control (see attribution theory below). Second, it is also useful to highlight any inconsistencies and conflicts between the client's short- and long-term aims and priorities and help the client to weigh up the evidence for the pros and cons of drug use. It can then be demonstrated how beliefs are linked to emotional and behavioural consequences and alternative beliefs. Clients can also be taught new skills and coping strategies, from a decision matrix to reminder cards and self-talk or cognitive restructuring.

Attribution theory and application

Psychological approaches to addiction include the application of attribution theory. The first attempt to examine the influence of the client's beliefs about dependence on their consequent behaviour was that of Eiser and colleagues in the late 1970s (Eiser and Sutton, 1977; Eiser and Gossop, 1979; Eiser, 1982). The most comprehensive exposition of the application of this theory to drug use as a whole is that of Davies (1993). Davies argues convincingly that drug users use drugs because they like them and that if they are taught to attribute difficulties in giving up to a 'disease' it will simply make it a lot more difficult to give up. Davies used data similar to those in the chapters on user views to clarify the influence of the subject's own beliefs on their behaviour, within a psychological model. He too identified different categories ('chronic' and 'sporadic') of drug user from subjects' subjective understandings (Davies, 1993: 135).

The previous chapter has used these data within a different methodological framework (a sociological-phenomenological perspective) to gain a greater understanding of the phenomenon of drug use and dependency itself. Both sets of research data can be seen to emphasize the relevance of the client's subjective beliefs. It is unclear how far the subject's subjective understanding contributes to the social reality of their own drug use and how far it can be seen as a function of the interaction between attributional style, (other aspects of social cognition or group belief systems are discussed in Chapter 7), but there can be little doubt that the individual's beliefs influence future drug use behaviour.

Brief interventions

Minimal or brief interventions have been used for people with alcohol problems for many years, before being developed for drug users. Robertson and Heather (1986) and Miller, Sovereign and Krege (1988) provided the first manuals for use. Dunn *et al.* (2001) update these versions. Miller has shown that this intervention can produce a 20 per cent reduction in the amount of alcohol used and, perhaps more significantly, a 7 per cent reduction in 'peak intoxication levels'. Miller *et al.* (1988) suggest that the essence of effective minimal intervention is an objective assessment of problems, an empathic quality of intervention and feedback to highlight discrepancies between desired goal and present state.

Brief interventions vary from self-help pamphlets to structured cognitive behavioural interventions by a psychologist. Heather (Heather *et al.*, 2002; Heather, 1989) has argued that the personal contact is an important aspect of brief interventions, but there is little evidence for the necessity of psychologist input. Within the field of brief interventions there is some blurring between what is considered cognitive behavioural psychology and what is simply giving information. Information and advice giving can involve cognitive behavioural methods such as behavioural monitoring (Heather, 1989) whereas basic education techniques can be described in cognitive behavioural terms.

There is also debate about the aims of brief interventions. If 'early intervention' methods, such as information and cognitive behavioural techniques, are seen in a preventive light this itself raises methodological issues. It should perhaps be asked whether epidemiological population measures of incidence and prevalence might not be more appropriate to assess early intervention methods rather than studies of treatment outcome. Although research indicates that non-serious drinkers can be helped to control their drinking at an 'early stage' (Edwards, 1986), the research cannot distinguish between those who will progress to a 'later' stage and those whose drinking would not become harmful at all. Edwards himself was increasingly unsure of the comprehensiveness and validity of early outcome data and the wisdom of excluding many aspects of dependence in favour of those emphasized by the now popular cognitive behavioural perspective (Edwards, 1989a).

However, despite the influence of the cognitive behavioural perspective, the notion of sequential stages of dependency, which seems integral to behavioural notions of early intervention, is not derived from social learning theory itself. It is here, as might be expected, that psychologists would question the integrated approach. Hodgson, in an article entitled 'The alcohol dependence syndrome: a step in the wrong direction' (Hodgson, 1980), criticizes the notion of a syndrome as too medical (although he does concede that the concept of a dependence state is valid) and yet if there is no sequential syndrome then the rationale for early intervention is less apparent. Not all academics feel that the concept of a continuum of dependence is necessary to prove the worth of brief interventions. Heather (1989) argued that if these techniques serve to reduce drinking at any time then they serve a useful purpose, whether or not dependence was a likely outcome.

Relapse prevention

Cognitive behavioural techniques have also been developed to help prevent relapse. These include self-monitoring, relapse fantasies and behavioural assessment methods to assess the relative risks of particular moods and situations. Clients are informed about the immediate and delayed effects of substances. Information is gained from clients through descriptions of past relapses and rehearsal of possible future relapses. In addition to teaching clients to be self-aware and able to assess risks, relapse prevention techniques also offer skills and coping strategies including relaxation training, stress management and efficacy-enhancing imagery (Witkiewitz and Marlatt, 2006; Heather *et al.*, 2002; Dunn *et al.*, 2001). These methods are discussed in Chapter 9.

The disease perspective

This perspective has developed from the belief that alcoholism is a physical and spiritual disease, which was the cornerstone of the creation of Alcoholics Anonymous in the United States in the 1930s. The concept was later enlarged and expanded to include all chemical dependence and the model is now encapsulated in the philosophy and methods of the Narcotics Anonymous groups in Britain and America and has been developed into what is called the Minnesota Method of therapy. The essence of this approach is that the affected individual has to experience a spiritual conversion and a moral transformation to cure the 'disease'. The cure can only be achieved through total abstinence.

Some 25 years after the creation of Alcoholics Anonymous, Jellinek, in his book *The Disease Concept of Alcoholism* (1960), argued that alcoholism could be regarded as a physical disease and treated accordingly: although his analysis was not entirely consistent with the philosophy of AA, it was incorporated into their perspective. Jellinek is therefore often understood as providing the evidence for the spiritual disease model. He categorized some forms of alcohol problems as diseases but also stressed that there were many different kinds which did not fit into these categories. Jellinek's notion of the 'gamma' form of alcoholism became most influential in the field, together with the idea that alcoholism was a unitary disease. These concepts reinforced and maintained AA, but the success of AA itself also helped; the mutually reinforcing elements of Jellinek's work and AA are of interest as it is these that kept the disease model alive. Some of Jellinek's work was taken further by Glatt (1972) and incorporated into a wider treatment programme.

Recent trials have given more indication of the success of the 12-step, disease approach (Groh *et al.*, 2009; Walitzer *et al.*, 2009; Zemore and Kaskutas, 2008; Timko and Debenedetti, 2007; Moos, 2007 and Bodin and Romelsjo. 2006). The model has been found to be particularly successful in building social networks (Davey-Rothwell *et al.*, 2008) and in providing social support (Gyarmathy and Latkin, 2008), and particularly in supporting the whole family (Copello *et al.*, 2009; Elliott *et al.*, 2005a, 2005b). However belief in this approach has been found to increase drop out from other types of programme (McKellar *et al.*, 2006).

The basic beliefs of the Anonymous Fellowship can be found in two texts, *Alcoholics Anonymous* (Anonymous, 1976) and *The Little Red Book* (Anonymous, 1970). Narcotics Anonymous is one of five self-help groups within the Fellowship. The other four are Alcoholics Anonymous (for alcohol addicts), Al Anon (for families of alcoholics), Alateen (for the teenage children of alcoholics) and Families Anonymous (for the families of drug addicts). Alcoholics Anonymous is by far the largest and has a longer history (founded in 1935); others have developed more recently as offshoots from the original Fellowship. Dependence on any type of drug is referred to as 'chemical dependency' and Narcotics Anonymous is recommended by American authors for a variety of different types of drug use. For example, Elliot *et al.* (2005a) and Millman (1988), recommend this approach for cocaine abusers.

The premise underlying this approach is that the 'addict' is not normal, that they suffer from an illness of the whole person. The addict is seen as having three characteristics: a physical allergy to alcohol and/or other drugs, an 'addictive personality' (described as immature and self-centred) and a spiritual sickness. The client is seen as an addict rather than a person who has an alcoholic disease. Chemical dependency is defined as a primary disease which causes other problems; it can involve dependence on one or a range of drugs.

Members of NA are recommended to attend regular meetings of the Anonymous Fellowship, to read regularly its approved literature and to work the Twelve Steps for recovery. As noted above, the disease model of addiction can be applied to families. It is important to emphasize that addictive disease is conceived of as different to physical addiction and therefore also identified in different ways. Only a certain proportion of the population are considered vulnerable (approximately 10 per cent). Various authors have attempted to describe the programme; perhaps the most accessible account is that of Kurtz (n.d.) *'Not God': A History of Alcoholics Anonymous.*

The Minnesota Method is founded on the basic premises of Alcoholics Anonymous and Narcotics Anonymous. This method is usually applied in residential settings and only five of the Twelve Steps are used before the clients are discharged into the community, where they then attend Fellowship groups in order to complete the remaining seven. There are slight differences between the emphasis of the two approaches but these are largely concerned with the intensive residential elements of the Minnesota Method. Information concerning this can be found in Lefevre (n.d.) *How to Combat Alcoholism and Addictions: The Promis Handbook on Alcoholism, Addictions and Recovery,* and Anderson (1981) *The Minnesota Experience.*

The basic assumptions are that addiction or chemical dependency is a disease and that all addicts 'should receive treatment within the same basic programme framework' (Lefevre, n.d.). The disease concept of addiction is considered relevant to gambling, risk taking, relationships and other forms of compulsive behaviour. The addict is not held personally responsible for having the illness but is held responsible for their own recovery. Initial denial is seen as symptomatic of the illness. This illness or 'addictive disease' is assumed to 'originate as a disease of the human spirit' and 'this predisposition may be genetically determined'. This disease of the spirit 'leads to a disorder of mood' and 'affects intellectual processes' (Lefevre n.d.: 45–7).

The philosophy of the Anonymous Fellowship emphasizes the contribution that non-professional ex-addicts make to the recovery of others in both residential and day-care facilities. There is much controversy about the working relationship between professionals and non-professionals in non-statutory agencies and in residential treatment. Zemore and Kaskutas (2008) and Kostyk *et al.,* (*1993*) found that non-professional ex-addicts can be effective co-leaders in therapeutic groups and provide useful role models by offering hope and optimism, however McKellar *et al.,* (2006) and Orford *et al.,* (2009b) found problems in people believing dogmatically in the disease approach.

The Twelve Step treatment process

The following gives a brief description of the Twelve Steps of the therapeutic programme based on this model. The quotes are taken from anonymous booklets and pamphlets published in connection with Narcotics Anonymous and the Anonymous Fellowship, generally published by Hazelden, City Centre, Minnesota.

Step One: powerlessness   Step one is probably the most significant part of the process. The essence of the step is that clients should believe or accept that they are an addict and that they are powerless over their lives as a result (i.e. admit that their lives are unmanageable). If clients do not accept this interpretation of their experience the treatment process cannot proceed. This stage is often referred to as 'breaking denial'. The beliefs of clients in the initiation stages of treatment appear to be of particular relevance to later attitudes and behaviour (Keene, 1994).

Step One refers to 'the foundation of recovery' and involves members coming to an understanding of their own powerlessness. 'We admitted we were powerless over drugs and that our lives had become unmanageable.' The notion of disease and powerlessness is also linked to the notion of responsibility for one's own recovery. This may appear to be paradoxical, but is explained within the NA philosophy in the following way: 'personal responsibility for addiction occurs when we have recognized it in our self, or others have pointed out the symptoms to us, and we realize we are afflicted with a disease. It then becomes our responsibility to start a recovery programme'.

Step One then integrates the concept of unmanageability with the notion of powerlessness. 'Personal unmanageability relates to our attitudes and beliefs ... In many cases, personal unmanageability was present many years before chemical addiction.' The concepts of powerlessness and unmanageability are linked to the idea of an 'addictive personality' which can only be controlled through adherence to the programme and abstinence. 'Some examples are temper tantrums, not sharing feelings and emotions honestly with others, insisting on having one's own way and the like. Such behaviour patterns enlarge and gradually take over a large part of one's personality.'

Step Two: hope   This step involves recognizing and 'coming to hope' that one has the need to and ability to change, with the help of the programme and, more importantly, with the help of a 'higher power' or 'power outside of oneself'. This step is a necessary follow-up to acceptance of powerlessness, as without hope and faith in outside help, little progress can be made. In effect the first step in isolation could be worse than useless. The notion of a higher power does not necessarily involve Christian or religious beliefs. Some solve this problem by defining their higher power as being the Anonymous Fellowship itself or their therapeutic groups, that is, without recourse to ideas of a spiritual god.

Step Three: commitment to change   This step involves not only making a commitment to change, but also 'handing yourself over to others in the programmes, that is, learning to *trust* others'. This stage involves an effort on the part of the client to stop 'controlling or manipulating others', that is, relinquishing control over both themselves and over others.

Step Four: the moral inventory   This stage involves the client writing a list of their previous character or personality defects prior to treatment. This list is referred to as a 'searching moral inventory'.

Step Five: confession   This stage involves sharing this 'moral inventory' with someone else. This is often referred to as the 'confessional' step. The benefits felt by clients are often described as very similar to religious practices.

The final steps (6–12) do not form part of the inpatient or day-centre treatment programmes, but they are part of the continued experience of the majority of those who complete the programme successfully. They take place in self-help groups after the structured treatment period. In effect, the Twelve Steps can be split into two stages: the first five steps concerned mainly with changing or converting the client, the last seven steps concerned with maintaining this change or conversion. The programme of treatment is not therefore complete without the second stage (that is, the Narcotics Anonymous equivalent of relapse prevention).

Step Six   This involves emphasizing the willingness to change and to have the higher power remove defects.

Step Seven   This step involves putting the initial commitments into action.

Step Eight   This involves becoming willing to make amends to people one has harmed.

Step Nine   Step Nine involves actually making amends, as far as this is practicable.

Step Ten   This step involves learning to take a personal moral inventory on a regular basis, that is, continually monitoring and evaluating what happens in one's life, admitting when one is wrong and changing if necessary.

Step Eleven   This involves building and improving on faith and improving one's relationship with one's higher power.

Step Twelve   The final step is considered of extreme importance, as it demands helping others, consistently reminding oneself of how bad one was and reminding oneself of the principles of the programme by teaching them to other addicts. 'Twelfth Stepping' is thought to give members 'a purpose, a social identity and self-respect' and is seen as an integral part of recovery and sobriety.

Although this description attempts to give an overall picture of the Twelve Step process, at present we have little understanding of what actually happens in these programmes or why an approach at odds with both the methods and beliefs of contemporary British academic and professional consensus should survive and flourish alongside its scientifically credible opponents (Moos, 2008; Moos *et al.*, 1990). Information is usually acquired experientially by 'working the programme', with the consequent internalization of the belief system on which it is based. Reports by 'insiders' are often more concerned with promulgating this philosophy than objectively analysing the perspective. Those who have not gone through this process themselves are often critical, citing lack of research evidence, but have little understanding of how the treatment functions. The exception is the work of Moos *et al.* (1990) and Denzin (1986, 1987a, 1987b) who carried out intensive qualitative studies of Alcoholics Anonymous. The outcome research carried out by 'outsiders' has done little more than show that this approach is no more or less effective than any other (Cook, 1988; Moos *et al.*, 1981, 1990).

The disease perspective incorporates an essential commitment to abstinence and there is some evidence to indicate that commitment to abstinence influences likelihood of relapse; Hall, Havassy and Wasserman (1990) followed up subjects for twelve weeks after treatment for alcohol, opiate and nicotine dependence and found that commitment to complete abstinence was related to lower risk and a longer time until relapse.

The wider interest of this perspective is, however, that it deals specifically with the factors known to be correlated with relapse: emotions, relationships and social norms. It also takes into account the social factors correlated with successful treatment and long-term maintenance of change, such as relationships with family and social support systems. The programme also emphasizes the importance of the sequential nature of the individual recovery process. In addition this approach has identified issues such as uncontrollability, poor impulse control and lack of restraint, which have been highlighted in studies of the effects of drug use on the brain through developing neuroscience research.

It is important to point out that the Twelve Step model combines those components which have been found to be useful with those which have not. For example, the ideology of the Anonymous Fellowship has been unacceptable to many of those who have sought its help. The author's research indicates that the 50 per cent drop-out rate can largely be attributed to this source (Keene and Raynor, 1993) and the moral/spiritual content can also prevent initial self-referral and noncompliance during treatment (Keene, 1994). In addition, the evidence for the effectiveness of the following aspects of the programme is limited: group therapy (Frank, 1974), individual counselling (Miller and Hester, 1986a), lectures/videos and attendance at AA/NA self-help groups (Miller and Hester, 1986b). The success of AA and the Minnesota Method is therefore, as might be expected, no greater than any other treatment approach (Project MATCH Research Group, 1997; Moos *et al.*, 1990).

The consensus of professional opinion in Britain is similar to those professionals and public health campaigners of the late nineteenth and early twentieth centuries, who disagreed with the developing moral/pathological approach to addiction. The situation is different in North America where the 'spiritual disease' model and the Minnesota Method provide the dominant theory and method (Sanchez-Craig, 1990).

There is a substantial body of literature which criticizes this particular disease perspective, for example, Heather and Robertson (1981, 1986) and Fingarette (1988). Robinson (1979) has discussed AA self-help groups in detail and Cook (1988) has reviewed the literature. Frank (1974, 1981) and Antze (1979) have taken a more independent view of the therapeutic processes. Kurtz (n.d.) and Denzin (1987a, 1987b) have attempted overviews, but these texts can seem to be biased in favour of the underlying assumptions of the perspective itself. In contrast Moos (2008) and Moos *et al.* (1990) have attempted comparisons which indicate that this approach may be as effective as the alternatives because of the social support and after-care offered.

However, as the notion of dependence as a unitary disease is questioned by both the psychiatric profession and behavioural psychologists, Jellinek's theory and AA therapy have become less influential in some countries and are seldom referenced in contemporary British journals. As Lindstrom (1992) points out, 'Jellinek's working hypothesis had a salutary effect on alcohol research. Today many researchers regard it as a principal obstacle to the advancement of knowledge and the emergence of interdisciplinary approaches to alcoholism' (p. 54). This is unfortunate as Jellinek had identified important aspects of alcohol dependence and treatment which have been largely ignored in statutory British services.

It is interesting that much of the literature criticizing this approach is largely preoccupied with examining the theoretical reasons why it should not be effective, rather than considering the reasons why it is effective in many cases. The approach is poorly represented in British journals or edited collections and only mentioned in passing in literature reviews. Yet the Anonymous Fellowship and the Minnesota

Method underpin much American treatment and AA has established self-help networks in most countries (Alcoholics Anonymous, 1981). It therefore seems strange that the concept has been subject to so little study. As Bratt (1995) stated, 'writing about alcoholism and leaving out what the Americans have to say on the matter would be like writing about Communism and ignoring the lessons from Russia' (quoted in Lindstrom, 1992: 10). Twelve Step advocates are themselves equally dogmatic in their criticism and dismissal of alternative approaches, particularly behavioural psychology, as Marlatt and Fingarette found out to their cost in the USA, when their early work was heavily criticized.

Different drug treatment models: doing the same things but defining them differently?

For those clients who do want to reduce or stop using drugs and are looking for drug treatment, it will be apparent that any of the main approaches will provide a great deal of help and support. Those clients who want to learn to control their drug use and to reduce their dosage over time may prefer a psychologically based or medical service; those who can accept that they are addicts and become abstinent may prefer to comply with the demands of the Twelve Step programme and receive the long-term social support offered by the Narcotics Anonymous self-help networks.

Those in statutory services in the UK seldom use the word 'addiction', but are concerned instead with control of drug use and the associated problems. This is in direct contrast to many self-help and other services in the residential and private sectors which are usually abstinence orientated and may utilize a Twelve Step or similar abstinence model, dealing with the 'primary' problem or disease of 'addiction' itself.

This strange coexistence of contradictory approaches is better understood when the short-term objectives and methods of both are examined. Most drug counsellors of whichever persuasion have an eclectic approach to treatment, using a range of different counselling methods. The objectives and methods in different models are to some extent very similar, though the sequence of steps will vary, the abstinence-orientated models insisting on abstinence first, rather than as the ultimate goal.

The aims and beliefs of each service are obviously of some interest to clients, but whether they are of practical significance is less clear. Drug workers will be well aware that many clients have used a wide range of different types of service and will often use two types one after the other (for example, moving from day centre to residential agency) or two types together (if they need drug treatment from a community drug team once a week, but also want the 24-hour support offered by self-help NA networks). This is a curious situation which has for a long time passed unquestioned by workers in the field: that whereas a single consistent theory is very important to professionals, it is not particularly important for clients themselves.

This is may be partly explained in terms of the practical services provided by each different approach. In effect what clients receive is actually very similar, whichever agency they attend. This is because most services provide the same core components of treatment, together with psychological and social support, whichever model provides the rationale.

Theoretical and research issues

Treatment effective in the short term, but not in the long term

Whilst a range of treatment models are relatively successful in reducing dependence in the short term, these changes are often not maintained at follow-up. Researchers have not yet succeeded in distinguishing between the efficacy of different treatment perspectives, in identifying the effective components of successful short-term treatment or in explaining the reasons for relapse (loss of treatment gains) in the period following treatment.

Drug treatment programmes have been shown to work best if they have adequate staff levels and quality assurance procedures (Keene *et al.*, 2004), but most significantly, if they have adequate follow-up (McCaughrin and Price, 1992). It is well documented that addictive problems are highly susceptible to recurrence following successful intervention (West and Gossop, 1994; Somers and Marlatt, 1992). This lack of evidence for long-term treatment effects is similar in both the drug and alcohol fields. Lindstrom, in reviewing alcohol treatment, states that, 'Controlled studies of outcome criteria have generally demonstrated only weak and short-term effects of alcoholism treatment ... with virtually no effects remaining after one or two years' (p. 30). Lindstrom points out that the studies of treatment with positive results are those with little treatment follow-up. He lists a range of studies illustrating loss of treatment effect over time (for example, Valliant, 1983). A comparison of studies from two distinct time periods (1952–72) and 1978–1983) by Riley *et al.*, (1987) could find no evidence in either period, amongst old or new treatment models, of long-term treatment gains.

Little difference in effectiveness between treatment models

There are difficulties in distinguishing between the effects of different models, as all appear equally effective (Project MATCH Research Group, 1997). The major American MATCH study in the 1990s found little or no difference in effectiveness between the major treatment models. As early as 1977, Edwards and Orford found little difference between different treatment approaches with alcohol problems and this work is often cited as the best example of an outcome study illustrating no difference between the two options of 'treatment' and 'advice'.

Overall, variations of outcomes tend to be large within treatments and small between treatments, (Lindstrom, 1992) Although there is some indication that certain methods may be more or less effective (Hodgson, 1994), there are few data to indicate that one overall approach is better than another. Although the disease perspective requires more intensive input than a behavioural or social learning approach (see Mash and Terdal, 1976; Goldfried and Bergin, 1986), ongoing Narcotics Anonymous support is free, in the form of a countrywide network of self-help groups. On the other hand, the cognitive behavioural approach is likely to be more accessible to a wider range of clients with drug problems and to generic professionals such as health-care workers and social workers, as a social learning approach to drug and alcohol abuse and treatment often forms part of their basic training. It should be mentioned, that all therapeutic approaches can to some extend limit the type of help provided and perhaps more importantly the length of time it is provided for (Keene, 2000).

Work on individual differences and matching individual clients to different treatment models has been largely inconclusive (Project MATCH Research Group, 1997; Moos *et al.*, 1990; Keene, 1994; Marlatt, 1988). Glaser (1980) considered the implications for treatment and the possibilities of matching clients to different services, stating, 'The question is not whether similarities and differences between individuals exist – they do – but which is pre-potent in determining the outcome of treatment?' (p. 178). He makes the point that: 'In most circumstances at the present time, the similarities between individuals are assumed to be pre-potent, and hence all individuals presenting are dealt with in the same way ... which is perhaps why the matching hypothesis in most fields remains a hypothesis.' Although early researchers stressed the influence of individual differences in treatment process and outcome (McCrady and Sher, 1983; Caddy and Block, 1985), discussion of client matching has remained largely abstract and the practical implications for treatment allocation remain vague.

Core components of treatment process

There is a need to identify the influential treatment components in each different treatment approach and there has been less success in defining and comparing different treatment perspectives than in measuring other variables, perhaps due to an inability to identify the core components which differentiate between them. Although much is known of the theory and practice of cognitive behavioural models, very little is known about the core components of both 'treatment' and continuing 'recovery' in the Twelve Step model. Because of this gap in basic knowledge, very few comparative studies have yet been carried out. The exception is the MATCH study in America (Project MATCH, 1993), which itself suffers limitations in design partly due to difficulties in identifying and isolating the relevant differences between treatment models. In order to facilitate future research it may be necessary to identify and define more clearly core treatment components in each model.

Little understanding of development or aetiology

Treatment models often appear to have been developed independently of understandings of aetiology or development of dependency. As Marlatt (1988) explains, there are 'whilst various conflicting positions put forth to explain the aetiology of addiction... A one-to-one correspondence between models of aetiology and the effectiveness of various treatment modalities may not exist in the area of addiction treatment ... there is no consensus of opinion or convergence of evidence concerning the underlying cause of addiction.'

A distinction can also be drawn not only between aetiology and treatment but also between initial change and maintenance of change. Marlatt himself is particularly concerned with prevention of relapse (1985). Working in America where the disease concept of alcoholism has widespread professional acceptance, he has utilized these arguments to adapt a behavioural theory of relapse prevention to fit with the disease concept of treatment. Whatever the practicalities determining the focus of Marlatt's work, it does seem possible to distinguish the process of relapse itself from that of initial change or 'stopping' use. Relapse prevention techniques can be used to reinforce abstinence or controlled use strategies.

Importance of treatment process

In the same way that there is a lack of a coherent overview of the process of developing drug dependency and recovery, there is also a dearth of longitudinal research examining the relationship between pre-treatment, during-treatment and post-treatment factors. This has resulted in a lack of knowledge about the treatment process as a whole.

The importance of process in treatment has been emphasized by DiClemente and Prochaska (1985), Davidson and colleagues (1991) and Prochaska and DiClemente (1994), who argue that sequences or stages in the process of individual change over time may be significant in determining effectiveness of interventions. Attempts have been made to identify and measure stages of this process (Rollnick *et al.*, 1992). The negative outcomes of treatment studies and the absence of conclusive outcomes in comparative studies have led to much controversy about the relevance of the methodology which limits the subject matter to treatment outcome. The major proponent of British treatment research in the past two decades, Griffith Edwards, has himself questioned the 'usefulness of predictors of treatment outcome and indeed of the usefulness of treatment outcome as a measure at all.' (Edwards, 1988).

In the light of these findings (or lack of them), it may be important to re-focus research and adopt a different methodology, to concentrate on the two subject areas that look most promising, that is clinically useful therapeutic components and social factors within treatment and post-treatment recovery processes.

The importance of social factors

Reviews of outcome studies suggest that 'social treatment' programmes seem more successful than others (Moos 2008; Moos *et al.*, 1990). In the alcohol field, Holder *et al.* (1991), Lindstrom (1992) and Hodgson (1994) identify aspects of treatment that appear to be more useful than others, particularly social factors and improved social functioning, which prove significant in terms of pre-treatment characteristics and treatment outcome.

Feigelman and Jaquith (1992) have argued that day care should be structured to treat drug abuse as a family problem, in that it requires behavioural change in all family members. Galanter (1993) emphasizes the effectiveness of involving family and peers in a cognitive behavioural programme. Gibson *et al.* (1992) have demonstrated that family problems as a whole decrease in the first few months of drug treatment of one family member, when the patient relates better to their family and there are fewer difficulties and problems within the family. This is substantiated by Spear and Mason (1991), who compared medical insurance claims for families two years before and after treatment of one member. They found that there was a significant decrease in health claims in the whole family.

Recent reviews suggest that social programmes focusing on individual functioning, such as social skills, family relationships, etc., seem more successful than other programmes (Holder *et al.*, 1991; Hodgson, 1994). Similarly, community reinforcement programmes seem successful (Fishbein and Ajzen, 1985). Treatment gains appear to be only short term. However, while within-treatment processes are qualitatively different from maintenance of change processes, it is important to emphasize that the short-term benefits of treatment could be kept up if that treatment were continued indefinitely in some form. Maisto and Carey (1987) found that staying in treatment seems to be associated with benefits that may be maintained for some time.

The importance of social factors in after-care

While the distinction between treatment change processes and long-term maintenance of change is useful, much research indicates that social variables may be more important in long-term maintenance of change than during treatment process.

It is significant that researchers cannot identify pre-treatment and during-treatment variables which predict post-treatment functioning. Catalano *et al.* (1990/91) report that pre-treatment factors have accounted for only 10–20 per cent of variance in post-treatment relapse and that during-treatment factors have accounted for 15–18 per cent. In contrast post-treatment factors have accounted for 50 per cent of the variance in outcome. These findings indicate that post-treatment variables may be more influential in treatment success than the treatment itself. There is much evidence to suggest that the most significant post-treatment factor are social skills and social support (Cronkite and Moos, 1980; Finney *et al.*, 1980; Simpson and Sells, 1982 and Simpson and Marsh, 1986).

As Catalano *et al.* (1990/91) point out, if post-treatment factors are important, there will be a need to change the emphasis of research on to post-treatment predictors of outcome in order to address the factors which are potentially critical to post-treatment success. Catalano and his colleagues found that lack of involvement in active leisure and education and an inability of treatment clients to establish non-drug-using contacts in work and educational settings and drug cravings were all important in relapse. They suggest that cognitive behavioural skills training will help clients develop the interpersonal skills necessary in developing new social networks.

Cognitive behavioural psychologists have also found that relapse within the two years following treatment is correlated with social and emotional factors. When the psychological reasons for loss of treatment gains were examined (Marlatt and Gordon, 1985, 1980; Marlatt, 1985; Wilson, 1992), the main precursors of relapse were identified as negative emotional states, interpersonal conflict and social pressure. This provides more evidence to suggest that maintenance of treatment gains may be correlated with psychological and social factors rather than treatment variables themselves (Moos *et al.*, 1990; Lindstrom, 1992).

It may also be useful to ask which in-treatment strategies interact best with which follow-up post-treatment strategies. Saunders and Kershaw (1979), Valliant (1983), Nordstrom and Burglund (1986) and Edwards *et al.* (1987) have presented findings that indicate that social relations are a major precondition for the persistence of whatever the severely dependent drinker may have gained from treatment.

Differences between drugs

Finally, although this section reviews work from the drug field, it should be remembered that much of the literature and research on dependence and treatment is based on early work in the alcohol field. This is for several reasons: first, because theories of drug or 'chemical' dependence are largely derived from theories of alcohol dependence; second, because drug dependency treatment models are often based on models of alcohol treatment, whether behavioural or disease models; and third, much of the early research and literature in the field of dependence is concerned with alcohol. The following proviso is also necessary: to generalize about all drugs or to make generalizations on the basis of one (not necessarily representative) drug, may be problematic. Theories of dependence assume that all drugs (including alcohol) share the same characteristics whereas, in fact, drug dependence encompasses an extremely wide range of different types of dependence. It may be unwise to make statements about drug treatment as a whole and particularly to generalize, for example, from alcohol treatment to heroin or amphetamine treatment.

Fresh complications are also introduced by those clients who use a variety of different drugs (polydrug use). Although it is probably the case that some clients will prefer certain types of drugs, there are also a large proportion of polydrug users. The problems of dependence are then compounded. For example, it is fairly common for certain drugs such as depressants to be used interchangeably, for example, heroin, Methadone and alcohol. Work by Stastny and Potter (1991) and Carroll *et al.* (1993) indicates that heavy alcohol use is not uncommon among opiate addicts and cocaine users respectively.

A longitudinal study of heroin addicts twelve years after treatment shows that a quarter of a group of 298 were classified as heavy drinkers, indicating a form of substitute drug taking (Lehman *et al.*, 1990). Iguchi *et al.* (1993) have also identified illicit benzodiazepines and sedative use amongst Methadone maintenance clients. San *et al.* (1993a) found that benzodiazepine use (particularly Flunitrazepam) was common among heroin addicts. However, these authors report elsewhere (San *et al.*, 1993b) that clients on a drug-free programme consumed more of a variety of illicit substances than those in Methadone maintenance.

It seems likely that certain types or combinations of drugs are preferred by different people. This seems clear from the qualitative data earlier in the book. Other researchers have also identified this phenomenon. For example, Kidorf and Stitzer (1993) found that patients had preferences for particular groups of drugs and not others, for example, Methadone patients did not particularly like cocaine. Craig and Olson (1990) compared cocaine and heroin users and found that the latter were more likely to have anxious personalities and evidence somatic distress, whereas cocaine users demonstrated antisocial personality traits. The authors conclude that there were clear personality differences between the two groups. Unfortunately it is difficult to determine causal direction, that is, to distinguish between the effects of long-term use and the reasons for using. The qualitative data in the previous chapter indicates that some users prefer opiates to stimulants (or vice versa) but also suggest that people mix cocaine and heroin to accentuate the effects, or use heroin to ameliorate the effects of crack and some cocaine users use cocaine to ameliorate the effects of being drunk. These data do not demonstrate that users are right in their interpretations of the effects of drugs, but do indicate that users themselves attribute a range of different effects and interactive effects to different drugs.

Limitations of research

This brief overview of research above has demonstrated the controversial and in many ways unsatisfactory state of knowledge of drug use and its effective treatment. There is simply a very poor fit between research and practice. This is perhaps most evident in those issues which challenge the autonomy of the different treatment perspectives and the notion of dependence treatment itself such as the dispute between controlled drug use or abstinence. There is very little research concerned with the controlled use of drugs, even though Methadone has been prescribed for long periods, little research has been carried out on the effects of this in terms of increasing dependency or entrenched use. Whilst we know that less than one in ten long-term maintenance prescriptions lead to a treatment outcome of abstinence, we know little about the reasons why. We know little about whether controlled maintenance prescription increases or decreases entrenched use, craving, compulsion or dependency (Keene *et al.*, 2007). While it is true that outcome research on drug use where behavioural hypotheses can be tested demonstrates that these techniques can be effective in changing behaviour, it does not follow that other therapeutic regimes are less effective or ineffective. It is possible that both professionals and non-professional helpers tend to rely on what works rather on the evidence of one particular theory. Clinicians may develop their own understanding from experience rather than academic theories and scientific research. It is this experience that has led to increasing emphasis on the process of change and the importance of social factors in the maintenance of change.

It seems clear that within the field at the present time there are theories of the aetiology of dependence, treatment and relapse prevention. It cannot be taken for granted that practitioners use corresponding theories for each stage in the client's treatment process. It may be that they can select several different theories for each client, describing the development of the problem in terms of a particular theoretical perspective, and then, perhaps independently of this initial understanding of the aetiology, choose a particular understanding of a treatment process to structure their practical response. While it is no doubt true that academics would require some degree of 'fit' between a theory of aetiology and one of treatment, it is not necessarily true for either practitioners or clients in the field. It seems possible for clients to work both with therapists who take a cognitive behavioural approach and those who work with the disease perspective: it is also possible for 'eclectic' practitioners to use both. The cognitive dissonance which would be generated in many academics is also problematic for many practitioners and clients but for a certain proportion of individuals these discrepancies are not important, if they are recognized at all.

In summary, it may be useful to conceive of three layers of theory: first, that of the aetiology or development of the phenomenon; second, that of initial change or treatment; and third, that of maintenance of change or relapse prevention. These considerations have some relevance in considering the possibilities of matching clients to different treatments. In practice, perhaps the two significant stages in treatment are those of initial change and maintenance of change. It is only recently that the second stage of maintenance of change has been given serious attention.

Implications for practice

Core components of treatment

It can be seen from the descriptions of the three different models that they define problems and solutions differently. It should also be noted that they share similar objectives and have core components in common.

Common objectives

- Encourage the client to identify drug use as a serious problem and to recognize that it causes other problems.
- Examine the problems underlying and perpetuating drug use.
- Use a process model of change (either the Twelve Step process or the motivational change models of Miller and Prochaska and DiClemente).
- Encourage the client to weigh up the pros and cons of drug use and come to a decision about change.
- Encourage the client to change drug use behaviour and other aspects of their lifestyle.
- Use recognized counselling and therapeutic techniques.
- Have a structured programme involving the setting of a series of concrete goals.
- Use cognitive behavioural techniques to change attitudes and beliefs and modify behaviours.
- Offer practical help and support concerning health, housing, welfare rights, child care problems, etc.
- Teach skills and strategies for coping without drugs.
- Encourage clients to develop new leisure interests, occupations, social contacts and support networks.
- Provide some kind of relapse prevention support and teach the client relapse prevention.

Common methods

- Client-centred counselling.
- Task-centred counselling.
- Relaxation, stress management and anxiety and anger control.
- Cognitive behavioural techniques for monitoring behaviour, behaviour change and relapse prevention.
- Diversionary activities and the development of new social skills and social networks.

A major difference between the different approaches is the sequence of steps to change, in effect the abstinence-orientated approach requires abstinence to be the first step in the treatment process, whereas the psychological approach will often see abstinence as the long-term aim after a series of earlier steps designed to bring drug use under control.

It is also significant that abstinence orientated models such as the Twelve Step are unlikely to offer additional harm minimization services, either alongside or independently of treatment. Both the medical and psychological models are likely to include the option of harm minimization before and during treatment, and again if and when the client relapses (see Chapter 5).

If generic professionals choose to refer, it is sensible to consider the client's aims, and perhaps also beliefs, in recommending an appropriate agency. It is then necessary to discuss with the client whether they are likely to benefit from the more intensive therapeutic intervention and aftercare support of Twelve Step or the counselling and prescription drugs of a community drug team. Having made these decisions, they can be fairly certain that the methods used will be similar.

The importance of treatment process and motivation

Research has shown that any of the three main treatment interventions can be effective in the short term. Different methods can be used in conjunction with each other but treatment process is important, independently of the treatment model used.

The efficacy of treatment is improved if the stage of a process of change is identified and monitored for each client, as each stage requires a different intervention. It is important in assessment and treatment itself to respond appropriately at different stages in the process of developing and dealing with drug problems (see Chapter 8).

Researchers did not initially consider the significance of the **process** of therapeutic change, simply because this is difficult to measure and evaluate within the confines of behavioural science or medicine. However theories of 'motivational interviewing' and processes of change were developed by Miller (1983), and the related idea of 'stages of change' by Prochaska and DiClemente (1983, 1986). Methods of interviewing and counselling in the field were developed in the late 1980s using notions of individual change processes, apparently in the absence of any coherent theory or testable hypotheses. The notion of the importance of individual change processes was first identified in 1983 in Prochaska and DiClemente's much quoted paper 'Stages and processes of self-change of smoking: toward an integrated model of change'. Prochaska had also published a more complex account, *Systems of psychotherapy: a trans-theoretical perspective* (1979), and with DiClemente, built on the idea of trans-theoretical therapy (Prochaska and DiClemente, 1982). This work was paralleled by W.R. Miller's development of the concept of motivational interviewing. Miller's work was published in the journal *Behavioural Psychotherapy* in 1983 and again (with Sovereign and Krege) in 1988.

Whilst ideas of change process and motivational interviewing have been criticized on the grounds that they have no underpinning theory and that they are not testable (see *British Journal of Addiction*, letters and articles 1992/9), the popularity of these methods among practitioners spread rapidly in the early 1990s and now form a base for specialist and non-specialist training in drug counselling techniques (Robertson, 1991).

As a consequence of the gap between psychological researchers and Twelve Step advocates, the 'stages of change' model of Miller and Prochaska and DiClemente was been hailed as an entirely new concept in substance-use treatment. In effect the Twelve Step approach incorporates a similar theory of stages of change in the therapeutic process. Many academics were unable to explain the popularity of these two unproven methods but their relevance to practitioners can be easily understood in terms of the importance of individual differences and individual change processes to clinicians. The motivational model offers a means of integrating notions of long-term individual change with more general theories of aetiology and treatment.

It can be seen that treatment process is particularly significant in the drugs field. Chapter 8 examines in more detail the sequence of stages in treatment change process and practical methods of motivational interviewing within this context.

Aftercare: the importance of psychological and social factors in relapse prevention

It will be evident that some kind of aftercare service is essential for preventing relapse. This can involve helping clients develop psychological and social skills and/or providing a range of social support systems in the community for follow-up maintenance of treatment gains.

The implementation of coherent aftercare models is however often not an important consideration for many treatment agencies. This lack of focus on the post-treatment period may be because much treatment theory and research is based on medical or psychological models of therapeutic change and outcome, and therefore does not seriously consider how psychological skills might be developed to maintain change and prevent relapse, nor how social relationships and social context might influence both treatment and relapse.

It is important to consider the effect of social factors, not only on drug users' ability to respond to treatment interventions, but also on their ability to maintain change and prevent relapse. Perhaps the clearest exposition of the relevance of social factors in the overall picture has been that of Rudolph Moos and colleagues (1990). Moos illustrated the influence of social functioning and social environment in the maintenance of change and there has been much evidence to suggest that methods aimed at social factors and improved social functioning, are also significant in terms of both pre-treatment characteristics and treatment outcome (Hodgson, 1994; Keene, 1997b; Baer and Carney, 1993; Moos *et al.*, 1990). As early as 1975, Baekland *et al.* (1975) reviewed 400 studies and noted higher socio-economic status and social stability among clients who succeeded. These factors are discussed in detail in Chapter 7.

Social factors and the social context are particularly relevant in aftercare and it is therefore necessary to consider social theories of drug use and the implications for treatment in terms of social factors, including the influence of old and new networks of family and friends (Steinberg *et al.*, 1994). (See Chapter 9.)

The study of post-treatment relapse highlights the factors connected with treatment failure over time. Although the medical definition of dependence involves tolerance, withdrawals and craving, research has provided little evidence that any of these factors are correlated with relapse or more generally with attempts to stay off alcohol and drugs (Somers and Marlatt, 1992; Wilson, 1992; West and Gossop, 1994). Craving itself has not been found to be a primary precipitant of lapses (Ludwig, 1972; Marlatt and Gordon, 1985; Drummond *et al.*, 1990). Instead, the main precursors of relapse have been identified as psychological and social. This is reflected in the reasons given for relapse among users themselves, the respondents in Chapter 2 clearly believed that the main influences on relapse were social, whether personal relationships with friends and partners (Steinberg *et al.*, 1994) or wider issues such as homelessness and unemployment. These issues are examined in more detail in Chapter 7, and the implications for practice outlined in Chapter 9.

The first element of relapse prevention and after-care is the development of individual cognitive behavioural skills (Marlatt and Gordon, 1985). The second element is the development of social support networks with social skills training (Catalano and Hawkins, 1985). Both elements rely on an accurate assessment of each individual's needs and resources post-treatment, and the consequent ability to help with a range of social, psychological and health needs. These can range from teaching clients to recognize drug-taking cues to improving housing and employment prospects, from building up social networks to dealing with stress or avoiding stressful situations. Risk of relapse is highest in the first 6–12 months after treatment, particularly in the first three months. There are different kinds of relapse, from one slip to a full return to old patterns of behaviour and social groups. There is more chance of success with swift re-intervention after the relapse (Brown, 1979; Brown and Ashery, 1979; Hawkins and Catalano, 1985). There is also evidence that self-help groups, networking and skills training help minimize relapse (Nurco *et al.*, 1983; Hawkins and Catalano, 1985).

As emphasized earlier, we have something to learn from each of the different treatment perspectives. The contribution of the disease perspective of NA is knowledge about the importance of social context in after-care. In America the Twelve Step programme of the Anonymous Fellowship integrates after-care into the actual treatment process and extends the period of 'treatment recovery' over several years (the average length of attendance at AA is 5–6 years). This period of recovery includes the provision of structured social support networks in the after-care or post-treatment period. In Britain we lack any structured pattern of after-care provision and need alternatives to the self-help after-care of the Anonymous Fellowship, which will fit better with the cognitive behavioural and harm minimization approaches.

It is important to remember that it is possible to use cognitive and behavioural methods for relapse prevention, irrespective of the theoretical interpretation of the problem (see guidelines in Chapter 9.) In the same way it is possible to give social and life skills training and help in developing social support networks independently of any theoretical beliefs about dependence.

Additional notes

Co-morbidity or dual diagnosis

Co-morbidity or 'dual diagnosis' is generally understood to mean a mental health problem and a substance misuse problem together. Professionals became concerned at the incidence of 'co-morbidity' in the 1980s (Kandel, 1982; Deakin *et al.*, 1987) and have increasingly focused research on drug use and mental health problems (Woogh, 1990; Brach *et al.*, 1995; Luke *et al.*, 1996; Mueser *et al.*, 1998). Interest has also broadened to include the wide range of multiple psychological and social problems encountered by dual diagnosis patients in terms of psychological, social and community functioning (Luke *et al.*, 1996).

For example, Mowbray *et al.* (1999) found that dual diagnosis patients had serious economic and employment problems, poor living arrangements, family and social relationships that were limited or subject to conflict and many had criminal records. Sloan and Rowe (1995) also found that dual diagnosis was associated with high rates of homelessness, disconnection from social support systems, unemployment and vocational disability and treatment chronicity.

There is difficulty in identifying causal direction between these problems. That is, one type of problem, such as depression, may be seen as a consequence of another, such as drug use or *vice versa*. For example, it is possible that drugs prescribed for mental health reasons can lead to dependency problems. Landry *et al.* (1991) suggest that patients attending treatment for anxiety disorders are commonly prescribed psychoactive drugs which can lead to dependence if not carefully monitored. Similarly, Khantzian (1985) suggests that illicit drug users may be self-medicating (knowingly or unknowingly) for problems of anxiety or depression and that individuals use drugs adaptively to cope with intensive adolescent-like anxiety. He formulates a self-medication hypothesis, proposing that drug users will select drugs which will 'medicate' their dominant painful feelings. It is also possible that illicit drug users may be self-medicating for behavioural problems such as aggressive and/or violent behaviour. Again there are problems in determining whether behavioural problems are an effect of drug use and withdrawals or whether they predate them. For example, Powell and Taylor (1992) showed that hostility and anger were common among opiate users after withdrawal. It does not, of course, follow that there is a causal relationship at work here. Substance misuse may result from mental illness, it may cause a mental illness or a common factor may be responsible for both, or a reciprocal relationship may exist in which the two sets of problems influence one another in a synergistic manner (Toombs, 2000).

It is perhaps the relationship between depression and substance use that is most significant to practitioners (Paton *et al.*, 1977; Deakin *et al.*, 1987). Many clients will say that they used drugs (or alcohol) because they were depressed and that therefore it is the underlying depression that needs to be treated, whereas others will see depression as a consequence of their drug use. It is of course likely that each contributes to the other in a worsening spiral of problems but in terms of practical assessment, it is very important to distinguish between the two as the type of problem will determine the type of intervention (Ilgen *et al.*, 2008). Although there are difficulties in determining the causal relationship, many professionals are concerned at the incidence of 'co-morbidity' (Kandel, 1982) and the increased incidence of depression. Deykin *et al.* (1992) have shown that among adolescents in drug treatment, the rate of depression is three times higher than in a control population and that this is linked to a very high incidence of physical and sexual abuse and neglect in the histories of depressive drug users. Magruder-Habib *et al.* (1992) have shown that those at highest risk of suicide were women using a range of non-narcotic drugs. They found that if clients felt suicidal tendencies soon after treatment these would be more likely a year later and that this was related to relapse.

Co-morbidity or dual diagnosis is associated with poor prognosis, higher relapse and more non-compliance, service costs are greater and clinical and social outcomes are worse. (Kranzler and Rosenthal, 2003; Crawford *et al.*, 2003; Keene 2001, 1997b). Co-morbid patients have traditionally received care from two different sets of professionals in parallel treatment systems (Drake *et al.*, 1998). This has practical implications in terms of therapeutic intervention, as what is believed to be good practice for dealing with dependence may be at odds with treatment of depression and other mental health problems where pre-scribed drugs are considered beneficial. There are particular treatment issues concerned with the psychiatric models of care and the disease/abstinence approach to dependence. Dermott and Pyett (1994) recom-mend that conflicts over conceptualization should be resolved; while this is most improbable, it is important to recognize the likely conflicts between psychiatrists and disease model adherents, and negotiate working relationships that take the differences in belief and practice into account. In addition to these problems, Kofoed (1993) outlines the difficulty of working with these complex patients over time, sug-gesting that different types of treatment intervention should be planned in a structured way through the treatment and recovery process.

The issue is sometimes (though rarely) resolved by providing services for both problems (Ilgen *et al.*, 2008). Saxon and Caslyn (1995) exam-ine treatment and conclude that dual diagnosis patients may initially perform more poorly than substance-only diagnosis patients in sub-stance dependence treatment. However, in the presence of psychiatric care they eventually exhibit comparable success. Whilst Hall and Farrell (1997) examine possible future developments that highlight the importance of maintaining and developing existing mental health services, Bellack and Gearon (1998) point out that whilst there is wide-spread agreement of the need to integrate psychiatric and substance abuse treatment, there are at present no programmes based on reliable empirical findings. Though some evaluations of coordinated service pro-vision have shown this to be more effective (Ilgen *et al.*, 2008; Moggi *et al.*, 1999), there is little substantial evidence to support this claim, particularly for evidence in relation to populations with severe psychotic disorders. A recent Cochrane review of treatment trials for this group highlights the lack of evidence for specialist co-morbid teams over standard mainstream care (Cochrane Collaboration).

Proposals for future development include new patterns of joint working between mental health and drug services (Holland 1999; Hall and Farrell, 1997). Hall and Farrell propose an approach of closer working, where there is greater skills sharing and liaison between agencies. It is has been suggested that in the light of extent of co-morbidity and of potential dual agency service use, it may be useful to develop a more broad based response to this client group and develop capacity in 'mainstream' services. For example, it may be effective to develop and evaluate specialist substance misuse services within mental health services, (focusing on inpatient populations and those clinical sub-groups where the incidence of co-morbidity is found to be greatest). However, the proportion of mental health clients in substance misuse agencies is far higher than the proportion of substance misuse clients in mental health agencies. It would therefore also be necessary to prioritize, resource and develop services within substance misuse agencies themselves.

Mainstream systems for developing inter-agency and inter-professional collaboration might include case management and care pathway approaches. Weaver *et al.* (2003) and Marsden *et al.* (2000) highlight the opportunities that exist for improved coordination between addiction, general medical and specialist mental health services. A first step to improving mainstream services would be to provide substance misuse training (including identification and management of co-morbidity) for staff in mental health services and mental health training for staff in substance misuse agencies. These developments would be facilitated where a single organization encompasses both mental health and substance misuse services. Finally, whilst evidence for the effectiveness of specialist teams is equivocal, there is little research on other forms of intervention. There is a need for longitudinal and comparative studies of a range of different types of intervention and a range of different outcome measures including harm minimization, Methadone mainte-nance, and/or treatment aftercare.

How common are co-morbidity and dual diagnosis?

The present combination of fragmented and uncoordinated services provides not only challenges to treating the problem, but also to researching it. Clinical studies have identified co-morbid clients receiving treatment in mental health populations at approximately 3 per cent (Watkins *et al.*, 2001; Brach *et al.*, 1995; Woogh, 1990). The alternative approach using epidemiological methods and general population studies, has resulted in a variation of findings (Luke *et al.*, 1996), though it is clear that all studies show much higher rates of co-morbidity than would occur by chance (Crawford *et al.*, 2003; Regier *et al.*, 1990).

The methodological limitations of research in co-morbidity have been summarized by Crawford *et al.* (2003). These include: differing definitions of co-morbidity and criteria for diagnosis of both mental illness and substance misuse; different settings for studies and different definitions of treatment and interventions (resulting in many different combinations of problems, setting and intervention). For these reasons little is known about the present extent of co-morbidity, as many agencies do not assess clients and may be unaware of which clients attend other agencies (Weaver *et al.*, 2003; Keene, 2001a.) That is, whilst we know something of the extent of clinically assessed co-morbidity in a range of different treatment populations, we know little about the numbers of co-morbid clients in substance misuse agencies actually receiving psychiatric care, or of co-morbid mental health patients receiving substance misuse agency care.

Conventional methods of monitoring co-morbidity have traditionally been limited to treatment samples in particular agencies (Kranzler and Rosenthal, 2003), or wider public health surveys of geographical populations. Reviews of research identify a range of studies of the extent of assessed need, but there is little work on overall shared care populations across different agencies or service take-up (Havassy *et al.*, 2004; Crawford *et al.*, 2003.)

Keene (2005b) determined the actual extent of dual agency provision for co-morbid clients. Of the total population of drug agency clients in one English county (N = 1,206), 28 per cent had received mental health services. For a total mental health population (N = 19,029), 2 per cent had received specialist drug services. Two-thirds of 'dual agency co-morbid' clients were male, 40 per cent had attended A&E and half had been mental health inpatients.

For the mental health care population as a whole, Farrell *et al.* (1998) and Wright *et al.* (2000) estimate 10 per cent prevalence of substance misuse among a mental health population. Crawford *et al.* (2003) in a review of the co-morbidity literature conclude that many UK studies have similar estimates of drug use in mental health populations of approximately 10 per cent. This should be compared with 2–3 per cent in the mental health population receiving substance misuse services in the Keene (2005b) study and 3.4 per cent of drug users in the Weaver *et al.* (2002) study. The gap between need and service provision is partly explained by Weaver *et al.* (2002) who found that less than 5 per cent of mental health patients exhibited patterns of drug use likely to satisfy eligibility criteria for drug treatment programmes.

For drug agency care populations, approximately one-third (27 per cent) had attended mental health services. (In comparison with approximately 3 per cent of a general population attending mental health services overall (Keene, 2005b). Frischer and Akram (2000) examined a total health care population as a whole and found that 195,000 of 1.4 million had both substance misuse and mental health problems (14 per cent). Weaver *et al.* (2003) found that 75 per cent of drug agency clients and 85 per cent of alcohol agency clients had some kind of mental health problem in past year, Schukit *et al.* (1997) found that 60 per cent had a mental health or psychological problem and Regier *et al.* (1990) found that 5 per cent of those with a drug also had a mental health problem. When specific psychiatric disorders are identified Farrell *et al.* (1998) found that 45 per cent of drug users had a serious psychiatric disorder rather than a mental health problem. Marsden *et al.* (2000) found that more than a third of opiate users had some form of serious psychoticism and 20 per cent had had psychiatric treatment within two years.

Finally although many researchers have attempted to monitor levels of dual diagnosis, few studies have attempted to examine the extent of other health and social care needs associated with drug use. It is known that mental health and substance misuse populations have high rates of contact with Accident and Emergency departments; Keene *et al.* (2005) found that 29 per cent of the mental health population had attended Accident and Emergency departments, 40 per cent of drug agency and 4 per cent of alcohol clients had done so (compared to 11 per cent for the general health population). These findings may indicate a need for further research into the multiple problems and multiple service use of co-morbid populations.

Chapter 4

Drug Users' Perspectives on Health Risks

Introduction

Whilst the previous chapters have focused specifically on dependency, this chapter will examine different kinds of risks and problems associated with drug use other than dependency. Drug users here talk about harmful drug use, where there is a direct risk to their own physical and mental health and general well-being.

It should be remembered that the majority of drug users use on a recreational basis only and take few risks. However this book is concerned with those users who are a risk to themselves or others. There is a continuum from recreational to risky drug use and although most do not travel the distance from one to the other, some make the journey very quickly indeed. For example, some recreational users of cannabis or stimulants may be at no greater risk than a social drinker, but those who use many different drugs in an uncontrolled or chaotic manner are likely to be taking more risks than someone physically dependent on alcohol or opiates, whilst those who inject drugs may be taking life-threatening risks.

This chapter gives a picture of drug users who saw their own use as risky, chaotic or uncontrolled. These users were at risk from overdose and other physical complications but perhaps most significantly, they were particularly at risk from HIV and hepatitis B and C and also consequently at risk of transmitting these blood-borne diseases to the general population.

These respondents were drawn from different research projects over a period of several years and interviewed in many different environments, ranging from their own homes, cafes, pubs and night clubs to syringe exchanges, drug agencies and in prison. The respondents were all asked for basic information about themselves and their drug use. They were also asked how they understood the effects of drugs, why they thought they used drugs in a dangerous way, how problems developed and what kind of help they wanted.

Some recreational drug users restrict themselves to cannabis, stimulants and alcohol, and only used benzodiazepines to 'come down' after using other drugs. In contrast, the high-risk respondents used a wide range of both stimulants and depressants, sometimes using crack or cocaine and then using opiates to 'come down.' It was difficult for many of them to give an account of their drug use in the past week or predict it for the days to follow; there was often no sense of planned or controlled use. For some this was not the case at the time of the interview but they remembered recent chaotic periods when their use had been compulsive or uncontrolled. Many had periods of controlled use interspersed with periods of uncontrolled or dangerous use. It will become clear that during the latter they felt that they needed help and support.

Reasons for taking risks

Respondents were asked what they thought were the good things about drug use and the reasons why they used drugs. As with dependent users, many were confused about the causes and effects of drugs, finding it difficult to decide if depression was caused by drugs, and if so whether it was caused by long term use, the immediate come down, withdrawals or effects of long term abstinence. Most users used more than one type of drug and were often unsure what were the direct effect of each distinct drug. Similarly there was some confusion about side effects and interactive effects of different drugs.

Although users emphasized the positive physiological effects of drugs, as with dependent users, many were less concerned with hedonistic than with self-medicating functions, often saying that they used some drugs to deal with psychological problems or to deal with the side effects of other drugs. More significantly, they often described almost automatic or compulsive behaviour over which they felt they had little or no conscious control.

USING DRUGS TO COPE AND SELF MEDICATE

Respondents used drugs to cope and self medicate in the same way as dependent users.

> ❝It started when my marriage broke down. I can't see the kids. I lost my job. I feel depressed and can't cope at all sometimes. I can't face people. I feel frustrated and want to break things without drugs.

> ❝I think I am more anxious and depressed than most people, but it's a circular thing, I also get like this when I use too much.

> ❝[I use] because of depression. I take downers to take away the come-down and opiates to take away my body pain... Because I can't get doctors I have to rely on tablets because of my emotional and physical state.

Conscious reasons for use can be split into three categories – hedonistic, coping and self-medicating – although it is apparent again that respondents are confused about which are the causes and which are effects of drug use, often using some drug to ameliorate the short and long term effects of others.

RISKS OF NON-DEPENDENT DRUG USE

General risks

Most users told of bad experiences, such as feeling faint or sick and having panic attacks, while many had more serious continuing paranoia and health problems.

> ❝It depends on what you are taking. With some drug use there are only legal and health risks. If using drugs in a chaotic manner, then there are risks, for example, crime to get money, needle sharing; however, needle exchanges are open so this can be done safely. There is always the risk of AIDS, injecting into an artery, a risk of job loss, a risk of not being able to get visas, the risk of going to prison, the risk of having a prison record, etc. It is relative, it depends on the circumstances. For example, parents, job, etc.

> ❝You always take risks when you take drugs because it is illegal and there are always health risks. It is not risky if you buy off people you know and don't take too much and stop when you have had enough. I have had problems associated with drug use. I have been busted for possession and have had health problems. I always smoke at home and I don't carry drugs with me. I have seen lots of other people with problems because of drugs and I have seen people being busted, people have died who have overdosed, suffered relationship breakdowns and beaten up.

Compulsion and lack of control

Most of these respondents had experienced some kind of drug-related difficulty. The main fears were of contracting HIV or hepatitis and other health hazards. These were followed by compulsion, uncontrollability, changes to personality or behaviour and changes to relationships and social life.

It can be seen below that the respondents were aware that their drug use was risky, many giving graphic details about risks they had taken. But it is less easy to determine if they have an accurate view of the particular risks associated with, for example, using drugs while intoxicated and mixing drugs.

> 66Once you've injected you can't take it any other way. I want it more and more but I hate the drug now, I'm ashamed of doing it. I can't walk around with a T-shirt on [injection sites visible].

> 66If I pick up any drug, whatever it is – alcohol, drugs, computer games, gambling – I don't know when I'll put it down and it will mess up my life in the meantime. Something triggers me off, but I do not know what it is.

> 66It is not just giving up the drugs but it is getting out of the drug circle. I feel like a coward. I am not addicted to speed, and can give it up. I have always prided myself on my fighting ability but I can't say no.

Health-related risks

> 66Infections on the arms and legs where you inject.

> 66You mess up veins and get veins blocked with bad drugs. I had thrombosis and my leg swelled up and was extremely painful.

> 66Overdosing, people also buy stuff that they don't know what it is mixed with. I was always getting ill.

> 66At one time I let someone inject me with amphetamines and I was taken to hospital as a result and almost died. I thought he was injecting me with street speed but I just don't know what it could have been.

> 66Afraid to go to bed in case I go unconscious and then am sick.

> 66You get lot of trouble with chest infections and lot of flu.

HIV and hepatitis

> 66I got jaundice and went yellow. We all got hepatitis before they gave free needles and things.

> 66I've caught hepatitis B from unsafe sex and I thought I had AIDS. But I never take any risks. I always clean spoon before and after jacking up. I have shared needles but I was lucky. Don't use same needle. I know so many dealers from prison I know who to trust.... the ones that use speed themselves are the ones to watch.

Many respondents gave reasons for sharing needles and syringes:

66I had no money for clean works and I missed the needle exchange.

66The chemist was closed.

66We were stoned.

66I was in prison.

Psychological risks

66I have suffered from depression from taking drugs.

66I have had paranoia, I suffer regularly from paranoia when on drugs. I think all drugs can cause paranoia.

66[When I was taking drugs] I had voices in the head, paranoia, fear. I was still having panic attacks up to six to eight months ago. They've stopped now.

Social risks

66The loss of my marriage; wariness of friends. Unpredictability, that type of thing. Paranoia, people are wary of me. Family problems, in loss of communication with my family.

66I was doing criminal offences, burglary, to get money for drugs. It would have got me into trouble in the end.

66I'm afraid all the time. I can't pay back what I owe. I have to deal because I owe money to make it up.

66There is a risk of falling into debt and getting threatened.

66If something goes wrong you can't call the police like normal people.

POSSIBLE SOLUTIONS: WHAT CLIENTS THINK THEY NEED

The following section examines the views of respondents about the kinds of help needed for the problems identified above – health problems, risks of HIV and hepatitis, periods of chaotic uncontrolled drug use, underlying problems and problems of coping generally. Once the different types of problem have been identified, it can be seen that a different solution may be appropriate for each. The respondents themselves suggest a range of possible solutions for different problems, from prescriptions to help stabilize drug use to basic health care facilities. The first section examines the previous attempts respondents have made themselves to change their drug use; the second considers the help they think they need from professionals.

Self-help

In contrast to dependent users, these respondents talked much more about how they could help themselves. This may be because services were often seen only as treatment for dependency and therefore they were not aware of what was available for those who were not physically dependent. However overall they had less to say about specific harm minimization services and more to say about how they could make themselves safer and take less risks and use in a less harmful way if they had access to basic information and support services.

Many respondents had made changes and most were concerned with making their drug use safer, protecting themselves from HIV and other health hazards and bringing uncontrolled drug use back within their control. Self-help here also refers to service provision such as syringe exchanges where drug users can get the information and equipment to enable them to help themselves.

HIV and hepatitis C prevention

❝Less injecting, [I] smoke or snort instead.

❝I don't share works, needles, syringes, spoons, anything.

❝I use the needle exchange.

Avoiding physical dependency and uncontrolled use

❝I withdraw myself when it gets too much, I cut right down and get back in control.

❝Cutting down due to high tolerance levels.

❝I've been wanting to stop injecting for a while, but I don't think I want to enough yet.

WHAT PROFESSIONAL HELP DO YOU THINK YOU NEED?

It can be seen that these risky drug users were concerned with reducing the risk of HIV and hepatitis B and C by ceasing to share equipment or inject. They attempted to reduce other risks associated with drug use by controlling the amount and quality of drugs used and being careful about hygiene and health issues. What they wanted was the support and resources to help them do this. When asked about medical support and healthcare, many respondents said that they did not have a GP or had not informed their GP because of fear that they would share information with other professionals, some were reluctant to attend Accident and Emergency departments where they were already known.

In essence, most drug users emphasized that they wanted information about drugs (including the interactive effects of different drugs), basic health-care support to help them to reduce the risks and damage and more intensive support at particular times when their drug use or life-style got out of hand and became too difficult to manage on their own. Most saw themselves as fairly independent and in control of their lives most of the time, but dependent on the provision of clean equipment and health care support.

Respondents attending drug agencies for harm minimization also described their need for prescription to regain control of their drug use, help them to cope and self-medicate. They also felt that prescribed drugs were useful to help them stabilize their drug use and stop using in risky, chaotic or uncontrolled ways. Several individuals appreciated access to a psychologist for anxiety and anger control, but the majority wanted some kind of help and advice for social problems particularly welfare benefits, debt management, training and employment.

It should be emphasized that many comments below reflect respondents' ambivalence about drugs, seeing them as a solution yet also causing further problems. Although some clients did not know what was wrong with them or what kind of help they needed, if they were not physically dependent, they often wanted help to reduce the risks rather than give up drugs.

Information

❝I was pretty ignorant, did not know what was happening

❝I started to use [heroin] to come down from crack, I didn't realise what was wrong.

Reducing the risk of HIV and hepatitis

❝I need clean works, that's all, nothing else, no counselling, no do-gooding.

❝I just need clean works and perhaps a script when I get into trouble.

❝I go down the chemist's to buy needles and syringes or I get them off my friends.

Basic health care

❝It would be good to be able to see a nurse when you need some help, the GPs are no good, they won't ever believe you about anything.

❝The veins can get blocked and infected, it would be useful to be able to get antibiotics and painkillers without the usual trouble with doctors … in fact it would be good to have a doctor in the first place!

❝Abscesses are a problem, but you don't like to go and get something as people will know.

Practical help

❝I have never been homeless, I'm not a junkie, but it would be useful to get some practical help with prescriptions even if it's just Temazepam, when you need it.

❝I need to move from a one-bed-roomed house that's like a shoebox. I want someone to help me manage my anger. I don't really know what's going on.

Prescription drugs to stabilize and maintain safer drug use

The majority of these respondents thought their primary aim was to reduce the risk of HIV., hepatitis and other risks such as infection and overdose. Respondents also wanted to stabilize their drug use. Many felt that prescribed substitute drugs would help them do this. Maintenance was seen as serving different purposes for different types of drug users. It was seen as enabling those using drugs in an uncontrolled or chaotic way to regain control of their drug use and to order their lives so that there was less risk of harm. It was also seen as providing injecting drug users a regular supply of oral drugs to help them stop injecting, and enabling those who use drugs to cope or to self-medicate to do this in a safer way.

❝I need stability. I need to be stabilized. That's why I went for a Methadone programme. I don't have to worry about drugs or money or not having enough.

❝With prescribed drugs you know what you are using, on the street it could be mixed with anything.

❝To stop me burgling chemists. To keep me out of jail because that's where I would have ended up.

Help with psychological problems

Respondents' opinions differed radically when asked about counselling services and social support. Non-dependent users did not see counselling in such a positive way as some dependent users. Those who did not attend agencies usually felt strongly that this kind of help or therapy would be very unwelcome and made many disparaging comments, whereas those who had received help with anxiety and depression felt more positive.

> 66I'm less anxious now. If I do feel uptight, wherever I am, I do my breathing exercises. If I'm in the house I listen to the tape and it does work.

> 66I've done anger management courses. It was a three-way meeting with probation. It was planned for me, with me there. It's so that if I'm ever out, it will teach me to control my temper better. They stimulate situations that might occur. They look at what started the argument, where you could stop. Every argument is either win or lose. They said it could also be win/win where both sides are happy but I can't understand this.

> 66She [clinical psychologist] allows you to own the damage done to you. She looks at messages from childhood, feelings of abandonment, patterns and how I allowed all these things to happen. It relieves the blaming of myself.

> 66She's giving me faith in myself. It's nurturing, gentle – very different. She gives me support and invites me to see my own way. I'm looking at childhood issues and core issues ... I'm dealing with the emotional crisis.

Irrelevance of counselling and psychology

> 66The groups are really naff, nobody takes it seriously, what's it for anyway?

> 66I don't want to offend him [syringe exchange worker], after all he's only trying to help, but I can't see the point. [laughs]

> 66We have a chat, he gives me the week's works [needles and syringes], he asks if I want any counselling ... I want a script but I don't want all the rest of the palaver, so I don't bother with the script.

> 66[A friend] gets our works for us each week, he doesn't mind going to [drug agency], but most of us don't go, it's for nutters really.

THE IMPORTANCE OF A HARM MINIMIZATION SERVICE

Despite criticisms of some aspects of service provision most respondents were very clear that harm minimization provision was an essential part of their lives.

❝Before I used to share [needles and syringes] at least sometimes, now I know I've got works at home, I can wait.

❝At least the nurse will clean up wounds and things and give me antibiotics.

❝My confidence, my self-esteem. I've put on a lot of weight and I feel 100% better.

❝I plan things more, I don't run out of works or store drugs so I don't take unnecessary risks.

Discussion

This chapter has examined the reasons why people use drugs and the damage associated with this use. Although it is clear that many risky drug users still use for pleasure this is complicated by other reasons for using. Many say that they no longer get any pleasure at all, that the drug use is purely functional. Respondents explained risk taking in two main ways, first a feeling of compulsion to use and lack of control over their own behaviour and second, the need to use in order to cope.

The feeling of craving or a compulsion to use was often difficult for respondents to describe, many saying that they did not understand themselves and often did not remember making the decision to use:

❝It just sort of happened and there I was... I don't know, can't explain.

The use of drugs to cope or self-medicate may lead to more serious problems, as the user may become psychologically dependent on the drug as a remedy or solution and so use increasing amounts on a regular basis. This in turn leads to problems caused by the drug itself and the consequent self-medication of these problems by using more drugs. So, for example, respondents may use more drugs to compensate for the paranoia caused by initial drug use:

❝I haven't been drug free for so many years, it [being drug free] just makes me paranoid.

Not surprisingly, this circular, interactive process of drug use as a solution and as a problem causes much confusion about what are the causes and what are the effects of drug use:

❝I haven't got a clue [what the problem is]. I went off the rails – I don't know why. I was crying, suicidal, taking everything, buying off

the streets to deal with it. I went to the doctor, but he wouldn't prescribe – he sent me here [drug agency].

This chapter has been concerned with the views and beliefs of users
who take drugs in a risky way and attend agencies of some kind for
help. Of these, many saw themselves as in the grip of some kind of
compulsion or interpreted any problems as precursors of drug use and
the use itself as a coping mechanism or form of self-medication. They
were aware of the risks involved but considered these necessary evils.
Some were confused about what was the cause of their drug use and
what was a consequence. Many had periods of extremely unpleasant
and chaotic drug use during which they took risks they regretted. They
were afraid of getting infected with HIV and hepatitis or overdosing.
Those who injected had often developed infections from unhygienic
equipment and dirty injecting sites. Some got into debt and were afraid
of violence as a consequence. Most fell into difficulties at times, but felt
that on the whole what they needed was more control of their own
drug use, together with basic health-orientated help such as clean needles and syringes and health care advice.

Once these problems and needs had been identified, respondents discussed the potential solutions. These included a basic accessible, health-
care service (often denied to drug users), easy access to clean needles
and syringes, prescriptions for substitute drugs to help stabilize and prevent further damage. In addition, if drugs were used to cope with
psychological and social problems, psychotherapeutic and cognitive
behavioural interventions were thought to be helpful to some. However,
the majority of respondents wanted help to reduce drug-related harm,
but on the whole they did not want to change and as a consequence
could not see the relevance of therapeutic interventions. Whilst they saw
a clear need for harm minimization for both non-dependent and
dependent drug use, most of the respondents saw no need at all for
treatment for non-dependent drug use. At times the therapeutic option
appeared counterproductive in that it deterred them from attending
harm minimization services.

Finally, one of the main limitations of this type of qualitative
research is that respondents may not have had enough knowledge
themselves to understand the effects of different drugs or which problems were associated with which drugs. It is very significant that users
themselves often felt ill informed and confused about the effects of
drugs, but in interviews they were not able to articulate the reasons
why or what it was they needed to know. For example many people
mixed different types of drugs, but did not know about side-effects and
interactive effects of different drugs. Perhaps some did not have enough

basic knowledge to realize what it was they did not know, particularly in terms of the effects of long-term use and abstinence effects. Users were often unable to explain how or why drug use became entrenched. Similarly, users were often unable to describe in detail their feelings of craving, compulsion or loss of control. As with earlier groups of respondents, it is possible that this lack of information reflects an equivalent lack of knowledge of these phenomena among academics and professionals themselves.

Chapter 5

Harm Minimization and Public Health

Introduction

The previous chapter provided the users' perspective on their drug use, risk taking and needs. Whilst there is less conceptual or theoretical analysis of non-dependent drug use, this chapter examines the research evidence and outlines the type of services available for reducing health related harm among non-dependent and dependent users. Again it is useful to keep the users' views in mind, as these enable not only a clearer understanding of the problems and issues, but also give an indication of the limitations of service provision and potential for future developments.

This chapter is divided into four parts. The first, an introduction, examines problems of definition; the second briefly outlines the development of harm minimization services; the third considers different types of problems and harm minimization solutions; the fourth gives practical guidelines. A final section compares and contrasts harm minimization and treatment.

Harm minimization: what is it and what is it for?

For the purposes of clarity, the term 'harm minimization' will be used to refer to strategies for reducing the health-related harm associated with drug use; it will not be used to refer to the treatment of drug dependence. There are two kinds of health-related harm. First, harm to the individual drug user themselves and second health related risk to wider populations. Harm minimization is concerned with helping drug users limit the damage caused by drug use. The aims of drug treatment are, in contrast, concerned with helping users deal with the drug dependence itself.

The methods of harm minimization range from basic health care and drug prescribing to issuing clean needles, but they do not necessarily involve therapeutic change or reduction of drug use. Whilst some behaviour change may be necessary, particularly during periods of uncontrolled or chaotic drug use, this will be kept distinct from psychotherapeutic treatment for drug dependence. The term 'drug treatment' will be used to refer only to methods for stopping, reducing and/or controlling drug dependence as outlined in Chapter 3.

Both the aims and the methods are therefore different – harm minimization involves health-related interventions to reduce health-related harm and treatment involves therapeutic interventions to control or stop drug dependence. In practice, however, the terms 'harm minimization' and 'treatment' are often used interchangeably. This is partly because the term 'harm minimization' is itself ill-defined and partly because the concept of 'treatment' has been broadened to include a wide range of activities, from simply talking to people or helping with problems to withdrawal programmes. Harm minimization and treatment may both be accompanied by attempts to deal with a range of other client problems, from housing to anxiety and depression; multidisciplinary teams often employ psychologists and social workers to deal with specific psychological and social problems respectively.

It is necessary to clarify these three categories of 'harm minimization', 'treatment' and 'help with other problems' for practical purposes to ensure that the appropriate aims and methods are applied to appropriate problems. It is also important to add a qualifier. In reality, it is as difficult to categorize interventions here as it was to categorize people and problems earlier. In the same way that some people fall into more than one category of drug use, agencies often fall into more than one category of intervention. That is, they provide both harm minimization and treatment as part of the same package, reducing harm and treating dependence at the same time. This is because it is not unusual for clients to be both risky and dependent users. It is important therefore, to emphasize that agencies and generic workers can deal with both types of problems at the same time, by offering both harm minimization and drug dependency treatment.

This adds to the confusion in the field about what kinds of help are available for what kinds of drug users. While some methods can be used for both harm minimization and treatment, such as relapse prevention techniques and prescription of substitute drugs, it is important to remember that the purpose of each method is different in each context.

The aim of this chapter is to clarify the basic harm minimization provision necessary for risky drug users, independent of any kind of drug treatment. It gives the rationale for the harm minimization approach and examines when it is useful and why. It explains in detail the range of distinct methods that can be used independently of each other within this approach and gives basic intervention plans for professionals. Despite a lack of clear exposition of the theory and practice of harm minimization, it is possible to give an overview of both what it is and what it is for. Unlike drug treatment, there are few texts on harm minimization and no specific theoretical base. It is instead a pragmatic approach to reducing health-related harm among a large population of risky drug users, including those who use compulsively or chaotically and lose control of their drug use (Stimson, 2007).

Generic professionals are likely to become involved with many risky drug users who simply need basic health-care interventions and to know where to find clean needles and syringes. In addition, compulsive or chaotic drug users can also benefit from basic cognitive behavioural interventions for changing behaviour patterns and preventing relapse back into old risky behaviour patterns (see Chapter 9).

The basic premises of harm minimization assume that clients are rational beings who will make sensible decisions if given the information and support necessary to do so. The following models of health psychology offer reasonable interpretations of human attitude and behaviour change that can be applied to harm minimization practice: the health belief model (Rosenstock, 1966; Becker and Maiman, 1975), the theory of reasoned action (Fishbein and Ajzen, 1975) and the self-regulation model of illness (Leventhal and Cameron, 1987). These models conceptualize the individual as actively solving problems and see their behaviour as the result of a reasoned attempt to achieve a sensible goal. They emphasize the importance of the individual's cognitions or subjective understanding of the health implications of their behaviour and the efficacy of their own actions in avoiding harm. It should be noted that these models tend to downplay the importance of factors which may impede an individual's rational behaviour such as craving, compulsion or social processes.

The basic principle underlying harm minimization is not to change individuals themselves or make fundamental changes in their lives, but simply to give each person the information and the means necessary to enable them to make sensible decisions and behave in safer ways. The aims of giving information and practical help are to ensure that the situation does not deteriorate and if possible to enable the client to make small steps to improve their quality of life. Agencies and professionals using this approach will be more concerned with a client's exposure to HIV, hepatitis C and their health and social care needs than the degree to which they are drug dependent. This approach is easier to understand if placed in the context of other social and health care serv-ice provision in Britain. For example, the emphasis on psychodynamic change in social work became redundant some time ago and the major-ity of social work practice is seen as practical help and maintenance rather than diagnosis and therapeutic change (Davies, 1985).

It may not be realistic to try to make radical interventions in much social work or health care with the majority of clients. Instead of changing the client or curing the illness and getting rid of the problem completely, it may be more pragmatic to reduce environmental risks, lessen vulnerability and make life more comfortable. With recurring mental illness in the elderly, for example, instead of trying to achieve a permanent cure, professionals look at ways of improving social and individual circumstances. With child care, instead of trying to achieve perfect parenting or removing the child from home, social workers focus on maintenance and prevention services, offering support and help to families when necessary.

In common-sense terms, the harm minimization approach to health problems associated with drug use is the same as the professional's approach to any other social or health problem and drug users are no different from any other client group. In this sense, it can be seen that professionals should do with drug users what they are trained to do and have experience doing with any client group. The reason they do not is perhaps because emotions, morals and history get in the way.

Understanding the problem

Whilst it is likely that the majority of recreational drug users do not come to serious harm, a minority of drug users are taking greater risks, either by using many different drugs in a chaotic or uncontrolled way or by injecting illegal drugs. The type of drug used, the patterns and the methods of use all influence the amount of risk involved. This is reflected in the views of people who use drugs in a compulsive or risky manner (outlined in the previous chapter). It can be seen that their understanding of problematic drug use is very different from that of people whose main problem is physical dependency.

Much scientific research has focused on the physical aspects of dependency, particularly withdrawal symptoms. It was not so long ago that drug problems were understood only as a function of the unpleas-antness of physical withdrawal symptoms; that people continued to use drugs because they could not face withdrawal. It was only when the researchers emphasized high relapse rates and a growing depend-ence on drugs with no obvious withdrawal syndrome (such as cocaine) that people began to consider the relevance of other reasons for continued drug use.

Research reports now offer some understanding of the pleasant or hedonist functions of drugs, rather than simply detailing the withdrawal effects. The 'dopamine hypothesis' is generally held to offer the most useful explanation of all drug-induced pleasure. Much current research in the psychopharmacology of drug use is now focused on the effects of drugs on dopamine in human biology. Littleton and Little (1994) propose that the 'neurochemical basis for the rewarding effects of alcohol may be the potentiation of GABA at GABAA receptors (causing relaxation) and release of dopamine from mesolimbic neurones (causing euphoria)'. They add, however, that 'The adaptive changes in these and other receptors are unclear'. These authors suggest that a simple model of reinforcement can be useful, where the rewarding effects of drug use can be seen as positive reinforcers of behaviour, whereas withdrawal is seen as providing a negative reinforcer. (A similar theoretical model to behavioural psychology.) These authors also point out that research into depressants including alcohol has focused largely on withdrawal syndromes, which are easily measured. In contrast, research on stimulant use has concentrated on the hedonistic side of drug use, where effects on the central nervous system can be measured. This has led to an imbalance in our knowledge of the positives and negatives of both types of drugs.

The idea that entrenched or compulsive drug use may be due to chemical changes in receptors is controversial (Balfour, 1994). Although the reinforcing effects of drugs are seen as due to stimulation of the mesolimbic dopamine system of the brain, this may be only part of a complex reaction where a range of different receptors become sensitized and desensitized to particular drugs. Long-term drug use appears to result in a decrease in dopaminergic activity which causes disruption in limbic and prefrontal regions; the former making individuals more sensitive to the effects of drugs and less sensitive to the rewarding effects of natural reinforcers such as food, work and relationships, the latter impairs ability to control impulses to use drugs (Volkow and Fowler, 2000; Volkow *et al.*, 2003. These neuro-adaptions can persist for months, maybe years after abstinence (Volkow and Li, 2004).

There is little doubt that drug users show cognitive deficits in decision making (Bechara *et al.*, 1998; Yucel and Luban, 2007) and it is possible that these changes remain for a long time, even after abstinence for chronic drug users. Volkow and Li (2005) suggest that these changes in brain structure undermine self control.

This explanation fits with the experience of respondents in the previous chapter and also those who work with drug users themselves. Drug users vary the amounts of drugs they use, they may stagger drug-using sessions to ensure that they do not build up a tolerance or lose their sensitivity to a drug. They may regulate their use of a drug, leaving short drug-free periods between each dose in order to increase sensitivity or reduce need, or detoxify completely for similar reasons. One thing is certain: it is rare for drug users to steadily use a drug every day on a continual basis (unless they are receiving a supervised prescription). Instead, they are likely to control their drug use in various ways over time to increase the positive effects and decrease the potential costs of long term use.

This chapter is concerned with those drug users whose use is entrenched, chaotic or compulsive (but not necessarily dependent in the traditional physiological sense), where they take more risks than average and, as a consequence, need help to guard against possible harm. The harmful effects of drugs outlined by the respondents in Chapter 4 were not necessarily concerned with dependence but with a range of different types of drug-related harm. The kinds of help discussed in this chapter reflect the wide range of problems experienced by drug users and can range from protection against HIV and hepatitis to health care for abscesses and infections and housing for the homeless. Though it is less clear what type of help is available for dealing with compulsive use itself.

The development of harm minimization services

The early development of harm minimization in Britain was, to a large extent, the consequence of a pragmatic response to HIV prevention. Many statutory services were initially developed through central funding for HIV prevention. This has determined the type of service available, which tends to focus on drug injectors and the necessity to provide clean, accessible needles and syringes (Stimson 2007; Raistrick, 1994) rather than services for stimulant users and non-injectors. In contrast, the underlying philosophy of damage limitation was already present in some non-statutory drug agencies which offered social and health care support to drug users. These early non-statutory agencies have since been extended to include other forms of harm minimization (Judd *et al.*, 2005).

Harm minimization is a response to individual health risks, but also to the wider public health risks of HIV and the health-care costs engendered by risky health behaviours to the population as a whole (Des Jarlais *et al.*, 2009). As Stimson (1990) has highlighted, the period from 1986 to 1989 was a time of 'crisis and transformation' in British drug services, resulting in a change from the individual pathology model of drug use to a 'public health' model. This is best illustrated by the shift from trying to prevent or eradicate drug use to reducing the numbers of injectors sharing needles and other damage-limitation measures. Drug policy in many countries is a delicate balance between the social issues and the public health costs of drug-related harm. Erickson (1990) points out that social policy must find a means of reducing the health and safety costs to the lowest possible level and to implement and test a comprehensive public-health model for effective control of the demand for illicit drugs.

HIV prevention

Researchers highlighted the correlation between HIV positivity and sharing of injecting equipment in the late 1980s (Raymond, 1988; Van den Hoek *et al.*, 1989; Des Jarlais and Friedman, 1988; Schoenbaum *et al.*, 1989; Siegal *et al.*, 1991). Drug injectors, were also exposed to HIV infection through unprotected sexual intercourse and could transmit HIV into the general population in this way as many were sexually active and involved in prostitution (Donoghoe *et al.*, 1989).

As a consequence funding was allocated to develop syringe exchanges and harm minimization strategies in the late twentieth century, in an effort to reduce the spread of HIV. (Stimson, 2007; Strang and Stimson, 1990; Gould, 1993). Although there were dissenters (Raistrick, 1994), there was much evidence to suggest that this programme was effective (Wodak and Cooney, 2006; Stimson *et al.*, 1988, 1990; Keene *et al.*, 1993). Research indicated that if drug users receive information about HIV they modify their risk behaviours, initiating changes in their needle sharing and, to a lesser extent, their sexual behaviour.

There are still large differences between risk recognition and risk reduction (Stimson *et al.*, 1988; Huebert and James, 1992; Frischer *et al.*, 1993), but there is much evidence to show that drug injectors have knowledge about the transmission of HIV and are concerned about the risk (Hope *et al.*, 2005; Lungley, 1988; Stimson *et al.*, 1988; Des Jarlais *et al.*, 1990). Drug injectors have been shown to adopt various measures to prevent HIV transmission such as using new needles, cleaning needles, reducing needle sharing, marking personal syringes (Burt and Stimson, 1990). In many western countries the syringe sharing that remains is largely between sexual partners, close friends, relatives and small social groups (Bloor, 1995) and Burt and Stimson (1990) reported that many people who injected drugs no longer viewed sharing syringes as normal behaviour.

HIV and hepatitis prevention and drug treatment

In Western Europe drug services were tremendously influenced by the public health response to HIV, a response which was largely apolitical and pragmatic, as highlighted earlier (Stimson 2007; Judd *et al.*, 2005; Wodak and Cooney, 2006) The advent of HIV and later hepatitis C, in effect, actively changed the focus and priorities of many drug agencies and reinforced and made respectable the earlier non-statutory harm minimization agencies, through an influx of central government funding. For example, in the UK, the Advisory Council on the Misuse of Drugs declared early on that 'The spread of HIV is a greater danger to individual and public health than drug use' (ACMD, 1988/1989). This group recommended that 'Prevention of the spread of HIV infection amongst injecting drug users must be a priority for all drugs workers' and was extremely influential in limiting the spread of HIV among those drug users who came in contact with drug services.

Drug agencies were encouraged to change from treating drug dependence to providing individual health care and a public health service. Programme staff found themselves faced with the need to reduce sharing of equipment and change the sexual behaviour of their clients. They needed to encourage drug users to accept and use clean needles, syringes and condoms. They could provide these free of charge to their own clients but were also required to take a public health approach to the whole drug-injecting population rather than the small proportion of problematic IDUs they had seen previously (Hilton *et al.*, 2001). It is possible that the focus on harm minimization changed the beliefs and priorities of a generation of drug workers. If so this may have implications in the future, should the focus change back once again to abstinence-orientated recovery programmes.

At the end of the twentieth century, if workers were already concerned with preventing drug-related harm, preventing HIV and hepatitis infection often became an integral part of their everyday work (Judd *et al.*, 2005; Bloor *et al.*, 2006), whereas if the focus was on preventing drug dependence and encouraging abstinence it was less easy for workers to be seen to condone drug use (McKeganey, 2006; Neale *et al.*, 2007).

These differences are reflected in international variations in HIV prevention strategies. For example, in the United States and Eastern Europe where abstinence-based treatment programmes are common, there are few harm minimization services such as syringe exchange (though Methadone treatment is available for those who wish to modify their drug use). In Britain and other Western European countries harm minimization and HIV prevention strategies have been more readily accepted as they fit in with broader policies on controlling and minimizing the harm from drug use (Hope *et al.*, 2005).

Agencies in Britain dealt with this problem in various ways, sometimes incorporating harm minimization objectives into existing treatment regimes, sometimes using harm minimization provision as a low threshold entry point into treatment. These developments served as a means of rationalizing old services in the context of the new harm minimization objectives. In areas where drug agencies were unable to integrate public health-orientated harm minimization into their service provision, circumstances forced the development of community services based in pharmacies or health-care centres; though slower and more difficult to develop, these often proved more useful in the long term in reaching larger proportions of the community.

Existing drug treatment philosophies and policies therefore influenced the development of HIV prevention services (Keene and Stimson, 1997). This process also functions in reverse in that the syringe exchange philosophy reinforces and emphasizes the harm minimization message within the host agencies themselves. Thus in addition to providing a direct service for clients, HIV prevention services such as syringe exchange had a more general impact on services and service philosophy. In America the policy response is the inverse of the British approach; there is instead a responsibility put on HIV services to deal with drug use (Selwyn, 1991).

In Britain the changing priorities necessitated by HIV prevention resulted in provision of injecting equipment, health-care facilities and prescription drugs. The resulting amalgamation of harm minimization with drug treatment caused a growing confusion about which was which and which was best for whom. Although the new agencies reached more drug users by providing a package of services which included both harm minimization and HIV prevention, it became impossible early on to obtain a harm minimization service without drug dependency treatment (Keene *et al.*, 1991). In the same way that later it became difficult in some areas to obtain drug treatment without first receiving harm minimization and a fairly large, long-term Methadone script. As drug agencies became more 'user friendly' and more accessible to a wider range of drug users, this also resulted in easy access to long-term Methadone prescriptions for large numbers of people. Whilst this effectively reduced the transmission of HIV, it also increased the problems of entrenched drug use and dependency (Keene *et al.*, 2007; Hope *et al.*, 2005).

McKeganey is perhaps one of the most vocal critics of this approach in the UK. He has drawn attention to the widespread acceptance of the philosophy of harm reduction by professionals, yet his research demonstrates that slightly more than half of one thousand clients attending agencies wanted to be abstinent from drugs, rather than reduce the harm associated with their drug use (though reducing harm was seen as an interim measure by some (McKeganey, 2007; McKeganey *et al.*, 2006). This work indicates that users may view long-term prescribed opiates as more acceptable if this is seen as part of a cure for an illness, but less acceptable if seen as a preventive public health measure (McKeganey *et al.*, 2006). These findings reflect the work of Keene (1997a) who found that people with alcohol problems preferred to see their problems as a curable illness and often understood resolution of their problems as a cure, and Green and Sinclair (2005) who found that people with a history of deliberate self harm who had stopped harming themselves often understood their previous deliberate self harm as a symptom of untreated or unrecognised illness.

Summary

Harm minimization measures are aimed at encouraging drug injectors to change their behaviour to reduce their risk of infection from blood-borne diseases or of transmitting diseases to others. These strategies are based on the belief that the immediate public health task is to work with the people who inject drugs or are at risk of doing so in the future. The priority is to help reduce risk, whether drug users are willing to stop injecting drugs or not.

The methods include:

- information and clean equipment
- national and local informational campaigns
- advice
- information and counselling about risk behaviours and protective strategies
- the provision of needles and syringes
- providing information about syringe decontamination and providing decontaminants
- improved access to drug treatment
- adapting existing treatments (such as Methadone prescribing) to HIV and hepatitis prevention
- developing outreach to hard-to-reach populations
- encouraging changes in local drug-using communities (Strang and Stimson, 1990).

It is clear that harm minimization has been greatly influenced by HIV prevention, in terms of theory, policy and practice. However, it should not be forgotten that the aims of harm minimization are far more wide ranging than the prevention of HIV and the populations targeted far broader than simply those at risk through injecting drugs.

Contemporary programmes are as concerned with the transmission of hepatitis B and C, together with tuberculosis. These can be transmitted through shared equipment even if users are not injecting (such as crack pipes.) The remit of harm minimization has therefore become much wider and although there is no clear 'theory of harm minimization' in the sense that the approach prescribes anything that is effective in reducing the harm associated with drug use, the aims and target groups of this approach can be clarified.

The wider target group include all those drug users who take health related risks and a smaller group who lose control of their drug use and start to use chaotically for brief periods in their lives. Generic professionals are likely to become involved with both groups. Life-saving interventions include health care, clean equipment, stabilization prescriptions and basic cognitive behavioural interventions for changing behaviour patterns and preventing relapse back into old risky behaviour patterns (see practical Chapter 9).

Health and mental health care needs

Health care needs

The health problems described below are associated with drug use. It is useful for professionals to be able to recognize them and ensure that the client receives some form of health care (Zador *et al.*, 2008). Unfortunately drug users as a group can find it difficult to access help from health care professionals. These difficulties should not be underestimated and it is not unusual for a client to have no GP.

Problems related to method of ingestion

The largest category of health problems (other than HIV and hepatitis) which occur as a consequence of injecting drugs include skin infections and the detrimental effects of foreign bodies in the arteries and veins, such as thrombosis.

Hepatitis B and C are far more common among injecting drug users than any other group and they are the most commonly transmitted viruses. Hepatitis A is probably transmitted through other routes when hygiene is poor, but hepatitis B and C can be passed through sharing unsterile equipment and other drug-using paraphernalia. It is said that more than half of injecting drug users have had hepatitis B (Farrell, 1990). Farrell states that approximately one in ten of them will become a carrier and it is they who may develop active chronic hepatitis and liver failure. Most people with hepatitis B have only a mild illness, whereas hepatitis C is more worrying. Among drug users with hepatitis C, the virus can lead to chronic active hepatitis and chronic liver damage in up to half those affected.

Abscesses and/or skin ulcers are common in injecting drug users. Abscesses need not be infected but can simply be the result of injecting ground-up tablets and accidentally missing the vein. If unsterile injecting equipment is used an infected abscess may be the result. These can be treated with antibiotics unless they are serious enough to need incision and drainage. Some infections can cause cellulitis and if this inflammation extends along the vein it may result in thrombophlebitis. Septicaemia can also result as a consequence of a localized infection caused by unsterile injecting equipment and may result in cardiac lesions (Zador *et al.*, 2008; Farrell *et al.*, 1990; Banks and Waller, 1988).

Thrombosis develops from a sinus at a regular injection site and obstruction of the lymphatic drainage system (resulting in puffy hands) may be the consequences of long-term injecting. That is when drug users have either overused one site or moved on to more dangerous veins as they have used up the superficial veins. Arterial occlusion can be the result of one injection of particulate matter (resulting in a swollen pale limb) (Farrell *et al.*, 1990). Perhaps more serious is the gangrene that may occur if a user injects into an artery by mistake. This is why it is dangerous to inject into veins that are situated close to arteries, such as the femoral vein (Banks and Waller, 1988).

Finally, although injecting provides the greatest risks to health, other non-injecting methods of drug ingestion, while far safer, are not risk free. A recurring trend appears to be the mixing of a range of drugs including alcohol which greatly increases the risks associated with any one substance (McDermott *et al.*, 1992). Although non-injecting drug use is almost invariably safer, there are also various risks associated with other forms of ingestion, from swallowing a pill in a nightclub to heavy inhaling of amphetamine or cocaine. They range from a high incidence of asthma to more serious bronchial and heart problems.

Overdose

It is often not clear to either professionals or users whether overdoses are deliberate or accidental. These categories are not really of much use in understanding this phenomenon and it may be easier to appreciate that individuals who are suffering or depressed may be less concerned about overdose and so less cautious in their drug use. It is also likely that people who are living chaotic lifestyles or are too intoxicated to determine the amounts they are using may overdose without realizing it. Ignorance can lead to overdose, through lack of knowledge about the strength of the substance used or individual levels of tolerance.

Overdose results in coma with slow, shallow breathing. The unconscious person should be placed in the recovery position, with the airway open. Opiate overdose can be reversed by the administration of the opiate antagonist Naloxone, though this should be delayed until the arrival of an ambulance unless breathing becomes very shallow and the lips cyanosed (Strang *et al.*, 2006). There is also a serious risk of overdose with barbiturates (where there is a very small margin of safety between feeling the effects of the drug and overdosing) and an equivalent risk of fitting when withdrawing (Farrell, 1990; Banks and Waller, 1988).

Respiratory problems

Depressant drugs affect the respiratory system. Large quantities or mixtures of depressant drugs (for example, Methadone and alcohol) can cause death through respiratory failure. These drugs also have a depressant effect on the cough reflex, allowing secretions to gather in the bronchial tree, causing bronchitis and pneumonia (Banks and Waller, 1988). A possible complication of inhaling any drug (including stimulants) is asthma (and accentuation of the problem in previous asthma sufferers). If cocaine vapours are inhaled it can lead to lung damage and other respiratory complications. Solvent use can result in asphyxia or inhalation of vomit (Farrell, 1990).

Debilitating short- and long-term effects

Hallucinogens, such as LSD and the hallucinogenic mushrooms such as psilocybin, are not physically addictive but can lead to stomach and bowel disorders. Most importantly, intoxication with these drugs can lead to distorted perceptions and hallucinations, resulting in serious accidents.

The most significant effect of immediate or short-term use of depressants is the slowing down of reaction time and disorientation of psychomotor function. Cognition and memory are also affected. This has obvious implications for people engaged in difficult tasks, whether at work or not, such as driving or operating machinery. Any depressant drug use is therefore likely to have a debilitating effect on performance and increase the risk of accidents. Much commonplace drug use in small quantities, such as benzodiazepines or cannabis, can have serious effects, if dangerous tasks are undertaken, but there is little information available. The stronger depressants such as the opiates may also have serious effects but even here, continued use of steady amounts of opiate are unlikely to cause much trouble unless the user is falling asleep.

It is those users who are unaware of the effects of their drug use and those who are chaotic, using different types and quantities of drugs in a haphazard manner, that are most at risk. The most significant effect of long-term use is depression; it is also likely that depression will occur in the post-withdrawal period for drugs such as opiates.

Mental health needs

Contemporary drug agency-based harm minimization often includes reducing social and psychological problems associated with drug-related harm. Many agencies employ counsellors and psychologists to work with the relevant clients. Generic professionals may wish to deal with these problems themselves, refer clients or work together with social workers or psychologists if they identify problems in these areas.

Psychological problems

These can include the effects of compulsive behaviour and loss of control and chaotic drug use, together with depression, anxiety, anger and aggression. Drug users who present at drug agencies often do so for brief periods in their lives when they seem to lose control of their drug use and start to use chaotically. The data in the previous chapter illustrate these problems.

Generic professionals are also likely to become involved at this stage. Life-saving interventions include health care and stabilization prescriptions, but basic cognitive behavioural interventions can also be useful. These are particularly appropriate for aftercare maintenance, helping drug users not to relapse back into old risky behaviour patterns (see Chapter 9). In addition, the most common psychological problems in the general population, such as depression, anxiety and anger, can all be associated with drug use, either as direct effects, withdrawal effects of drugs (Pilling *et al.*, 2007; Keene and Trinder, 1995) or as precipitating factors leading to self-medication.

Methods derived from cognitive behavioural psychology can be used for general problems of depression and anxiety or specific drug-related problems, such as compulsive behaviour and loss of control. General behavioural techniques involve teaching clients to monitor and understand specific behaviours in terms of what causes or motivates each action (antecedents and consequences). Clients can then learn to modify their behaviour patterns by changing the controlling factors and trying out new behaviours and coping strategies. The methods include: assessment of antecedents and consequences: behavioural monitoring; schedules of reinforcement and punishment; stimulus control and generalization; de-conditioning and desensitization (cue exposure) and modelling and imitation.

Cognitive behavioural techniques are designed to modify both cognitions and behaviour. The essence of this work is again identification of problematic behaviours, antecedents and consequences. To this is added a comprehensive assessment of the maladaptive or controlling thoughts precipitating or following these behaviours. Clients are then taught to change and control their thoughts as a means of controlling behaviour. The methods include cognitive restructuring, self-instruction training, stress inoculation, thought stopping and basic self-control, self-talk methods and relaxation tapes. These methods are in widespread use for reducing anxiety and promoting relaxation, and so on. Tapes and instruction booklets are usually available from psychology and health promotion departments in health authorities. These techniques are often effective when used in conjunction with practical development of new coping strategies and development of alternative activities such as physical exercise and sport. However, it should be remembered that changes in lifestyle can also help reduce stress and anxiety.

Behavioural and cognitive interventions involve: assessment of individual problem behaviours and maladaptive cognitions together with the controlling conditions (antecedents and consequences); the development of structured interventions for cognitive and behavioural change aimed at achievable and measurable goals. These plans are carefully tailored to the individual; the active participation of the client; and comprehensive baseline measures of the problem behaviour and consequent changes.

There are many texts outlining cognitive behavioural techniques for both clinical psychologists and generic professionals and the following may be useful: Goldfried and Bergin (1986), Kanfer and Goldstein (1986), Egan (1990) and Trower *et al.* (1991).

Social needs

Social problems are discussed in detail in the following two chapters. These can include financial problems, debts and, perhaps more significantly, violence and intimidation for non-payment of debt, accommodation, employment, child care and legal problems.

Financial problems may be resolved by debt counselling, welfare rights advice or the provision of an alternative supply of prescribed drugs. Many drug users also find themselves under considerable pressure from dealers to whom they owe money, leaving them vulnerable to intimidation. The social environment in which a client lives may determine the level of risky behaviour that is normal. Help with new accommodation may avoid unhealthy, miserable conditions, where unhygienic drug use and injecting and/or sharing may be the norm. Sharing needles and syringes is more likely when clients are not in their own home. This type of risk is increased among the homeless.

Three harm minimization approaches

Prescribing substitute drugs

As described earlier, historically, illicit drug use was sometimes controlled by the judicious prescription of substitute drugs by doctors. The advent of HIV and serious strains of hepatitis have led to the revival of this medical prescribing policy, but for different reasons. Rather than control the availability and dependence itself, the aims are to control the spread of infections, maintain health and reduce crime. Crime and drug use will be discussed in the following chapter. This section is concerned with the effectiveness of substitute prescribing on personal and public health.

Methadone prescribing for harm minimization

The question for public health professionals is not whether Methadone maintenance programmes are a useful 'treatment' for heroin addiction, but whether they decrease health related harm in populations. Do they reduce the risk of HIV and hepatitis transmission among injecting drug users? Do they reduce general health risks? Williams *et al.* (1992) found that subjects in continuous treatment report less needle sharing and fewer needle-sharing partners than those not in treatment. (Though it is, of course, possible that those who shared less would be more inclined to attend treatment in the first place.) Longshore *et al.* (1993) and Chalmers (1990) both found less sharing of syringes when Methadone was prescribed. Caplehorn *et al.* (1993) report that the more Methadone that was prescribed, the less the chance that programme participants would use heroin as well. They found that the likelihood that someone would use heroin was reduced by *two per cent* for every one millilitre increase of Methadone.

Methadone maintenance over long periods of up to 18 years has been shown to be relatively safe in comparison with long-term heroin use, with no Methadone-specific effects which were not also visible in heroin use (Novick *et al.*, 1993). A univariate analysis of variables associated with HIV infection carried out by Serpelloni *et al.* (1994) indicates that long-term Methadone treatment reduces the chance of HIV infection. This is in all probability because of reduced injecting/sharing behaviour but may be due to other factors. It is possible that Methadone may affect the immune function, but a review by McLachlan *et al.* (1993) suggests that this is not the case and consequently they recommend that Methadone is safe to prescribe for people with HIV.

However there are clear problems with prescribing large, long-term Methadone prescriptions which may have been discounted by those concerned specifically with harm minimization. These are discussed more fully in the following chapter, but it is important to emphasize here that Methadone scripts can not only increase the degree of dependency and entrenched use, but can also create a physiological dependency if someone was not physically dependent before receiving a script.

One difficulty with Methadone prescribing for harm minimization is in determining who should and should not receive it. Traditionally Methadone has been prescribed for those dependent on heroin, rather than occasional users. However, with the increasing interest in HIV and harm minimization, Methadone prescribing is becoming more flexible. Bell *et al.* (1992) suggest that the traditional policy actually lengthens the period of illicit drug use for individuals by putting off treatment. It is unclear how many occasional heroin users stop spontaneously after short temporary periods of use. Similarly it is unclear how far physical dependence becomes more entrenched with a regular daily supply.

Prescribing for harm minimization among stimulant users

The risk of HIV, hepatitis and other health problems can therefore be reduced by the use of the method of Methadone maintenance among heroin addicts. But it is less clear what should be done for recreational heroin users and users of other drugs such as amphetamine, crack and cocaine. There is much less research on the prescribing of drugs to non-dependent users or on the use of stimulant substitutes such as Dexamphetamine, which is less commonplace.

However, a large group of high-risk stimulant users has been increasingly presenting at traditional drug agencies, partly as a consequence of diversion schemes for offenders, but also indicating changes in the general trends of drug use (Keene *et al.*, 2007). Stimulants speed up the body's functioning by increasing the levels of adrenaline and noradrenaline. Therefore they are often used to increase concentration and prevent the detrimental effects of tiredness, for example for long-distance driving or night work. Whereas depressants can lead to depression as a consequence of use, stimulants can help prevent depression (and were used as antidepressants in the 1970s) but depression is a consequence of cessation of use. There has been much debate concerning whether stimulant drugs are 'dependence inducing' or 'addictive' as many people appear to use them compulsively and to lose control over their personal usage, whether or not they experience any kind of withdrawal effects. Stimulant use can result in serious health costs. Continual use has a detrimental effect on overall health, as users get little sleep and often do not eat well. There is not a clear-cut physical withdrawal syndrome as with opiates but withdrawal can be unpleasant and lead to increased tiredness, lethargy and depression (Carroll *et al.*, 1993).

The main issues associated with these drug users are problems of engagement as they are unlikely to engage with services unless they also have a heroin problem. Whilst many of this group use heroin in conjunction with stimulants, either to intensify the effect by using a mixture of drugs concurrently or by using heroin after stimulant use in order to ameliorate the after effects during the come-down period (Keene *et al.*, 2007), they often break off contact with services unless receiving a Methadone prescription, as they do not see the purpose of drug services if they are not addicted (Strang *et al.*, 1990; Gossop *et al.*, 2002).

It is argued that harm minimization is equally, if not more, important for stimulant users as they are less likely to access traditional drug services (Decorte, 2001), though there is some controversy about whether providing help for non-addicted drug users to carry on using is justified in the same way as providing help for heroin addicts (McDermont, 2003).

Methadone can be prescribed in order to stabilize and maintain opiate users, to help prevent injecting, sharing and other dangerous and illegal practices. Dexamphetamine can be prescribed for the same reasons; to convert users to a legal, oral drug, to stabilize lifestyle and maintain contact in order to encourage use of other services. It is extremely uncommon for substitutes to be prescribed for cocaine or crack users. As with Methadone prescribing, it is difficult to determine which amphetamine users should be prescribed a substitute drug and which should not. Useful guidelines were developed by the Petersford Community Drug Team (reported by Peter Ford in the SCODA newsletter, Institute for the Study of Drug Dependence, December 1992/January 1993) These have been appropriated by many prescribing agencies today: the client must show evidence of regular frequent amphetamine use (at least every 72 hours), over a period of six months or more (this may be corroborated by their use and knowledge of effects, street terms and prices); the use of amphetamine should be problematic and abstinence not an option; and psychological and health problems should not be exacerbated (for example, blood pressure and paranoia).

Despite the increasing acceptance of harm minimization as a rationale for prescribing substitute drugs, there are many medical practitioners who still perceive Methadone prescribing only as a treatment for dependence and so cannot view amphetamine substitutes in the same light because amphetamine is not a physically 'addictive' drug. It is therefore often easier for clients to procure a heroin substitute such as Methadone than an amphetamine or cocaine substitute because amphetamines or cocaine are less easily justified within a treatment framework. Similarly, whilst many harm minimization services will provide equipment for heroin injectors, they may not be willing to provide clean equipment for non-injectors, such as crack pipes etc., even through there is a risk of transmitted infections through sharing this type of equipment.

This ambivalence in prescribing practice can lead to the wrong drug being prescribed for the wrong reasons, as when stimulant or polydrug users are prescribed opiates for harm minimization purposes, simply because these drugs are traditionally prescribed in drug treatment. It is therefore perhaps more important in this area than anywhere else to be clear about the purpose of prescribing; is a script prescribed in order to reduce drug-related harm or as a treatment for dependence? If the former, then the most appropriate prescription is a legal substitute for the illicit drug of abuse, whether this drug is physically addictive or not; if the latter, prescribing should perhaps be limited to physically addictive substances for physically addicted patients. A drug may of course be prescribed for both reasons, in which case there will be two objectives (harm minimization and treatment). The problem here is that the aims of the script become confused. If one aim is discounted (for example, treatment ends), this is then not a reason to discontinue prescribing (for harm minimization purposes).

Saliva and urine testing

A common method for testing for presence of drugs is the spit or saliva test. This can indicate the presence of different drugs in the body. However this will not demonstrate whether somebody is physically addicted or even a regular user. The danger is that an occasional heroin user may be identified in this way and prescribed a regular Methadone script and so become physically addicted for the first time on substitute drugs.

A common method for monitoring treatment compliance has traditionally been urine testing. However, the utility of urine testing when pursuing harm minimization purposes is less clear. Urine testing in the context of treatment prescribing may be useful to enforce contracts and the same may be true for harm minimization prescriptions; however, prescribing to reduce drug-related harm is more flexible and there need not be the same emphasis on hard and fast rules of 'treatment compliance'. It should be stressed that the least harmful drug, cannabis, remains in the urine for four to five weeks, whereas more harmful drugs such as heroin are not detectable after several days. Urine testing may, therefore, encourage clients to switch to more dangerous drugs to avoid discovery, for example, in custodial institutions (Keene, 1997a).

Syringe exchange

The method most clearly designed to reduce both HIV and drug-related health risk as a whole is needle and syringe exchange. This does not try to integrate harm minimization with drug dependency treatment and as a consequence is less confusing to professionals and drug users alike. Needles and syringes are offered free on an exchange basis or sold from pharmacists. The aim is to ensure that anyone who injects drugs will use a clean needle and syringe rather than share. Syringe distribution and syringe exchange programmes operate on the assumption that drug injectors share syringes because sterile syringes are difficult to obtain.

Syringes have been supplied through pharmacies, vending machines, outreach workers and through special syringe exchange schemes. They work successfully in many countries including Holland, Sweden, New Zealand, Canada and Australia (Stimson *et al.*, 1990). Syringe exchange schemes (as opposed to syringe distribution schemes such as pharmacy sales) are basically concerned with dispensing sterile needles and syringes to people who inject drugs and providing facilities for their disposal. These schemes often link dispensing and disposal, with the continued access to clean equipment being to some extent contingent on the return of used needles and syringes. This service is provided free and usually from a particular base at regular times during the week. Syringe exchange schemes are often based in drug services or have links with these services, which enables them to provide help and advice concerning drug problems, education about HIV risk behaviours, basic health care and access to other services (Keene *et al.*, 1993). However, these services often remain distinct from drug services themselves, having for example separate entrances.

Generally, syringe exchange attenders report less injecting and less sharing of equipment. They are also likely to be more knowledgeable about HIV and make harm minimization changes in their behaviour (Stimson *et al.*, 1992; Keene *et al.*, 1993; Frischer *et al.*, 1993). Needle exchange programmes can also function as outreach programmes, firstly in the sense that they make contact with at-risk groups in order to attract them into treatment (Ginzburg, 1989) and secondly in terms of public health aims as they deal with drug users as a whole population rather than just those individuals who present at treatment agencies. For example, individuals will often be given more needles and syringes than they need so that they can distribute them amongst other drug users. In some places drug dealers are given large numbers of needles and syringes to distribute when they sell drugs.

Syringe exchanges have been shown to reduce sharing rates in drug-using populations and to reach many people who are not reached by more conventional services (Donoghoe, Dolan and Stimson, 1991). Syringe-sharing rates in the UK and the Netherlands are lower than rates in many US cities where legal sterile syringes are unavailable. In seven US cities, a National Institute on Drug Abuse tracking study found continuing high rates of syringe sharing (in four of the seven cities 70 per cent or more had recently shared) and only modest risk reduction (Battjes *et al.*, 1991). Negative effects of increased syringe distribution have not been reported. In Amsterdam, the total number of injectors has not increased (Buning, 1991) and participants have not increased their frequency of drug use or of injecting (Van den Hoek *et al.*, 1989). The limits of syringe exchange are partly operational; they reach drug injectors but are not very successful in reaching women, younger injectors or those with a shorter history of injecting (Donoghoe *et al.*, 1991a).

Separating syringe exchange from drug treatment

If the public health objectives of harm minimization and HIV prevention are separated from the specialist skills and philosophies of the drug treatment professions, it is possible to see a wide range of possible participants and methods for tackling the problem. Pharmacists provide only one example of a health care profession delivering a harm minimization service for drug users. The development of syringe exchange schemes provides a useful service for a certain proportion of injecting drug users, but the integrated package presents obstacles for other service providers and the customers themselves. Drug agencies themselves attempt to separate their syringe exchange and drug treatment services as much as possible. It is also practical to use a wider range of health and social care professionals, including pharmacists and GPs, to dispense needles and syringes and organize various community-based disposal points together with education concerning safe disposal at home, while maintaining the specialist drug agency services and developing links between them.

Outreach projects

The growing evidence that many risky drug users were not attending drug agencies led to the development of outreach projects. An outreach project involves individual staff members gaining access to networks of drug users who would not normally receive any service provision.

Outreach can have one of two purposes: it can be a means of reaching whole populations or it can function as a low threshold entry point into an agency. The former public-health approach fulfils a widespread need for harm minimization amongst those who do not want drug treatment; the agency-orientated approach expands the role of the old agencies by developing projects to access new 'clients' and possibly link them into the agency itself.

The agency-orientated approach to outreach work

This usually involves working with small numbers of drug users directly in their own homes or in their communities. It can mean seeing clients only once or twice but it is more usual for workers to get to know a core of clients and see them on a regular basis, so obtaining introductions to others. Workers often see part of their task as encouraging these people to attend drug agencies. For example, in San Francisco outreach workers gave treatment coupons to high-risk drug users (Sorenson *et al.*, 1993) and succeeded in attracting them into treatment. McCoy *et al.* (1993) recommended that outreach programmes be incorporated into mainstream health and drug treatment programmes, to function independently and also as low threshold entry points.

Outreach work is difficult, dangerous and often unpopular. Outreach workers may take the more comfortable option of working closely with office-based services, which can be counterproductive. Bolton and Sellick (1991) found that using volunteers from the drug-using community itself proved a useful way of extending outreach work. Gilman (1992) points out that professionals may be more reliable but often have difficulties accessing target groups and may be vulnerable in ways that indigenous workers are not. He suggests that it is useful to involve indigenous workers to encourage a sense of social responsibility amongst drug users and to help change social norms related to risk behaviour. It is however often problematic to employ drug users for agency or outreach work, as they can relapse or become caught up in old networks.

The public-health approach to outreach work

It has now been demonstrated that outreach projects reach different populations from those attending drug agencies, particularly attracting younger users who inject infrequently (Wechsberg *et al.*, 1993). This led to a change in purpose for outreach projects, as many workers focused on educating wide networks of users and linking these networks into a range of health and harm minimization services. An example is the peer education project implemented by the Wirral Drugs Service to prevent HIV amongst drug users working as prostitutes (Hanslope, 1994).

This approach also utilizes social support by peers (Rhodes and Humfleet; 1993, Stimson, 1995) and is based on an understanding that the social networks through which HIV can be transmitted are the same social networks that can be co-opted for HIV prevention. Outreach services often use these networks as a way of targeting and encouraging changes among populations of drug injectors, using indigenous advocates, working within social networks, supported by community outreach workers.

Rhodes and Stimson (1994) argue that there should be a change in focus from the individual drug user to large social groups and communities. Rhodes *et al.* (1991), in a review of HIV outreach health education in Europe and the USA, propose that HIV prevention education should not be the province of specialist agencies but should focus instead on 'community change'.

The main problem with outreach is that it is by its nature difficult to evaluate without epidemiological studies of populations. Moreover, the difficulty in measuring outcome is increased by the tendency of outreach workers to attempt a very wide range of different tasks.

Practical guidelines for harm minimization

It is clear from this chapter that reducing the harm associated with drug use is constructive and that the aims of harm minimization are achieved by the current methods and techniques (Robertson, 1989; Hopkins, 1991; Davies and Coggans, 1991). The difficulties lie not with its effectiveness but with moral controversies concerning the damage done by enabling drug use and with the dangers of increasing dependency. This chapter has not been concerned with moral controversies but rather with providing health and social care professionals with practical information on the most effective ways to reduce the health and social damage associated with drug use.

The aims of harm minimization are to reduce drug-related harm and the basic aim of drug treatment is to reduce drug use. The former aims to help clients stay alive, stay healthy and perhaps also out of custody, whilst continuing to use drugs; the latter aims to help clients cut down or give up drugs.

The confusion between treatment of dependence and reducing health-related risks is widespread. It is important when planning interventions to be clear about aims and priorities, as the aims of treatment of dependence and harm minimization may conflict. There are many different tasks involved in a comprehensive harm minimization service and most generic professionals can be involved in carrying out one or more of them. It is important to stress that the drug treatment agencies provide the most efficient and comprehensive service and should be the first recommendation to drug users.

Targeting relevant information and help

Griffiths *et al.* (1992), in their 'drug transitions study', found that different patterns of drug use were correlated with different routes of administration and different types of health risks. They recommend that interventions should take into account the different routes of current administration of drugs and consider the potential for future transmission within continued drug use. Des Jarlais *et al.* (1990) identify three different target groups for preventing HIV: those who have not yet started injecting, those who want to stop injecting and those who are likely to continue. The aims and therefore the methods will depend on which group is targeted. The following aims can all be considered to be part of harm minimisation.

Aims
- To reduce the harm associated with all drug use.
- To stop people starting to inject.
- To stop people injecting.
- To stop people sharing (borrowing and/or lending).
- To stop people sharing with unclean equipment.

The following harm minimization methods are available to clients, whether or not they inject. The main task of the generic professional is to ensure that their clients have access to the full range of harm minimization services.

Information

The first step is simply to obtain as much information as possible about available services. Outreach, prescribing and syringe exchange are all examples of harm minimization services which ensure that clients have easy access to information, clean equipment and disposal facilities, health care and prescribing services. Professionals can find out from health and public health organizations and drug agencies which of these facilities are available and where. This information should be made available to clients. There is seldom any system of referral, as the significant characteristic of such service provision is a greater level of anonymity than usual. Clients buying or disposing of equipment do not have to give a name and many syringe exchange programmes may be happy with only a first name or similar token identifier. Professionals can offer clients this information and other literature on safe sex and safer drug use.

Information on safer injecting drug use: This type of information is concerned with two areas – transmission of HIV and hepatitis and basic health risks. The risk of HIV and hepatitis infection can be reduced by ensuring that clients always have their own needles and syringes and that they do not share these or other drug use equipment such as spoons or water for flushing syringes. General health risks can be reduced by encouraging clients not to re-use their own needles and syringes.

Information is now available regarding safer and more hygienic methods of crushing tablets and preparing powders and drawing up substances into syringes. Information can also be obtained about safer injecting techniques and safer injecting sites (for example, how to avoid arteries). The issue of how much information should be given to clients is controversial and depends largely on the training, experience and knowledge of the professional. Perhaps the most practical solution is again to ensure clients have access to this information, if they need it, through information leaflets.

Distribution of new needles and syringes

The main agencies and professionals involved are drug agencies, syringe exchanges, hospitals and community pharmacists. Lists of providers can be obtained from health organizations and drug agencies.

Safe disposal of syringes

The main provisions are containers for disposal, disposal bins and other disposal points, and safe home disposal containers.

Agencies and professionals involved include drug agencies, syringe exchanges, hospitals and community pharmacists. Disposal points or sharps boxes have been made available in hospitals, general practitioners' surgeries, probation offices, hostels, therapeutic communities, night shelters and police stations. These facilities are often not available in prisons. Generic professionals can also provide disposal bins and safe disposal tubes themselves (available from health organizations).

Provision of information and equipment for cleaning needles and syringes

This includes the provision of information about syringe cleaning techniques, the importance of cleaning spoons, needles and other equipment, information on syringe decontamination, bleach/cleaning containers, sterile water and decontaminants (disinfecting/sterilizing tablets). Agencies and professionals involved include drug agencies, syringe exchanges, hospitals and community pharmacies. Lists of addresses and contact names are available from local drug agencies and community pharmacists. Disinfecting/sterilizing tablets have been made available in hospitals, GP surgeries, probation offices, hostels, night shelters, police stations and prisons.

Health care provision

Many drug users find it difficult to obtain health-care services as health professionals have often had negative experiences of drug users in the past. It is therefore useful for professionals to mediate on behalf of their clients, whether in Accident and Emergency departments or with GPs or family practitioner authorities. Some agencies will provide first aid equipment and basic health-care equipment such as swabs and wound-cleansing packs.

Agencies and professionals involved include drug agencies, syringe exchanges, hospitals, community pharmacies and general practitioners.

Prescribed substitute drugs

The availability of prescribed substitute drugs is extremely variable. Some drug agencies and GPs are prepared to prescribe maintenance or long-term prescriptions of opiates or amphetamine substitutes for harm minimization purposes. A small minority will even prescribe injectable drugs. Many GPs are willing to prescribe drugs if a drug agency worker or health care professional agrees to monitor the client. In some areas specialist GPs will maintain caseloads of drug users.

Cognitive behavioural interventions for controlling chaotic behaviour

Many risky drug users will pass through periods when their drug use becomes chaotic and uncontrolled. These periods are usually brief, but clients are probably at greatest risk at these times. The cognitive behavioural interventions described in the section on social and psychological problems will be of help to clients in stabilizing their drug use and other behaviours.

Social support and help with general psychosocial problems

Social services, citizens' advice bureaux and housing associations can provide essential information about welfare rights, housing and financial problems. General practitioners and drug teams can provide access to psychological support and/or prescribe for anxiety and depression. Psychological counselling is recommended for drug users with a range of psychosocial problems (Pilling *et al.* 2007).

Low threshold entry into drug treatment and referral to other services

As many drug agencies are self-referral, it is not necessary for professionals to refer clients but they can give information and possibly contact names in the agencies. Clients may prefer to attend drug agencies informally at first and they can also use agency syringe exchanges without giving personal information; many agencies do not require a name but simply initials and date of birth. Once clients are attending drug agencies the agencies can often help in obtaining access to doctors and other services such as a psychiatrist, psychologist or HIV counselling, which they drug users often have difficulty accessing.

HIV and hepatitis prevention, testing and counselling facilities

These services are available from specialist agencies and genitor-urinary clinics. Drug agencies will refer clients for testing and for pre- and post-test counselling. Information on safe sex and condoms should be provided. There is now a wide range of information leaflets concerning safe sex and many agencies offer free condoms. There is always a danger that well known facts about drug use and sex will not be available to younger drug users.

Agencies and professionals that provide information on safe sex, HIV and hepatitis include; drug agencies, syringe exchanges, hospitals and community pharmacies, genitor-urinary clinics, general practitioners' surgeries, probation offices, hostels, therapeutic communities, night shelters, police stations and prisons (not condoms). Health promotion departments will often provide leaflets and information to both professionals and clients.

Work with HIV positive users

There is an increasing need to consider HIV seropositive users and those with hepatitis B or C. It has been shown that these people are not receiving early intervention. It is therefore necessary to target this group, particularly for early treatment of asymptomatic HIV infection (Solomon *et al.*, 1991). Drug workers now find themselves working with clients who are likely to die of AIDS and are having to develop new ways of working to reduce risky drug use and sexual behaviour (Des Jarlais, 1990). Des Jarlais suggests that drug treatment programmes have gone through four stages of response to this phenomenon: denial, panic, coping and potential burnout. However the majority of drug agencies now provide information, testing and services for clients with HIV, hepatitis B and hepatitis C.

It seems clear that as many social and health care professionals as possible should be involved in harm minimization. The wide range of tasks make it possible for generic professionals to work with each other and drug agencies to provide a comprehensive service for all drug users.

The main points arising from this chapter are:

- There is no need for 'treatment' in order to prevent drug-related harm
- There is a great need for direct health care to maintain individual health and prevent HIV and hepatitis
- There are a wide range of different professionals and agencies that can provide some of the elements of harm minimization service provision

This chapter has given an account of harm minimization. Chapter 3 gave an account of drug dependence treatment. It should be emphasized that whilst a client who needs treatment for drug dependence is likely to need harm minimization before, during or after treatment, a client who requires harm minimization input does not necessarily need drug treatment at all.

It is important for professionals to decide which goals and methods are most appropriate for which clients. They may decide a client needs both harm minimization and drug dependence treatment, but this should not be taken for granted. This multiplicity of different needs is partly what makes working with drug users difficult, but the essence of efficient practice is practical assessment of different types of need that can be met using a range of resources.

Conclusion: drug treatment, harm minimization or both?

There is clearly an argument for providing harm minimization services for clients in drug treatment and there is an equally valid argument for providing them for clients who do not need drug treatment.

The decision to try to cut down or give up drugs and engage in drug treatment is often not straightforward for clients, many of whom will refuse to accept the diagnosis of addict and/or refuse to become abstinent. As many drug-using clients are neither dependent on drugs nor ready to give them up, this should not come as a surprise. These clients do not need treatment for drug dependence at all. Instead they need harm minimization services and prescribed drugs, to protect their health and prevent the transmission of HIV and hepatitis.

Most statutory drug workers in the UK now integrate harm minimization goals with counselling and/or therapy with a long-term aim of reduced drug use and/or abstinence. The consensus is that drug use can be best dealt with, or treated, by initially controlling or stabilizing use, dealing with underlying problems and teaching new coping skills. These elements are seen as precursors or parallel interventions alongside counselling for therapeutic behaviour change and abstinence. The only answer for most drug users seems to be – if you can't get harm minimization services without drug counselling treatment then it is advisable to take both.

This chapter and Chapter 3 give an indication of the different goals and methods of each approach. It is important for professionals to decide which goals and methods are most appropriate for which clients.

Differences between harm minimization and drug treatment

It can be seen from Table 5.1 that whilst both harm minimization and treatment services offer health care, social support and HIV prevention,

Table 5.1 A comparison of harm minimization and drug treatment

Harm minimization	Drug treatment
Helping drug users reduce drug-related harm	Helping drug users reduce or stop drug use
Maintenance prescribing and flexible prescribing	Flexible and withdrawal prescribing regimes
No change in drug use necessary	Change in drug use (reduction or abstinence)
No change in lifestyle necessary	Change in lifestyle
No counselling or therapeutic input	Counselling or therapeutic input
No examination of underlying reasons for drug use	Dealing with underlying problems
Syringe exchange	No syringe exchange (though this may be available nearby)
Drug use equipment, sterile water	No drug use equipment
Health care and social support	Health care and social support
HIV information and support	HIV information and support

they have a great many differences. For example, the rationale for pre-scribing drugs for harm minimization is entirely different from that of prescribing drugs for treatment. A practitioner utilizing the former will prescribe on a continuing basis to help the drug user reduce the health and social problems associated with drug use. A practitioner utilizing the latter will not prescribe independently of a treatment regime.

Because people can be both risky drug users and dependent, most drug agencies provide both harm minimization and drug treatment as a complete package, thereby offering harm minimization services to help their clients at any stage before, during or after treatment. This has undoubtedly reduced a great deal of drug-related harm and prevented HIV and hepatitis infection among drug users in treatment.

However, it is not the case that because dependent drug users need harm minimization, risky drug users will need drug treatment. In essence, a harm minimization service should provide basic information, equipment and a health care service for the majority of risky drug users who do not want drug treatment.

Finally, it should not be assumed that there are no disadvantages to harm minimization. The introductory chapter highlighted the problems associated with long-term prescribed drugs whatever the reason for their prescription. Prescribed drugs are no different in their physiological effects to illicit drugs and it would therefore be unwise to see them as a general panacea for drug problems. Whilst abstinence-orientated drug treatment can result is a relapse which brings more dangers than ongoing dependence, it should be remembered that long-term prescribing for harm minimization purposes can bring more entrenched drug use and greater severity of physical dependency.

Chapter 6

Drug Users' Perspectives on Social Harm

Introduction

This chapter will examine the importance of social relationships in influencing drug use, whether starting, continuing, stopping or relapsing. It will explore the social harm caused to individual drug users themselves and also the harm caused by drug users to society. The first type of social harm to individual drug users includes social exclusion, unemployment and homelessness. The second type, social harm to the wider population, includes crime and risks to community safety.

Drug users' beliefs about drug use are not necessarily the same as those of academics or professionals, but individuals do not hold these beliefs in isolation from their social peer groups. MacDonald (2005) has shown that alternative belief systems generated by particular social groups and social cultures prior (or parallel) to service contact can reinforce different beliefs about the value and nature of drug use. It has been noted that individual beliefs about drug use can change as people contact professional service providers and move through different stages in the helping process (Keene *et al.*, 2007). So people contacting services may, then, start to conceptualize their drug use in the same way as professionals, although it is clear from these data, that this is not always the case.

Measham (2006) points out that drug and alcohol policies have been determined by a primarily medical model without reference to the wider cultural context of traditional and contemporary influences on users themselves. She suggests that for alcohol, there are serious problems in establishing classifications of drink-related harm based on medical consequences that are not necessarily grounded in the attitudes and behaviour of users themselves. The same may be said to be true for drug-related harm. It is very important therefore, to have a clear picture of how drug users understand their own use of drugs.

117

The following data are taken from an analysis of semi-structured interviews and questionnaires with drug users attending a range of different services and also more than 250 drug-using offenders, including those in prison, on probation and on Criminal Justice Drug Intervention Programmes. Most of the respondents interviewed had been involved in criminal activities at some time and were able to discuss their experiences of offending and their beliefs about the relationship between their offending and drug use.

This chapter examines the changes in relationships and social networks that accompany increasing drug use. It will explore the social life and criminal sub-cultures that that are associated with drug use. As drug use becomes more entrenched, inclusion in, and dependency on drug-using social groups also becomes more entrenched, highlighting the increasing importance of social life to drug users. Their lives become increasingly social as they are integrated into tightly knit exclusive social networks of drug users. These drug-using communities appear to provide social leisure activities, employment, accommodation, money and social support at the same time as excluding drug users from conventional sources of these essentials.

User views of the importance of social factors in drug use and crime

The data presented below first illustrate the changing relationships with friends and partners and second the social processes associated with starting, continuing, stopping and relapsing. The following sections then explore experiences of growing sociability and social involvement with drug-using communities and the relationship with offending and crime. At the same time there is an examination of the parallel exclusion from non-drug using society and conventional access to housing, financial and employment opportunities and the relationship of drug use to criminal activity.

Social relationships with peers, partners and parents are drug related

This section will examine drug users' views about relationships: peers, partners and parents. It will become clear that respondents believed that drug users and non-drug users do not mix and that relationships with friends and family are greatly influenced by whether they are continuing to use drugs or not.

Respondents associated longer-term drug use with an almost a complete absence of non-using friends or peers. Whereas non-using partners and family were associated with periods of abstinence (when drug using peers were absent).

PEERS

Peers were almost exclusively seen as supporting drug use and not supporting abstinence or treatment. There was an absence of non-using friends and therefore periods of abstinence were very lonely, with relapse often associated with (if not initiated by) a return to social life and old friends.

> ❝I suppose for me, I had people coming around every now and again and they had gear in their pockets and they'd share their stuff with me and when I'd got a bit of money I'd share my stuff with them, that sort of social thing. That's what it was.

> ❝It's social. I get myself into situations where the drug is there. I can sit down and watch you use for half an hour and not ask but then all of a sudden it's like 'I need it – sort me a bit out', you know? I don't know anyone not using, ha! not really.

> ❝It was just like what people knew about it was just myths. People make up their own stuff as they are going along and because they are lying to themselves they are lying to everyone else, and then everyone else is taking it in and they are believing the same things. It's just one big circle.

PARTNERS

Non-drug using partners were seen as supporting abstinence or treatment. However many respondents had drug using partners (co-dependents, spouses, girl-friends or boy-friends) who were seen as supporting and reinforcing drug use. It should be noted that it was not unusual for drug users not to have partners.

Partners supporting abstinence/treatment

> ❝I can come off crack like that. I've done it before. Like I've met someone new or... I didn't take crack for 6 months.

> ❝Well my missus is pregnant with my kid. Plus whenever I've come out of jail I've never had nothing to look forward to. This time I've got my missus, a house, a job, I've got everything and if I lose all that

whereas before I didn't have nothing to lose and now I've got too much to lose. Do you know what I mean.

Partners supporting drug use

❝To be quite honest with you I haven't had a partner that hasn't been on drugs, for many years, I always seem to fall into that field.

❝The men did the sorting for the women, you just accepted it.

❝My husband was doing drugs so I did. I think if he went fishing, I would have gone fishing.

PARENTS

Many drug users were not in contact with their parents, either because of negative experiences of parenting when children, present day parental problems and/or because their own behaviour had caused a breakdown in relationships. Non-drug using parents were seen as supportive during periods of abstinence or treatment. However, as with partners, drug using parents were seen as reinforcing drug use.

Parents supporting abstinence or treatment

❝At least I can go to my family and say look I'm clean, live with my family, start afresh, get a job and get my house back. That would be great.

❝So basically I got myself clean. My dad paid for the prescription privately and my family supported me while I was doing it. I stayed clean for nearly 4 years.

Parents supporting drug use

❝Yeah, my mum was an addict and a dealer, it's what I've grown up knowing. I'm 36 now. Stopping using was a bit scary – I've always been around it, I mean my mum was a dealer and that so I grew up with it.

❝My boy is on drugs – he is 25, on crack and smack – trying to talk him off it. That's another reason why I want to get off them is because I can't talk to him about getting off if I'm not off them myself. I don't want him to end up like me.

Starting, continuing and relapsing as social processes

Whilst those respondents using drugs recreationally often maintained non-drug using relationships within families, education and/or employment, those drug users who used drugs for longer periods of time found that their relationships and social lives became increasingly orientated around drug users.

Starting to use drugs was often seen by users as a process of integrating into a social network and stopping was seen an anti-social process breaking away from that social network, when individuals relapse they were re-integrated. (The opposite was true for non-using partners and family.)

Relationships appear to go through processes of social change as users start, continue, stop and relapse.

STARTING AS A SOCIAL PROCESS

Many respondents saw starting drug use as an inherently social process in that it enabled greater sociability and contributed to the development of social relationships between drug users. Drugs here are seen as a social lubricant, with socializing made possible or easier when intoxicated with others who are intoxicated in the same way.

> "They make you feel great, you can talk all night and whatever you want. People who are total strangers become your close friends overnight and that is what appeals to me.

> "It was social. I was at a party one night and they all went down and...I didn't even know what it was. They all started doing it and I started. It's cocaine, it makes you talk a lot doesn't it. It's quite funny to see me talk like that!

> "Yeah – well, not so much me but the people I was with were doing it so I did it along with them, being an idiot. So it wasn't so much what I wanted to do, it was what they were doing and I just thought they were all right.

ONGOING USE AS A SOCIAL PROCESS

Respondents described increasingly social lives, with greater reliance on drug-using communities. Everyday activities were described increasingly in terms of social interactions with drug-using peers which provide company, structure, leisure activities, social life and social support.

In effect, respondents appear to be describing increasingly full social lives, with increasing emphasis on the importance of company and social support of drug-using communities, alongside a increasing isolation from conventional non-drug-using social spheres. That is, the drug-using social networks may provide a very attractive sociable alternative to the increasing isolation and loneliness of exclusion from conventional social groups.

> ❝Then I got into drugs and the only people I knew were other druggies, so sod it.

> ❝You know other drug users, especially in your own area. Of course because you have got everybody coming in for their medicines, cause most people use the doctor don't they and most people are on some sort of benefit so all the locals are coming in with their scripts and you are sitting there waiting for yours and it is a bit (difficult not to talk about illicit drugs) sometimes, yeah.

> ❝No. What I find is, because the boredom... especially in weather like this [sunny], you start getting out and about, up and down the High Street and you bump into friends that you don't really want to bump into. Do you know what I mean? 'Oh I'm just going to get some, do you want to carry a bag out? And you just get tangled into it, where really, if I had a job – but I'm on the sick and not well enough to work.

STOPPING AS AN ANTI- SOCIAL PROCESS

Users emphasized the difficulties of stopping, because drug-using social groups tended to induce relapse in ex-users. Respondents also emphasized the problems of loneliness and social isolation when stopping and the difficulty of starting different types of (non-drug using) relationships and trying to integrate with new non-using social groups.

> ❝When I've got the opportunity of not seeing anybody, like now, I don't see anybody ever because I really want to come off it see.

> ❝Ummm, it's just hard work with having nowhere to live, you've got to find people to try and stay at and they are all smoking so it's just going to be another circle and I don't want it to happen.

> ❝I think anything they could keep us busy or active or occupied when you make the transition from junky to clean. When we change, when you are clean, we need something to do. Some people can't just go out and get jobs, walk straight into a job and they are left out there, with all the time on their hands and nothing to do, soon enough you could end up using again. So if there is something that could be done for people to keep them busy, some programme or something.

RELAPSE AND RE-INSTATEMENT AS A SOCIAL PROCESS

As might be expected where drug-using social groups and social processes contributed to ongoing drug use, they also contributed to relapse.

> ❝[Now I have stopped] now it's my family, my mum, my son comes to visit... I split my time between my girlfriend's house and my mum's house. Even then if I do bump into people in the street – there is always people saying 'What have you been up to, I've got some gear, come and have a smoke' – 'no, I'm alright', cause I know if I go off with them and have that little smoke, that's a top up to what I've already had, or what I'm gonna have and I'd rather not because I'm trying to cut it down. I don't stop on the street and tell people I'm trying to get off the gear cause people look at you funny – I don't know how to explain, its hard to explain, but if you start telling people you are trying to get off the gear, you're clean and this and that, I dunno – I've noticed this, its like... They try and trip you up. I've noticed this – when you are hard on the gear and you know the little circle that you are in and you ask people one day, you don't have the money and you ain't got the energy to go and make money so 'help us out, give us a bit of gear' and people will say 'No'. They will think about themselves. The day you tell them that you are clean they are' You're clean, that's great, are you sure you don't want a smoke?' Then they offer it to you more – I have noticed that. I'll say I've cut down to £10 bag a day and they will say 'seriously, I just went and got a bag, do you want some?' and I'll say, no you're all right, thanks for the offer – thinking to myself, if I was ill, you lot wouldn't be offering me, but now you know I'm not smoking as much so I might have more money in my pocket then that will benefit you more, so you will try and drag me in.

> ❝I was feeling a bit down and went to the pub after work and there was someone in the pub saying do you want to buy a bit of heroin and because I am a heroin user I introduced myself to the man and because I've been in jail a few times around the country I knew a couple of people that he knows so he took a chance on me and slowly pulled me back in.

> ❝Leaving the drugs alone is going to be hard, especially with nowhere to live, I'm going to have to crash around people's houses and do what they do – well you don't have to, but you know what I'm saying.

> ❝I made a mistake – one of the people that came to pick me up had drugs and I got in the car – I should never have done it, I knew I was making a mistake because I'd done so well and I was really healthy and everything – the moment I got in the car I thought what an idiot, all that work for nothing.

MEMBERSHIP OF DRUG USING SOCIAL NETWORKS EXCLUDES YOU FROM OTHER SOCIAL NETWORKS

Respondents saw themselves as excluded from other social support networks, partly because they were involved in drug-using groups.

> ❝It is shame [ful] doing drugs. People just don't want to know you and you get involved in the wrong crowd. All the right people that don't do the drugs, you don't see them people. When you come off the drugs and do normal things you see the normal people…and you've got to get out of that bad circle and socialise with people who don't do drugs, who do good things. It's quite difficult.

> ❝I have to drink my Methadone in the chemist. It is the new policy. I was drinking my script one time and my aunt walked in and caught me, now it has gone straight through my family and I haven't seen my mother for weeks.

MEMBERSHIP OF DRUG USING SOCIAL NETWORKS AND EXCLUSION FROM NON-USING NETWORKS EXACERBATES EXCLUSION FROM HOUSING AND EMPLOYMENT

Respondents saw themselves as more reliant on the drug-using social support network for accommodation, employment (albeit illegal) and money because they were excluded from conventional access routes to money, housing and employment.

> ❝Well, it seems the doors are already shutting. It seems I've got no help there – there's no one. You've done your sentence, out you go, carry on with the rest of your life…yeah but you've lost my accommodation, when I was told it was being kept open for me. What have I got to do – go and thieve and all that palaver – not to get the drugs but to get accommodation, because they want you to go and pay £400 a month or whatever it is. No one's got no money, everyone is in the same boat, everyone is skint. I don't know – I need a job. I've got to sort something out. The chances of getting a job are slim, because every time they ask about your criminal record. I know the past five to ten years have been petty things, driving and things like that, I have got burglaries on there from years ago to be disclosed. If you disclose you have got to disclose it all. I was working before…then the police blamed me for something I didn't do, so I had to tell them where I was working for them to check I was there on this particular day and time and then they turned around to the employer and said 'oh he's a drug addict and an ex criminal' and I got sacked from the job. That's what started me going again because I was on drugs and didn't have no way to pay for me drugs so it was back to crime.

Housing

Similarly, many respondents had found accommodation difficult at some time in their lives. Whilst some had been without a roof and sleeping on the streets, most had instead relied on friends during difficult times, often sleeping in temporary or Bed and Breakfast accommodation when friends could not put them up.

> 66 I'm just sleeping either in my friend's car or just some people's sofas. Till hopefully I can get some housing sorted out.

> 66 It's going round in circles. I've been to Shelter. They put me in a B&B down there and I got mugged, I said I'm not going back there. So somehow, if they only picked up the phone and dealt with it, it would be alright. This is my second eviction, I though I can't go through all this again, poor old Shelter bloke is doing his best so I thought I better go to the solicitor.

> 66 Yeah, but my rent should have been paid for 12 months on remand – I was only on three and a half months remand and then I've come out – and they said they were going to keep it and I paid money out of my own. I can't see how they can give it away in two weeks.

Employment

Whilst most respondents had hope of finding some sort of accommodation, even if this was only on a temporary basis, the great majority had no hope at all of legitimate employment. A criminal record, particularly if it involved a prison sentence was seen in effect as a life sentence of unemployment. The only possible employment was seen as criminal activity or possibly illegal short term jobs involving manual labour.

> 66 Well, I've been out of work for about two years now, cause everything got too on top of me and I couldn't keep a job down. I wouldn't mind getting back - I'm sitting on my arse at the moment, I've given up the gear and that's why I've started drinking again. I'm doing nothing all day and because I've been out of work for two years I can't get a job. Probation can't seem to do anything, they're useless as well. It's swings and roundabouts, because I've got a flat and everything – if I go back to work, my rent shoots up and if I'm only gonna get paid £5 an hour and pay my rent, and gas and council tax, I'll have less spending money than I have now on benefits. It's a catch twenty two, what can I do.

> 66 I haven't had a job for about eight years, since I left school, I haven't had a proper job. So I don't know what to write down in my CV,

> I don't even know what I would say in an interview – 'what have you done?' … 'ahhh' – you don't get a job like that.

Finance

It will be apparent that as most respondents believed legitimate employment was beyond their grasp, that legitimate sources of income were also not seen as accessible. Many could not understand how it was possible to live without criminal activity if they could not get legitimate work.

> 66Money – is easier when you are thieving and that, easy spent, easy come, when you are living that lifestyle.

> 66Because I can't survive – I get one water bill for £300 – how am I supposed to pay that? I get £44 a week, it just drives you to crime all the time.

> 66I feel I could live a pretty clean life if I could only get enough money to live on.

MEMBERSHIP OF DRUG-USING SOCIAL NETWORKS AND EXCLUSION FROM NON-USING NETWORKS IS ASSOCIATED WITH CRIME

Social exclusion is greater for offenders

Whilst offenders became increasingly dependent on social networks of criminals, they also became more socially excluded from conventional non-offending groups. The social consequences of belonging to drug-using groups appeared to include access to a criminal black-market with opportunities to make money from acquisitive crime, dealing and other illegal activities. This was seen as accentuating problems when drug users tried to break off from drug-using networks, as they would lose occupation, accommodation and income but would be unable to access new networks that could provide these resources.

> 66People use for certain reasons – me, I come here because I have been around these circles so many times, I have lost count. And I know how it starts, how it ends and how it starts again. I come out [from prison] and I really did think in my heart that I would be able to make it, that I would be able to be strong, stay away from it, do the right thing by my family and get on with my life peacefully. But, I got backed into a corner every time. Every angle or way I tried to get up that ladder, I got kicked down. Because I have a criminal record, because I needed training, because I needed experience,

because I never had a CIS card, I never had this, I never had that. I was always without a job, no matter how hard I tried to get a job, I could not get a job. I had too much time on my hands, I am at home, getting pressure off family, kids need school clothes, need this, need trainers.

66Going to prison, even for just a little while, gives you a life-sentence of unemployment.

66I had a job once and they never knew I had a criminal record because I never told them and they found out afterwards and I got sacked – it only lasted a week – they done a check after a week and I got sacked.

66Yes, most [offenders] don't have their own places, the people I knew, they were moving from place to place and I suppose having your own home, it makes you a bit more determined to want to come off it. When you are just sleeping rough, and from place to place, it's a lot harder to come off the drugs, you can't get a job, hold down a job being homeless.

There is a complex relationship between drug use, crime and social factors

Users found it difficult to explain the relationship between social factors, crime and drug use, however it is apparent that the lifestyle integrating these factors had positive attributes, perhaps in comparison with the alternatives.

66With my psychology, you get into a routine. Like my routine used to be get up, get my money and go and get my stuff. It is sometimes hard to break the routine. Obviously, I don't go out every day now, but still it is there.

66There is something in me that enjoys drugs, I like the lifestyle, I do like the risks I take and all that. I am weak...the first thing that comes into my head is I have got to get some money and that's it, I am dressed, washed and re-offending just to get drugs.

66It is an adrenalin rush. It's hard to explain, it's like a kick. It is like people who do credit card fraud – for them it isn't about the drugs or the money, it's about the kick they get from doing it. Mine was like that from doing the burglaries.

66Diazepam helps – at least it cuts out one half of it because I don't use nearly as much heroin, but I'm still offending to get the crack.

MOVING OUT OF DRUG USING SOCIAL NETWORKS INVOLVED IN CRIMINAL ACTIVITY IS A MAJOR FACTOR IN AVOIDING BOTH DRUGS AND CRIME

Users felt that the social relationships linked to drug use and crime could be as difficult to give up as the drugs themselves, but that it was necessary to break away from these groups and change lifestyles completely in order to break away from drug use.

> ❝Yes I still have a few friends, but I don't socialise with a lot of them any more because of their drug taking and I am not being judgemental against them, it is just that I do not want to be in that circle, that it why I do not socialise with them now.

> ❝Now I come out [of prison] – I've been given chances in the past that I've always messed up. I've done a lot of thinking lately and I've just got to sort myself out. A lot of the contacts I used to have, they are either dead, moved away or they are still stuck in the same routine, going nowhere fast and I just looked at myself one day, I am a father as well, I have got a wife and I just looked at myself one day and said I can't live like this no more.

> ❝I went to court, they sent me an appointment with probation. I went on a Monday and on the Tuesday I got a call from (criminal justice treatment service) and here I am today. So it is all pretty quick. It was left down to me, I don't think I would have done it. Not because of not wanting to do it, but cause of the lifestyle, the drugs and the lifestyle and everything else.

Discussion

These data illustrate how individuals understand themselves to be influenced by others and the importance of social relationships to their drug use. It is apparent that users themselves believe that the effects of drugs are important in different ways when starting, continuing and stopping and relapsing, but more importantly, that their relationships and social groups of drug-using peers are crucial in initiating, reinforcing, entrenching and reinstating drug use. Different types of drug effects such as physiological tolerance and withdrawal, psychological dependence, craving and compulsion have differing social impact at different stages in drug use careers.

Similarly social groups have different effects at different times in drug users' careers. Not only are drug-using social groups (peers) seen as providing support when users have no housing, work or money, but they are also seen as excluding individuals from other more conventional social groups and obstructing conventional routes to housing, work and money. So drug using social groups may provide informal sources of accommodation, money and work at the cost of inclusion in other groups which would otherwise enable conventional access to housing and employment. It may be necessary to use drugs and carry out crime in order to belong to an excluded group, but this then excludes you from others. Users identified the main social problem as the need for support during the transition period of giving up drugs, when they have little chance of accessing traditional routes to employment, housing or money. If there is not enough support in these early stages they felt that they would be likely to fall back on the old drug-using social support networks. It is believed that that these social networks will be proactive in re-recruiting old members by offering inducements to return to drug use. Users saw drug use as a social compulsion and social relationships as instrumental, not only in starting drug use, but more importantly in relapsing.

A social habit

This picture of how drug users understand their social worlds indicates that drug use is perceived to be associated with increasing access to inclusive social networks of drug users and decreasing access to exclusive non-drug using partners or parents.

Social relationships and social groups were seen as dependent on whether respondents were using drugs or not. Drug use was seen as a 'social habit' or a social compulsion. Starting and continuing were seen as social processes integrating users into a social support network. Similarly, stopping was seen as an anti-social process breaking away from that social support network, and relapse almost as a social compulsion or re-instatement of the social habit in that respondents were re-integrated. (The opposite would be the case for non-using partners and family.) Membership of drug-using social networks was seen to exclude users from other social networks and consequently also from housing and employment opportunities. Finally, crime was perceived as closely linked to both social networks and social exclusion, in that drug-using social networks provided opportunities for employment (crime) and accommodation (with friends), alongside exclusion from conventional opportunities for employment and accommodation.

It appears from this analysis that people transfer between social worlds when starting and continuing drug use, move to different social worlds when stopping and then go back to drug-using social worlds when starting again. It also appears that the drug-using and non-drug-using social worlds are incompatible. (Membership of one social group automatically excludes you from the other.)

If it is the case that social relationships go through a process of transition when individuals use drugs, which results in exclusion from non-using social networks, housing and employment; it is possible that these social relationships may need to go though an inverse process of transition when individuals stop using drugs, to enable access to non-using routes to social relationships, housing and employment. Similarly, if users associate relapse with drug-using friends, it would be important for them to avoid all contact with drug-using social groups in order to avoid relapse.

This may have serious implications for service provision, as it could be detrimental for some clients to mix with other drug users on agency premises.

Overall it is clear that users themselves view their drug use as a 'social habit' often associated with a process of social integration into drug-using social groups which then support users but exclude them from other social groups. The transition process from supportive drug-using social networks to non-using groups may be difficult and/or involve a period of social isolation, which few are equipped to cope with without help. These issues are discussed in the context of wider research literature in the following chapter.

Chapter 7

Reducing Social Harm: Social Inclusion and Crime Reduction

Introduction

The previous chapter has illustrated how starting drug use is seen, by users themselves, as a social process where they are integrated into a social support network. Similarly, stopping is seen as an anti-social process that involves breaking away from that social support network and relapse as a re-integration with the network. Respondents highlight the difficulty of leaving the drug-using social world, entering a non-using world and perhaps most importantly, the difficulty of transferring between social worlds and the problems of coping with the ensuing periods of social isolation that might be involved in this transfer.

This chapter examines the research evidence for the importance of social relationships and social cultures. It outlines the social disadvantages of this group and shows how wider social processes lead to deprivation and exclusion. It then considers how drug use impacts on the wider society itself though crime.

It considers the potential obstacles to drug users, particularly criminal drug users, moving between social worlds, and considers how people might be helped to make this transition. First, by substituting the anti-social process of leaving the drug-using world, with a positive social process through mentors and access to social support groups. Second, through education, voluntary or paid work and leisure activities. Though these conventional routes are much less accessible for drug users and it is important to be realistic about social constraints from stigma to legal restrictions on employment.

The relationship between drug use, social groups and wider society

How social groups affect drug use

Early sociological studies have focused on the effect of sub-cultures and small group processes on individual drug use, such as Becker (1964). Sociological research indicates that there are sub-cultures of drug use and that users are socialized into this way of life through engaging with these particular group cultures (Becker, 1964; Young, 1971; Parker *et al.*, 1988; Bloor *et al.*, 1994).

These small group sub-cultures reinforce different beliefs about the value and nature of drug use. For example some sets of beliefs may place a greater priority on short-term hedonism and greater status on acquired tolerance and the ability to function well when intoxicated. It is also possible that many recreational drug users are part of a cultural tradition of weekday restraint and weekend excess similar to the drinking patterns that characterize the UK drinking culture (Measham, 2006). Whilst there is little research in the drug field, in the alcohol field recent findings indicate that there is a distinction between the social cultures of wine, beer and spirits drinkers and that heavy episodic drinking is associated with weekends and celebrations in Northern Europe (Makela *et al.*, 2006). Similarly research in the alcohol field has shown that found that conflict between the values of different social networks can result in more at-risk drinking (Chalder, Elgar and Bennett, 2006) and that if use of alcohol is culturally sanctioned as a coping strategy this can result in more tolerance of excessive consumption (Tilki, 2006). Keene (1997b) has shown that similar sub-cultures exist amongst drug users and can have similar effects in condoning and controlling certain kinds of drug-using behaviours.

It is possible that beliefs about the value of hedonism and/or palliative functions of drugs are not only associated with particular social support networks, but also with a lack of conventional opportunities. For example, MacDonald (2005) found that locally embedded, social networks become part of a process in which poverty and class inequalities are reproduced in later life. She suggests that networks of friends generate a sense of inclusion and support but that the sort of social capital embedded in them can also serve simultaneously to close down opportunities and to limit the possibilities of escaping the conditions of social exclusion. Similarly, Tilki (2006) found that alcohol and the pub can be seen as protecting individuals from social isolation whilst limiting their social opportunities.

How drug use affects social groups

There is very little information about how drug use itself influences social relationships, though it is clear in Chapter 6 that drug users themselves believe that their drug use significantly affects their relationships with family, partners and friends.

Although most people have personal experience of how intoxication or heavy drinking affects their social relationships, whether through increased sociability or decreased social skills, there is remarkably little research on the way in which intoxication and drug use itself influences relationships, small group processes, social interaction, social networks or sub-cultures.

It can be seen that respondents in Chapter 6 believed that compulsion to use drugs and intoxication influenced their social behaviour and determined their social relationships. There is some evidence of this in literature on families and friendships (Kail and Litwak, 1989). Drugs and alcohol can be perceived in some groups as serving a range of functions from coping with physical and psychological pain and social stress to medicating the symptoms of mental illness (Tilki, 2006). But there is little consideration of the social consequences of intoxication and compulsive drug use in the research literature.

How the wider society affects drug users

Although there is a lack of research on small group social processes, there is a wide research literature on the significance of social context and social determinants of health which gives a clear indication of the social and societal problems associated with drug use for the individuals themselves (Solivetti, 1994). That is, how their drug use is related to social problems such as poverty, powerlessness and lack of opportunity. This section will explore this research, first examining how the wider society affects drug users and secondly, how drug use affects the wider society.

Social deprivation and social exclusion

Studies of social epidemiology and public health are concerned with the significance of social context and social determinants of health for deprived populations such as drug users, (rather than the effect of drug use on social context, which is the preserve of the criminological approach.) Drug use is more common amongst younger people, though it is important to note that the social consequences of youthful drug use may continue throughout life (Keene, 2005a). A key focus of population research is an investigation of the role of individual and social factors in determining social exclusion and health behaviour (Arbor and Khlat, 2002). It is difficult to develop methodologies that examine these interactions throughout the life course (Ford *et al.*, 1994), however, there are clear associations between socio-economic factors and health indicating that the effects of economic disadvantage are cumulative, with the greatest risk of poor mental and physical health seen among those who have experienced early social exclusion or sustained hardship throughout life (Everson, 2002). Public health and sociology of health research give an indication of the types of social problems associated with poor health and drug use in deprived geographic populations, such as poverty and lack of opportunity. There are clear associations between socio-economic factors and drug use (Green and Sinclair, 2005; Keene *et al.*, 2001b, 2005a, 2005b; Keene and Rodriguez, 2005).

The relationship between drug use and social exclusion through the life-course

Social exclusion is associated with different problems at different stages in life. Drug use, as one of the earliest problems to develop (often preceding crime, mental health problems and unemployment), may be particularly significant, if not formative in this process. Drug use is associated with a range of socio-economic factors, including violence, crime and poverty (Keene *et al.*, 2005; Keene, 2005b; Keene and Rodriguez, 2005), depression and breakdown of family relationships (Green and Sinclair, 2005). Drug users are more likely to suffer lack of contact with their parents or children, mental health problems, unemployment and homelessness (Keene, 2001b, 2005b). In addition, they suffer from lack of access to health care and other support services (Rodriguez, Keene and Li, 2006).

It is perhaps not therefore surprising that the drug users interviewed in the previous chapter found the social networks of other drug users very supportive, if not essential, to their daily survival, often in the absence of any other kind of social interaction or support. Whilst there is little research on drug users specifically, it has been demonstrated that those who are socially excluded are held back by social networks of individuals with similar problems. For example, as mentioned earlier, MacDonald (2005) suggests that networks of friends and family generate a sense of inclusion and support young people as they make the necessary transitions to adulthood in adverse circumstances. However for deprived or criminal groups, such as drug users, the sort of social capital embedded in them can also serve simultaneously to close down opportunities and to limit the possibilities of escaping the conditions of social exclusion.

Despite this, it is also possible that some vulnerable groups are excluded, when young, and become integrated in middle age (but then perhaps become isolated again in later life). There has been little research examining the ageing of socially excluded groups such as drug users throughout the life course: we therefore know little about 'ageing deviants' as opposed to conventional cohorts. However it is possible that deprived populations, whilst more likely to have drug problems when young, go on to have other problems in middle age and later life, or alternatively if they 'retire' from the drug use lifestyle and community, that they may establish more conventional lifestyles. This is reflected in population studies where problems and health and social care service use are greatest for the young and old (Keene and Rodriguez, 2005). Research indicates that drug users move between recreational and problematic drug use during 'drug careers' (Simpson, 2003), however rates of drug use, offending, self harm and violence decline rapidly in total populations after the age of 30 years (Keene and Rodriguez, 2005). In contrast, alcohol and mental health problems rise and then decline during the middle years (Keene and Rodriguez, 2005). Whilst these findings are very limited, they are interesting as they indicate that it may be possible to support drug users in what could be seen as 'early retirement' and development of new non-drug-using lifestyles in middle life.

Whilst there have been a series of recent life course studies such as the work of work of Evandrou and Glaser (2004) which track the impact of early family relationships on later life, Schröder-Butterfill and Marianti (2006) and Grundy (2006) point out that much research has focused on vulnerability in old age itself (whether drug use, poverty, poor health or social isolation) rather than examination of how specific vulnerabilities are created and distributed over the lifecourse. Grundy (2006) argues that lifetime circumstances lead to vulnerability in later life and Schröder-Butterfill and Marianti (2006) describe how vulnerabilities can be the outcome of complex interactions of risks throughout life, leading a to lack of resilience or resource later in the life course. Similarly, Krause (2005) found that the negative effects of lifetime trauma, lack of emotional support and negative inter-personal contacts are most evident in old age. These authors recommend that policy initiatives should aim to reduce vulnerability earlier in the life course so ensuring that people reach later life with 'reserve'. This includes healthy lifestyles, the acquisition of coping skills, strong family and social ties, active interests and savings, all areas in which drug users have deficits. Interventions to develop compensatory supports include access to good health care, substitute professional social and psychological help in times of crisis, long-term help and income support. It is clear that these services would be beneficial for drug users.

It therefore seems possible that drug users could be helped to over-come early problems and become less vulnerable throughout the life course. For example it is possible that those drug users who exper-ienced a more conventional lifestyle in their middle years would be able to continue this into old age in the same way that Ulrich and Brott (2005) found that the experiences of older workers who retired from long-term careers and took up transitional work prior to retirement, re-defined how they understood their retirement.

How drug use affects the wider society

Social harm to wider populations: crime and risks to community safety

The rate of problematic drug use is much higher amongst criminal justice populations than other groups (Bennett, 1998a, 1998b; Newburn and Elliot, 1999). Whilst it is difficult to interpret associations between drugs and crime, it is apparent that drug use is associated with higher rates of crime and that financing addiction can be a prime motivation for offend-ing for a certain proportion of people dependent on heroin (Gossop *et al.*, 2000b, 2001; Strang and Gossop, 1994; Home Office, 2001). It is also possible that criminal activity provides access to social networks where drugs are available and the means to buy them (Hammersley *et al.*, 1990).

The relationship between drug use and crime

It has been difficult to be clear about what kind of crime is associated with what kind of drug use. Whilst the link between criminal behav-iour and drug use is well established, research identifying predictors of crime amongst drug users has varied, with researchers producing con-flicting findings about the types of crime associated with different types of drug use (Solivetti, 1994). Similarly, whilst attempts have been made to distinguish between dependent and non-dependent users in research on offending populations, this has not been very successful, as Simpson (2003) points out the recreational/dependent drug use dichotomy may itself be too simple, if there are varying patterns of poly drug use or 'persistent drug use' which is non-dependent.

Killias and Ribeaud (1999) analysed data from twelve countries and confirmed that drug use has an important impact on property crime, although they emphasized that drug use did not necessarily precede crime. Drug users are not a heterogeneous group and different types and patterns of drug use are linked to different types of criminal behaviour. Grady *et al.* (2003) found that drug use was not one of the main predictors of greater severity of crime, but that it did predict a greater range of crime and more frequent crime. De Li *et al.* (2000) found that drug dealing increased violent crime while drug use itself was only related to property crime. Martin *et al.* (2004) found that cocaine use was not closely associated with either property or violent crime, in contrast they found that violent crime was associated with high drug dealing income for those marijuana users who did not use opioids or cocaine. Battjes *et al.* (2004) found that increased severity of crime was related to drugs other than alcohol and marijuana. However, Martin *et al.* (2004) found that alcohol is more likely than other drugs to be associated with violence and the association between the annual rates of alcohol use and violent crime are strong. It can be seen that different researchers have come to different conclusions, so for example, Steele *et al.* (2003) and Casey *et al.* (2004) found increases in criminal behaviour during periods of increased heroin use. In contrast, Day *et al.* (2003) found that during a period of decreased heroin availability there was an increase in both property and violent crime as a result of the heroin shortage.

It is clear that there is a relationship between various types of crime and various types of drug use. However, it appears as if both drugs and crime variables are mediated by a range of other social and psychological factors, which strongly influence the probability of both drug problems and crime, indicating a need for caution in identifying simple cause-and-effect relationships between crime and drugs (Keene, 2005a).

Research on drug use and crime has suffered the same type of methodological limitations as those for co-morbidity drug use and mental illness. There are very few large population studies combining information from drug use and criminal justice populations and therefore a lack of information about the characteristics, risks and service utilization of the drug use/offender population as a whole. Whilst the link between criminal behaviour and drug use is well established, most research has been limited to studies of samples within drug agency or criminal justice populations. Available data is often fragmented and incomplete, largely due to the difficulties inherent in comparing criminal and non-criminal populations, because of frequent sample bias in research (Pottieger, 1981) and lack of data for specific geographical areas (Frischer *et al.*, 2002).

There is a need for more detailed information concerning the associations between drug use and crime in total populations in order to inform effective policies. Accurate data can inform development, targeting and effectiveness of criminal justice intervention programmes, whereas inadequate data could result in projects targeting people without problems and to failing to reach those who need help (Edmunds *et al.*, 1996; Gossop *et al.*, 2003; Turnbull *et al.*, 1995).

At present what we know of the predictors of crime and recidivism in general offending populations is limited to previous custodial sentences, age at first crime and age of first use of alcohol and drugs (Benda *et al.*, 2001). Similarly, research identifying predictors of crime amongst drug users has not been that useful. Newcomb *et al.* (2001) found that polydrug problems in early adulthood predicted criminal behaviour, but that criminal behaviour also predicted later drug problems. There is however, some indication that early childhood abuse and psychological problems such as depression and anxiety may precede substance misuse (Downs and Morrison, 1998; Ladwig and Anderson, 1989).

It is therefore difficult to interpret associations between drugs and crime. It is clear that crime can be carried out in order to fund a drug habit and financing addiction is a prime motivation for offending for a small majority of heroin addicts (Gossop 1996; Hammersley *et al.*, 1990; Strang and Gossop, 1994; Home Office, 2001). It is also clear that crime can lead to drug use, as criminal activity can provide access to drugs and the means to buy them (Hammersley *et al.*, 1990). Alternatively Bean and Wilkinson (1988) suggest that the association may be due to common causes of both drugs and crime. Bean and Winterburn (1997), examining a group of chaotic polydrug users remark that 'respondents talked of their acquisitive crime as a means of buying drugs. But many of them also acknowledged a more complicated picture, in which drug use and acquisitive crime happened to co-exist, without any clear cut cause-and-effect mechanism' (p.4). As these authors point out, rather than the evolution of a new breed of drug-related criminal, their own respondents seem remarkably similar to those in a study of persistent petty offenders carried out previously (Fairhead, 1981). It is possible that less severe forms of drug use have simply increased amongst offending and non-offending populations in the past decade. This is reflected in studies of drug use among suspected offenders arrested by the police. For example Bennett (1998), found that 60 per cent were using illegal drugs, and as Corkery points out in the Statistics of Drugs Seizures (Home Office, 1998), 'It is clear that drugs recovered by the police mostly involve small amounts, typically from users or minor drug dealers.' Similarly the majority of offences are for possession rather than dealing (Home Office, 1998: 2).

In contrast, where serious offenders were concerned, Baron and Kennedy (1998) found that while many drug users, such as those above, fear legal sanctions, more serious offenders definitely do not. Their fear of punishment is reduced by their poverty, drug use, criminal peers, and missing normative constraints. They found that serious street youth offenders are immersed in a lifestyle where crime, drugs, and criminal peers feed off one another, isolating them from conventional society. The authors point out that traditional models of deterrence are of little use when dealing with these extremely 'at risk' groups.

The relationship between drug use, crime and social exclusion

Research on social exclusion throughout the life course is as relevant to offenders as it is to drug users. Foster (2000) argues that the social and economic factors that shape the lives of the socially excluded are associated with both drugs and crime. It is therefore also likely that the relationship between crime and drugs is mediated by the social factors associated with exclusion.

As drug-use patterns are associated with crime in different ways, and drug use varies throughout the life course, the relationship between drugs and crime also varies through time for any one individual. Keene (2007, 2001) has shown that a wide range of psychological and social problems are associated with increased frequency of crime, drug crime and drug problems. That is, when the relationships between drugs and crime are examined more closely, it can be seen that many social and psychological factors mediate these variables. This complexity is also highlighted by Bennett (1998a). Bennett demonstrates that this relationship is influenced by a range of social, cultural, and environmental problems. Similarly, evidence from the treatment field (see Chapter 3) indicates that the most effective treatment (and successful maintenance of treatment gains) is that which incorporates methods to deal with psychological problems and offers both social support and skills training. Methods aimed at social factors and improved social functioning, are significant in terms of both pre-treatment characteristics and treatment outcome (Hodgson, 1994; Keene, 1997a; Baer *et al.*, 1993; Moos *et al.*, 1990).

Keene (2001, 2005a) argues that additional forms of intervention for drug using offenders could include; help with housing, employment

and debt together with the strengthening of supportive social environments of family or peers and personal and social skills training. These
might all, therefore, be expected to contribute to the reduction of crime
overall. This reasoning has informed the development of inter-professional and inter-agency partnerships such as Youth Offender Teams
(Callaghan *et al.*, 2003) and Criminal Justice Intervention Programmes
(CJIP) for offending drug users, where practical help such as welfare
advice and housing support is aimed at a wider range of problems
associated with both drug use and crime.

The following section examines the effectiveness of these initiatives
in the UK, which are designed to break the link between drugs and
crime, by treating drug using offenders and combining care and control
functions in one drug treatment service.

Is drug treatment a solution to crime problems?

A case example: UK policy and practice

When the criminal justice population is examined overall in the UK, it
is estimated that out of a million offenders, only 100,000 have three or
more convictions and that this group is responsible for half of all
crime. The most active 5,000 of these are estimated to be responsible
for one in ten offences (Home Office, 2002). As mentioned earlier, the
rate of problematic drug use is much higher amongst criminal justice
populations (Collison, 1994; Newburn and Elliot, 1999), with rates of
up to 60 per cent among police populations (Bennett, 1998a) and a
small proportion of heroin-using recidivists are responsible for the
majority of general crime by drug users. Finally, whilst it has been demonstrated that treatment is effective in reducing crime among those
with serious drug problems (Gossop *et al.*, 2000a; Home Office, 1998,
2001) it has not been shown that most drug users commit most crime,
simply that there is an association between criminal activity and drug
use and that a small proportion of heroin users commit a larger proportion of offences.

However, in response to identified associations between drugs and
crime, the UK Drug Strategy (Home Office, 1998, 2002, 2004) proposed a policy of targeting the total population of drug-using offenders
in order to reduce drug-related crime and drug-related health problems,
rather than treating drug use *per se*. amongst problematic users. The
consequent development of drug services targeted at offenders has been
extensive. The Drug Strategy (2002) involves a major expansion of
services in partnership with the Criminal Justice System. There was a

50 per cent increase in the drug treatment workforce between 2002 and 2007. Between April 2003 and September 2004, 8,000 drug-using offenders entered treatment (though almost three-quarters of those who tested positive did not enter or remain in treatment). The financial expenditure for 2005/6 was £1.5 billion, with £219 million extra funding for treatment services.

Alongside the increased expenditure on treatment, came a series of control measures extending the powers of the courts to increase compliance with drug treatment. The Crime and Disorder Act (1998) prioritized treatment for offenders and encouraged information sharing. The Criminal Justice and Court Services Act, CJCS (2000) gives courts the power to order drug testing. Courts can now enforce a range of treatment orders including *Drug Treatment and Testing Orders* (DTTO), requiring the offender to undergo treatment for up to three years. Section 19 of the Criminal Justice Act (2003) amended the Bail Act 1976 to allow *Bail Restriction* for those who test positive for drugs but do not agree to assessment and treatment follow-up, reversing the normal presumption (Home Office, 2004).

The 2003 Act also gives new powers to the police, including the power to drug test detainees (extended to 14–17 year olds in 2004) who had been charged with a 'trigger offence'. Trigger offences include the majority of minor and major acquisitive offences such as shop-lifting, burglary and robbery. Failure to provide a drug test sample becomes a criminal offence punishable with a large fine. The test result is made available to the court to assist with bail and sentencing decisions. This test is given in the police station and if the result is positive, the detainee will be encouraged to see an 'arrest referral worker' (based at the police station) immediately. The worker will assess and, if appropriate, immediately refer the offender to a 'gateway' drug treatment project for periods of up to twelve weeks or longer, whilst they wait for an established drug agency place as part of the Criminal Justice Intervention Programme (CJIP). This gateway project will provide prescription drugs (usually Methadone for those who test positive for heroin, whether or not they are dependent physically) and key worker support. Most projects are non-statutory and overseen by a local inter-agency advisory bodies; 'Crime and Disorder Reduction Partnerships' (CDRPs.)

All police forces in England now operate pro-active Arrest Referral schemes (employing 74 arrest referral workers overall). These screened 49,000 people between October 2000 and September 2001 of which more than half were referred to treatment (although due to high drop-out rates only a quarter (5,500) of those referred actually entered treatment). Alongside this initiative 'Caution Plus' schemes introduced a 'deferred caution' for a thirty day period pending attendance at a drug agency. 'Enhanced Arrest Referral Schemes' were introduced in March 2004 through the 'Prolific and Other Priority Offenders Strategy' (PPO). These police initiatives are designed to target particular individuals identified by police forces, rather than those identified by health-care agencies. Whilst national criteria for selection include severity of drug problems or dependency, the nature and volume of crimes is often the priority. Local criteria can vary, as the Home Office points out, each local Crime and Disorder Reduction Partnership (CDRP) will identify a small number of individuals who they think are 'The most prolific offenders, the most persistently anti-social and those who pose the greatest threat to the safety and confidence of their local communities. [In this way] the police intelligence-led targeting approach and the PPO schemes will add the stick of enforcement to the carrot of treatment currently being offered by the Criminal Justice Intervention Programmes. Data sharing protocols are agreed locally between police and the treatment providers within the legal framework' (Home Office, 2004).

It will be apparent that resources for drug treatment may be targeted at the most serious offenders, rather than the most serious drug problems. This raises questions about the allocation of resources within government departments and the appropriateness of criteria used for allocation of treatment resources overall. Some would argue that resources should be allocated in terms of clinical need, some that community safety criteria should be the priority. Of this latter group, Godfrey *et al.* (2004) argue that the decision about allocation of resources should be seen in terms of economic efficiency. That is, whether the predicted reductions in crime are worth the costs of investing extra resources in expansion of treatment services.

Therefore, it is perhaps first of all important to establish whether treatment services for offenders will actually be effective in terms of reducing crime, reducing drug use, reducing health related harm or reducing dependency.

Are treatment services for offenders effective?

Most research findings concerning the overall effectiveness of these drug treatment programmes in the UK provide some evidence of the effectiveness of Methadone treatment in reducing illicit drug use and associated offending behaviours among individual opiate users (Edmunds *et al.*, 1999; Sondi *et al.*, 2002; Home Office, 2004, 2001). The strongest evidence includes social outcomes such as reduced debt, but relates almost entirely to Methadone maintenance programmes rather than detoxification treatment (Seivewright and Iqbal, 2003). In the National Treatment Outcome Research Study (NTORS), Gossop *et al.* (2000a) monitored 75 clients and found that a very small proportion (10 per cent) had committed more than three-quarters of all offences. They demonstrated that at one year, the number of crimes was reduced to one-third of intake among the whole group, and criminal involvement was reduced by about half. Reductions in regular heroin use were strongly associated with reductions in crime.

There were no significant gender differences in treatment outcome, though women reported more frequent cocaine use and more health problems prior to treatment (Stewart *et al.*, 2003). These findings are reflected in the work of Anglin *et al.* (2003) who found that longer treatment retention was associated with crime reduction at follow-up. They also found no gender differences in substance misuse at treatment follow-up, but found that men reported more crimes than women. Reduction of crime was also linked to legal involvement for women, and legal involvement, use of multiple drugs, and living with children for men.

Whilst these findings indicate successes in crime reduction, Gossop *et al.* (2002) highlighted an unforeseen outcome regarding the use of crack. They found that although crack use halved at follow-up amongst initial users, a quarter of non-crack users had starting using this drug during the follow-up period. Crack users reported worse acquisitive crime and psychological health outcomes. This raises some concerns about the reasons for use of different types of drugs highlighted in the views of respondents in earlier chapters. For example, Haynes (1998) also found better rates of attendance at drug agencies and reduced re-conviction rates, but that more than half of this sample had used cocaine or crack. The comparatively high incidence of violent offences (17 per cent) was related to the misuse of non-opiates (and sole use of opiates was a reliable predictor of non-violence). These findings concur with those of Grady *et al.* (2003) and Battjes *et al.* (2004).

Whilst it is clear that Methadone is effective in reducing criminal activity in some groups, findings indicate that there are problems in terms of treatment gains. Keene *et al.* (2007), Home Office (2001), Edmunds *et al.* (1996), Gossop *et al.* (2003), Turnbull *et al.* (1995) all found reduction in crime, but problems in the use of long-term opiate prescriptions and on-going stimulant drug use.

These problems perhaps partly explain difficulties in both client and professional engagement. For many programmes client uptake was low and drop-out high, and many professionals were ambivalent or refused to become involved (Sondi *et al.*, 2002 and Edmunds *et al.*, 1999). Sondi *et al.* (2002) found that approximately three quarters of potential clients chose not to be tested or dropped out of the scheme in the early stages, almost half (45 per cent) of clients lost contact within two weeks and less that a third of this group (28 per cent) remained in contact after six months. These researchers identified the main reason for drop-out as the 'concerns about the independence of the scheme from the police, and in particular the extent to which information given to an Arrest Referral worker will be kept confidential and not used for police intelligence' (Sondi *et al.*, 2002: 46.) This is perhaps reflected in the position of defence solicitors who would not recommend that their clients accept the arrest referral to treatment option at the point of arrest and charge (Sondi *et al.*, 2002).

Generic professional engagement could be equally problematic. Leason (2002) found that doctors were concerned about providing maintenance services for those who might otherwise achieve abstinence anyway, and Duffe and Carlson (1996) identified practical problems where there was insufficient treatment provision and not enough debate about who should benefit first. Edmunds *et al.* (1999) evaluated arrest referral schemes and concluded that innovative schemes involving partnership working could be derailed by organizational culture clashes, role conflicts and differences in values between criminal justice and treatment agencies. The main problem was identified as 'scope for role conflict between helping agencies and those concerned with public protection' (p. 42). The researchers found that 'some drug project workers saw themselves as advocates for client interests and believed that the drug treatment projects were moving away from a treatment-based approach towards an inappropriate coercive model. [In contrast] some criminal justice professionals saw drug treatment as an unwelcome "soft option" for serious offenders' (p. 42). Finally, despite the fact that the Crime and Disorder Act (1993) legitimized information-sharing within the constraints of the Data Protection Act (1998), one of the most problematic aspects of the Criminal Justice schemes, has been the sharing of data between treatment and criminal justice agencies. This aspect of partnership working has caused much controversy in pilot projects and it has not been resolved at a national level, perhaps reflecting underlying differences between agency partners.

Crime reduction

It is clear that a high-dose, long-term Methadone prescription will reduce offending among severely dependent heroin users, if they don't use other illicit drugs. Both Gossop *et al.* (2003) and Godfrey *et al.* (2004) reported clear economic benefits to treating drug users and stressed that increasing time in treatment was cost effective in terms of reducing crime.

It has been pointed out earlier that there are similarities between the public health objectives of reducing disease in populations and the criminal justice objectives of reducing crime in populations. Both of the aims can be achieved through the harm minimization approach of providing substitute prescribing of opiates to heroin users.

However, whilst it has been demonstrated that there is a direct link between needle sharing and transmission of blood-borne diseases (which can therefore be prevented by substitute prescribing and clean injecting equipment), the link between crime and drug use is less clear. While there is evidence that a small proportion of heroin users commit a significant proportion of acquisitive crime, there is no evidence for a direct causal link from the majority of heroin use to the majority of crime as there is between the sharing of infected injecting equipment and transmission of blood-borne diseases. It should also be noted that there has been little attempt to measure prevalence and incidence of crime against drug treatment provision for a total population, as there would be in a public health study of the effectiveness of substitute prescribing as a public health measure to prevent HIV. There is therefore little evidence linking declines in crime with drug treatment for offenders in those populations overall.

This difficulty is partly because the causal direction of associations between crime and drugs has not yet been demonstrated in the straightforward way that the transmission of blood-borne diseases has been. If crime leads to drugs, or both crime and drugs are mediated by social and psychological problems, then stopping illicit opiate alone use may be less than effective. Lack of success in linking overall crime reduction to Methadone schemes may also be because only a very small proportion of recidivist heroin users are responsible for a large proportion of acquisitive crime (Gossop, 1998) and therefore changing the drug-use patterns of the larger proportion of offending drug users may not achieve measurable reductions in crime overall. It is also partly because opiates are only one of the illegal drugs used by most drug users (Keene *et al.*, 2007, Gossop *et al.*, 2002b), and they may be likely to continue their previous lifestyles if they continue using other drugs such as crack or cocaine.

Problems of medicalizing crime and criminalizing illness

Criminal Justice Drug Treatment programmes, in effect, bring together the aims of the criminal justice system with the models of health professionals, by 'medicalizing' drug related crime and providing maintenance prescription drugs, yet keeping this within the context of criminal justice through incentives and disincentives at each stage of the criminal justice system (perhaps best seen as 'criminalizing' treatment non-compliance or illness).

The theoretical implications of 'medicalizing crime' in the drug use field are similar to those raised in the mental health field. They include widening the theoretical conceptualizations of drug misuse and broadening the practical definition of compulsion to change the relationship between treatment, coercion and compulsion effectively.

The ethical implications of 'medicalizing' crime are less clear, though ethical dilemmas are apparent in conflicts between health and criminal justice professionals. These dilemmas are similar to those faced by mental health clinicians asked to control those with medical problems using coercion or compulsion. The Royal College of Psychiatrists and public bodies such as the Mental Health Alliance have made it clear that mental health professionals prefer to keep care and control functions separate. This reflects the tradition of civil liberties in the UK, which has historically kept separate health care and social control and developed distinct, hermetically sealed, health and criminal justice systems in order to maintain individual rights to treatment without compulsion.

These new policies signal a move away from established traditions to develop new forms of policy and practice in the drugs field which blur the distinction between care and control, perhaps without clarifying either the theoretical conceptualizations or the ethical principles which underpin this debate.

A conflict of care and control?

This innovative approach to the integration of crime reduction, harm minimization and drug treatment in the UK appears to offer an effective means of reducing crime among some offenders and also of providing fast access to much needed support among others. However it raises a series of theoretical, ethical and practical questions which are reflected in the ambivalence of both clients and professionals towards the scheme, not only in the UK, but also in Europe and the US (Solivetti, 1994; Burke, 1992).

First, different definitions of drug dependency and drug-related harm result in different definitions of treatment and harm minimization. These definitions will also influence the type of care provided and how long it is provided for and determine targets for evaluating success or failure. For example, the UK Department of Health, *Models of Care for the Treatment of Drug Users* (NTA, 2002) sets out very broad definitions of substance misuse and treatment:

> Substance misuse is drug and/or alcohol taking which causes harm to the individual, their significant others or the wider community. By definition those requiring drug or alcohol treatment are substance misusers. This term [treatment] describes a range of interventions which are intended to remedy an identified drug-related problem or condition relating to a person's physical, psychological or social (including legal) well being. (NTA, 2002: 2)

This extremely broad definition encompasses a range of different rationales for interventions such as prescribing opiates, ranging from the cure of physiological dependency to the reduction of drug-related harm in wider populations (whether health-related harm or crime). As a consequence, drug services now deal with greater numbers of clients and offer prescription of substitute drugs as part of a less treatment-oriented, longer-term harm minimization service (NTA, 2002; DoH, 1999.) In effect, long-term maintenance prescribing of Methadone can be seen as a means of reducing crime or public health problems, rather than a treatment *per se*, as a consequence, the rationale for prescribing drugs may sometimes be unclear. Future changes in policy emphasis from maintenance to recovery (NTA, 2008) will raise similar issues if abstinence orientated treatment is also seen as a means of controlling crime rather than caring for drug users.

It is not therefore surprising that there have been disadvantages to integrating Criminal Justice and treatment services. The Criminal Justice treatment programmes provide harm minimization and treatment services within a structured framework of 'compliance conditions', in which the client is expected to use prescribed, but not illicit, drugs and to change various lifestyle behaviours. If these conditions are adhered to, the client may become more dependent on opiates and so also dependent on services. One of the consequences has been to greatly increase numbers of long-term drug agency clients, as 90 per cent of clients on long-term Methadone prescriptions have not become abstinent and this has greatly increased caseloads (Keene *et al.*, 2007). If the conditions are not adhered to, the client may be discharged and prescription drugs terminated. This can leave the client worse off, if they have physiological withdrawals, go back to illicit drugs or if they revert to a chaotic lifestyle in the absence of service support. In addition clients may feel that information shared with the police will make it more likely that they are put under surveillance and/or penalized in the future. The problems shed some light on the ambivalence to the schemes among both offenders and staff (Sondi *et al.*, 2002).

In summary, this chapter has highlighted the underlying conflicts in care and control of drug users. In order to understand the conceptual complexity and ethical dilemmas, UK policy and practice has been examined in some detail. It will be remembered that Chapters 3 and 5 highlighted the confusion in the health field between the terms 'harm minimization' and 'treatment' showing how public health interventions such as harm minimization maintenance scripts, designed simply to reduce health-related harm in populations, could be re-defined as 'individual drug treatment'. This chapter has shown that when the health fields and criminal justice fields are combined there is a further confusion about whether public health models of disease prevention in populations can be utilized for crime prevention (that is, that disease prevention and crime prevention can be understood in the same way). These theoretical and ethical issues have caused much controversy amongst clinicians who still see their prime task as treating individual illness, rather than preventing HIV or increasing community safety (Keene, 2005; Strang and Sheridan 1998; Burke 1992).

There are no simple solutions to these dilemmas. It is apparent that drug-using offenders form a particularly high-risk section of the drug-using population and would benefit from help for drug problems and social and psychological problems, whether these cause, contribute to, or maintain crime. However these conclusions should not automatically lead to the assumption that developing services should be targeted at drug users within the criminal justice system itself. It may be more effective to separate care and control functions and confine treatment initiatives to drug-using offenders in health care services where there is less control and therefore less ambivalence among both clients and staff.

Chapter 8

Working with Users: Motivation, Maintenance and Recovery

Introduction

The use of drugs is now so widespread that most social and health care professionals are likely to have drug users on their caseload. The previous chapters have given an understanding of the problems and solutions in the field. The following two chapters will address the practical implications for professionals.

Health and social care professionals have reported a lack of confidence in their ability to deal with drug problems and an ambivalence about their role or responsibilities in this area. They need to know which of their own professional skills are appropriate and what specialist skills are necessary in order to enable them to deal confidently and competently with drug problems.

Whilst generic workers have knowledge and experience of the problems associated with drug use and the practical skills necessary, users do present additional problems.

- How do I ensure the safety of my clients?
- How can I motivate my clients?
- How do I make an assessment?
- Are harm minimization or treatment methods more appropriate ?
- What should I do about aftercare and preventing relapse?

These questions will be resolved through the development of a helping process incorporating generic and specialist skills. The answer to each question will provide a separate step in a sequential programme incorporating safety precautions, motivational interviewing, assessment, harm minimization and/or treatment and aftercare, in this order.

- Safety is concerned with giving clients information and contacts.
- Motivational interviewing is a specialist skill.

149

- Assessment and care plans require generic skills and specialist knowledge.
- The aims and methods of harm minimization and treatment are distinct.
- Aftercare and relapse prevention include both generic and specialist skills.

This chapter will describe this sequential helping process (outlined in Figure 8.1). The following chapter will outline the importance of after-care and relapse prevention. These chapters are designed to inform readers how to use their own professional skills in conjunction with some specialist methods, within a sequential helping process designed specifically for work with drug users. They will outline the use of generic and specialist skills, focusing on motivational interviewing and counselling and relapse prevention skills which form an integral part of this process.

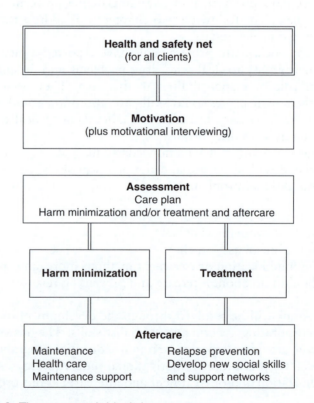

Figure 8.1 The sequential helping process

New beginnings and no end

In order for professionals to utilize their generic skills in working with drug users, a framework is outlined and additional specialist skills introduced. Effective work with drug users requires the professional to work through a sequence of steps and tailor interventions at each stage. The stages at the beginning and the end of this sequential process assume particular importance in this field; at the outset, health and safety precautions and motivation and, at the end, maintenance of change and relapse prevention. Specialist methods are necessary at these stages and these will be examined below in the context of the sequential helping process as a whole.

Although many of the methods and skills necessary for working with drug users are similar to those used in all health and social care work, the helping process itself is different for three reasons:

- Clients are often uncertain about reporting drug use
- Clients are often ambivalent about changing their drug use
- Clients often relapse within a short period

For effective working, these differences must be taken into account.

The need for motivation, maintenance and aftercare

The need for client motivation before assessment
Because clients are uncertain about reporting drug use and ambivalent about changing, motivation becomes the first step, changing the order and emphasis of the generic helping process. The initial stage is not assessment, as would be the case with many clients, but motivation and an early emphasis is on development of a working relationship with the client.

The need for health care maintenance support for those who do not want to change
This is followed by assessment and the negotiation of aims. In this field the client has a choice of two aims, either maintenance (harm minimization) or change (treatment). The choice must to a large extent remain with the client, though the professional may influence the client to move from harm minimization to gradual changes in drug use and/or lifestyle.

The need for aftercare

Work with drug users is coloured by the high proportion of clients who relapse. It is therefore necessary with this client group to spend a good deal of time and effort on the aftercare period. This involves completing assessments and care plans for the post-treatment maintenance period as an integral part of the treatment process. These plans should contain clear cut procedures in the event of crisis or relapse.

The sequential helping process

The sequential helping process incorporates the core elements of work with drug users cited above, within a structured framework. The essential first step for all clients is the provision of information and health and safety precautions (the 'safety net'). This is followed by the task of motivating some clients to use drugs more safely or to change their drug use in some way. As emphasized, motivation is a primary task when working with drug users, as many may not wish to seek help or to change. This stage involves building a good relationship with the client before asking questions about drug-use problems. In contrast to most work in the helping professions, motivation comes before assessment, as clients who are not motivated to deal with drug issues are likely to resist accurate assessment.

Following effective client motivation a comprehensive assessment and care plan will include the client's problems, skills and resources together with a review of appropriate assistance available through health and social care agencies. It should include assessment of the client's ability to change and also their ability to maintain any changes in behaviour, whether these be safer drug use or stopping dependence. The assessment will determine the intervention (harm minimization and/or dependency treatment) and it forms the basis for agreement of goals and the development of a care-plan. The care plan will include the basic services and methods described in Chapters 3 and 5, together with planned aftercare maintenance including continuing support, relapse prevention skills training and a clear cut procedure for immediate intervention in the event of relapse.

Assessment and help will vary depending on stage in the sequential helping process

No assessment is necessary for the initial 'safety net' stage; it could indeed be counterproductive. The help given should consist largely of information and contacts for easy access to services and resources if necessary. For those clients seen as at risk, assessment of health-care needs is necessary. Help may include the provision of needles and syringes, prescribed drugs and health-care support. Counselling for therapeutic change is not necessary at this stage unless specific psychological problems are identified independently of the drug use, or chaotic drug use points to an immediate need for cognitive behavioural change. The majority of clients will want to give up drugs at some time. For those clients assessed as dependent, it is necessary to determine whether change is likely (does the client want to change?) and whether it is sensible (is the client capable of changing and do they have the ability and resources to cope after treatment?) It is only when there is a likelihood of change, and when clients are assessed as capable of maintaining change, that a therapeutic change process should be undertaken. Even then, it is probably not helpful to undertake this process without an aftercare programme.

The safety net

The first stage of the helping process consists of education, providing a safety net of information about safer drug use, HIV and access to services such as syringe exchange. The aim is to prevent unnecessary risk taking or harm. This first phase establishes life-saving precautions for all clients and must be carried out for everyone, before anything else. Many drug users will not want or need anything more than these simple safety precautions, information and access to safety equipment such as needles and syringes. This phase can be seen as a pre-assessment stage of damage limitation. While completely distinct and separate from health care and treatment itself, it is a necessary precondition of any intervention. Providing information leaflets and contact names is less intrusive and more efficient than other interventions. It involves giving general information to protect the individual and others, as such it is a public health or health promotion measure. This information should be made generally available to all clients as posters or leaflets. It should include the range of services and products available, from syringe exchanges to health care and prescribed drugs. It should also provide contact points at different levels of confidentiality from outreach and drop-in to drug agencies, so that the clients can decide how much they are prepared to reveal to whom.

The safety net should be seen as a public health or health promotion measures designed for whole populations rather than aimed at individual clients. Many drug users will benefit from basic information about safer drug use and local service provision and some will ask for further help.

Intervention: harm minimization and/or treatment

For those clients who want help for drug problems, a full assessment is necessary, in order to determine which type of intervention is appropriate.

Harm minimization

This intervention involves the stabilization, support and maintenance of drug users as detailed in Chapter 5. The aim is to reduce the social and health damage of drug use. This intervention is enough for those whose drug use is temporary and/or non-dependent. Occasionally some clients may have short periods of chaotic drug use and at this time changes in behaviour or lifestyles are also necessary.

Treatment

This intervention is used to facilitate therapeutic change; it includes different models of treatment, from psychological techniques and controlled drug use to medical prescribing regimes, as described in Chapter 3. The aim is to end or curtail drug use. There are therefore two distinct pathways in the helping process:

The harm minimization sequence:

- Motivation to reduce risks and/or seek help
- Assessment and assessment of needs and resources for safer drug use
- Harm minimization
- Aftercare maintenance support to avoid risk taking in the future

The dependency treatment sequence:

- Motivation (motivational interviewing method)
- Reassessment of needs and resources for drug-free life, during and after treatment
- Treatment intervention (cognitive behavioural and/or medical prescribing schedules to reduce or stop drug use)
- Aftercare and relapse prevention skills and development of social support systems

Aftercare

Continued support (regular phone calls, meetings and/or group support) and immediate access and availability at relapse should be built into the aftercare phase. At present it is not uncommon for client and worker to see the end of a treatment phase as the final 'outcome' and therefore clients may well feel any relapse is a failure and should be disguised from the worker. This mistake stems from the medical concept of treatment as a distinct time-limited programme with a clear outcome, rather than the notion of a recurring disorder or disability, where there is no 'outcome' as such, only a continued monitoring of progress and availability of support when necessary.

Old generic skills and new specialist methods

Whereas most social and health care professionals are familiar with counselling and helping skills, some practical guidance is necessary concerning the introduction of two new elements into general counselling practice: pre-intervention motivation and post-intervention maintenance or relapse prevention. These elements are critical when working with drug users as both address the issue of high failure rates in this field. Clients are unlikely to respond in the first place if assessment and/or counselling takes place when they are unmotivated and they are likely to deteriorate or relapse if there is no maintenance or relapse prevention.

The research literature has demonstrated that initial relationship building and ongoing minimal aftercare maintenance are of particular relevance to drug users for harm minimization purposes. As we have seen, two specialist methods have been developed to deal with dependent drug users before and after treatment. The motivational change models of Miller and Prochaska and DiClemente and the relapse prevention model of Marlatt and colleagues. Both have been developed specifically for work with substance users but can be used independently of any particular model of dependence.

Generic counselling skills

Counselling skills of some form or another are part of the basic training and experience of most social and health care professionals. The term 'counselling' is rather vague and can mean anything from chatting to a client to a structured programme of behavioural change or intensive psychotherapy (Pilling *et al.*, 2007). Most structured counselling programmes use a mixture of psychodynamic client-centred methods with cognitive behavioural techniques. The skills developed from these programmes are outlined below, but for practical guidebooks and exercises the following are useful: Egan (1990) and Kanfer and Goldstein (1986).

The important distinction between different kinds of counselling is the aim. Many are designed to achieve therapeutic change, such as the cognitive behavioural and therapeutic programmes for dependent drug users discussed in Chapter 3. However, not all drug-using clients are likely to respond to such programmes. It is therefore necessary to distinguish between those counselling techniques aimed at change and those simply designed to build constructive helping relationships and to clarify problems.

Much has been written about non-directive, client-centred counselling – how to listen and help the client to understand their problems. This is useful for building relationships before offering support and practical help. It can also result in changing the client's attitudes and in their desire to change their behaviour. Though, if the aim is to bring about actual changes in behaviour through counselling techniques, it should be noted that attitude change alone is unlikely to be sufficient.

Much less has been written about translating attitude change into behaviour change. The therapeutic guidelines outlined in Chapter 3 addressed this problem by offering specific cognitive behavioural programmes (psychological approach) or straightforward step-by-step guidelines and social support networks (disease model). Both approaches have in common a clear-cut definition of problems and practical solutions. For generic professionals this difficulty is best addressed by not only helping the client to understand the problem and the possible solutions, but also by assisting them to understand the ways of achieving the solutions. The essence of goal setting is to clearly define the sequence of steps necessary to achieve the aims; that is, to define exactly how a goal will be achieved.

Qualities of a good counsellor

Much research has been undertaken to identify which are the factors that effective counselling sessions have in common. The most significant is the counsellor. The qualities of a good counsellor have been variously listed as warmth, genuineness, empathy, respect, caring, together with the use of feedback, confrontation, self-disclosure, commitment and careful listening. Carl Rogers (1951) has suggested that warmth, empathy and unconditional positive regard lead to a more genuine and authentic relationship; however, he was not convinced that these qualities could be learned. Gerard Egan (1990) points out that, though some personal qualities lead to a more effective working relationship, many counselling skills can be learned and practised. Particular emphasis is placed on empathy and the ability to communicate understanding of the client's feelings and point of view, followed by a stress on genuineness, unconditional positive regard, respect and a non-judgemental attitude.

Skills of a good counsellor

The ability to demonstrate the qualities of empathy, respect and genuineness can be improved by good listening and feedback skills and the ability to confront clients and negotiate contracts.

Collecting information: Careful listening or attending is important. Body language is significant, together with appropriate eye contact and smiling, nodding, and so on. It is important to concentrate, ask open-ended questions, identify significant issues, ask for specific detail and prevent too many deviations in the conversation. An integral part of collecting information is to remain silent for much of the time and allow the client to fill awkward pauses.

Feedback: An essential part of counselling is accurate empathic feedback. This involves the ability to paraphrase what the client has said (rephrasing or active listening) and to be specific and identify significant issues. The object of paraphrasing is to avoid misunderstandings and clarify issues. It also serves as clear indication to the client that the professional is listening and taking seriously what is said. Feedback also includes empathic responses in terms of attempting to understand what the client may have felt in certain situations and asking specific questions about emotional states. Positive comments and questions are an integral part of feedback but it is important to be brief. Summarizing is similar to paraphrasing but can be used specifically to clarify what has occurred so far and to determine what issue or direction should be pursued next.

Challenging and confrontation: Challenging a client's point of view can only be constructively attempted after the initial stages of listening and feedback. It involves introducing a new perspective on the client's problem or situation, usually taken from the professional frame of reference or that of a significant other. It includes suggesting possible patterns or themes and pointing out discrepancies. Confrontation often requires self-disclosure or giving the client information. Information giving is a skill in itself which, at its most effective, uses simple words, short sentences and explicit categorizations. It is necessary to be concrete and specific, avoid jargon, summarize and ask for feedback from the client.

Clarifying the concrete steps necessary to achieve goals: The counsellor should clarify the practical means of achieving goals, step by step, so the client not only knows what they are going to do, but how they are going to do it. They need to know who will do what, what will happen when each stage is completed, what will happen if a goal is not achieved and what will happen in the event of relapses. The more specific and concrete each step can be, the better. So, for example, the main goal may be to stop sharing injecting equipment outside the home. The practical steps to achieving this goal may be to ensure that injecting equipment is always available at home, by developing links with local pharmacists and the local syringe exchange.

Basic counselling within the sequential helping process

Counselling skills can be used at different stages of the process. First, for the motivation stage, when attempting to understand the client and develop a working relationship; second, at the assessment stage, when understanding problems and needs; third, at the care plan stage, when helping the client to work out what choices are available, make decisions about which to choose and develop strategies for achieving these goals, and fourth, for therapeutic change in drug treatment.

Client-centred listening skills are the essence of motivation and assessment, whereas more directive and confrontational skills are an integral part of therapeutic change. Cognitive behavioural interventions are useful for therapeutic change and relapse prevention (Pilling *et al.*, 2007).

So in the sequential helping process, initial client-centred, reflective and non-directive counselling precedes the more task-orientated later stages. If there is a need for therapeutic change, the therapeutic component (whether cognitive behavioural or psychodynamic) follows initial non-directive listening. Finally, the emphasis on maintenance of change and relapse prevention requires further cognitive behavioural counselling skills.

It should be emphasized that, although the interventions in the following framework form a sequence, there is no necessity for all drug users to progress along it, as the earlier steps can be used independently of those that follow. For instance, it may be decided that information and provision of pharmacist contacts is the most appropriate intervention. It is quite possible that this is all that is necessary or practicable.

If, however, the professional decides to embark on a working relationship to deal with drug problems, the total sequence becomes necessary. As clients progress through the motivation stage to assessment and harm minimization or treatment, these interventions should lead inevitably to continuing aftercare maintenance. In effect, harm minimization does not have a 'treatment outcome' as there is a continuing possibility that the client will take risks if services are removed. Likewise, with treatment, although there is an 'outcome', it is the following two years of after-care support that are most critical in maintaining treatment change. If no such after-care support is available, research indicates that clients will relapse to old behaviours. The answer is to develop a system of minimal maintenance support which not only guards against relapse but allows for rapid re-establishment of contact in the event of crisis or relapse.

Motivation to change: the process model and methods

The importance of motivation has long been understood by professionals working with drug users. Although there is little research in this area as the phenomenon is difficult to measure, lack of motivation is often cited as a primary reason for treatment failure.

Motivating the client is the first step of the sequential helping process. It necessitates developing a working relationship or 'linking the client in' to the helping process. This should take place before assessment in order to ensure cooperation. The main aim at this stage is to build understanding and trust, by listening to the client's view of their problems and being clear cut about the professional position. It is particularly necessary to develop the relationship by clarifying what services are available and what you can and cannot do. This stage should be designed to remove any blocks to client help-seeking by establishing rules of confidentiality and clarifying professional responsibilities regarding children or criminal activities. The first thing is to greet the client in a non-judgemental way and make them feel at ease. This is particularly important with drug users who will expect to be judged adversely, if not treated badly, because of their drug use.

The use of motivational interviewing (Finney 2009; Miller, 1983) and the change model (Prochaska and DiClemente, 1986) in the drugs and alcohol field has become widespread. This model has been shown to be useful for specialists working with drug users and drinkers (Finney 2009; Davidson *et al.*, 1991). The more traditional Twelve Step model also focuses on the importance of motivation and the change process, structuring therapeutic change through twelve separate stages. There has, however, been little research into motivational factors or the use of this type of approach. The exception is perhaps the work of Murphy and Bentall (1992) who carried out a factor analysis and revealed three main components of motivation to withdraw from heroin: private affairs, external constraint and negative effects of heroin use.

Using motivational change models for drug users

The best known authors writing about the importance of individual moti-vation in dependency treatment are Prochaska and DiClemente, who out-line a process of individual change. Whilst a model of process can be used alongside a range of different theories of dependence, it is most closely aligned with a cognitive behavioural approach and the interventions sug-gested are concerned with cognitive and behavioural change.

The authors developed a model of change processes from their work with smokers, incorporating the notion of a sequential change process. They then modified it to develop a practical motivational counselling method for work with drug and alcohol users. The model consists of five stages (Prochaska and DiClemente, 1986):

- Pre-contemplation
- Contemplation
- Action
- Maintenance of change
- Relapse

Pre-contemplation

The model predicts that people in the pre-contemplation stage of the change process will respond less well to information and advice than people in the contemplation stage. It is therefore suggested that counsel-ling for clients in this stage will be more effective if it is designed simply to raise the client's awareness of the possible issues connected with drug use (rather than attempting to offer information and advice), in order to move them to the next stage. Intervention at the pre-contemplation stage is seen as less constructive than at the contemplation stage.

Contemplation

At the contemplation stage information and advice are more likely to be assimilated and utilized. The interventions suggested at this stage include cognitive techniques such as awareness raising, information, decisional balances, re-evaluation of life events and drug-related problems. Clients at this stage are more receptive to alternative observations, interpretations and confrontation. Behavioural assessments and analysis of the functions of drug use as a coping strategy can also be useful here.

Action

This stage is sometimes split into two, the decision stage, including a firm commitment to change, which can be of very short duration, followed rapidly by the action stage, where treatment interventions are most effective.

Maintenance of change

This stage follows treatment and indicates that achieving change involves ongoing maintenance.

Relapse

The authors have demonstrated that smokers progress through this whole cycle on average about three times. They have therefore incorporated a relapse phase into the overall model.

Although the later stages of maintenance and relapse are integral parts of the model the emphasis is on the pre-contemplation and contemplation stages and the later stages are less well developed. The model is therefore particularly useful for initial assessments and appropriately timed treatment interventions, but perhaps less helpful for working in the maintenance and relapse stages.

Uses of motivational interviewing

This work was paralleled by W. R. Miller's development of the concept of motivational interviewing. His work was published in the journal *Behavioural Psychotherapy* in 1983 (Miller, 1983) and again with Sovereign and Krege in 1987 (Miller *et al.*, 1988). This approach has been evaluated over time and shown to be effective in some respects, it is however difficult to demonstrate outcomes (Finney, 2009). It has the following key principles: the client must be accepted in a complete and unconditional way; the client is a responsible person; the client must be ready for change and not forced into it by the counsellor; the goals and the forms of treatment must be negotiated.

The stages are:

- Assessment, to determine if a client wants to change or is 'ready' for change
- Increasing motivation by encouraging the client to recognize that the drug use is a problem and/or causes other problems
- Helping the client to understand the functions and effects of the drug use itself in order to weigh up the advantages and disadvantages
- Monitoring progress through the cycle of change from pre-contemplation, contemplation, decision and action to maintenance of change

Miller worked with clients with alcohol problems and argued that it was possible to increase motivation and reduce denial among them by placing emphasis on the 'decisional balance' or helping clients to weigh up the pros and cons of their drinking; by clarifying the range of choices open to them and by highlighting the discrepancies between their beliefs and behaviour. (There are similarities here between the decisional balance of Prochaska and DiClemente and the more confrontational 'breaking denial' of the Twelve Step approach, although Miller's work is not often compared with the latter.) The basic underlying premise is that change is a process with clearly definable sequential stages. The helper can be more effective if they identify which stage the client is at and make the appropriate intervention for that stage.

Limitations of the motivational change model for recreational drug users

Motivational interviewing is only for those clients who need to change: it selects from this group those who want to change. It should be remembered however that clients apparently at the pre-contemplation stage may not consider their drug use a problem, because it has not yet become one. In addition, the client whose drug use is problematic but who has decided not to change cannot simply be equated with the pre-contemplation stage of Prochaska and DiClemente, as many drug users have actually contemplated the risks and weighed up the pros and cons and already made the decision to carry on using drugs. An individual process of change may therefore actually involve several options at any one stage, rather than simply progressing from one to another along a continuum. As Nick Heather (1991) remarks, 'one wonders whether the process of change is quite so smooth and unidirectional as it seems to suggest or whether change is often more fluctuating and inconsistent'.

Despite the limitations of using motivational interviewing and the change model for clients who do not need to change, they are very useful as assessment tools, allowing professionals to determine if the client is 'ready' and 'contemplating change' or not and determining which interventions are likely to be most effective at the pre-contemplation and contemplation stages. They also help make the crucial distinction between those who need harm minimization alone and those who are more likely to respond to treatment.

Why a process model is useful

A process model of change enables professionals to understand two important factors: that clients may not be ready to change and that if they do change, they will pass through a process (several times) and interventions should therefore be tailored to their current stage.

It is interesting to examine why a process model of motivation and change should achieve such popularity among professionals in the absence of research evidence of its effectiveness. Academics and other researchers have tended to focus on outcome studies of particular interventions (as a scientific methodology is designed for this purpose), rather than study the individual processes of change. The practical relevance of a model of change processes has highlighted the limitations of this approach.

In contrast, clinical experience is often based on a different kind of knowledge, that of individual cases over time. In other words, clinical experience resembles qualitative, rather than quantitative data, providing the necessary in-depth understanding of process, individual differences and subjective interpretation. Clinical experience indicates that a change model is useful for understanding an individual's progress over time and that motivational interviewing is a useful therapeutic tool.

The concepts used in the Twelve Step approach come from a different conceptual framework and as such are not accessible to some professionals and clients. However, the essence of this approach is that a person with experience of the therapeutic change process guides an inexperienced person through stages in the correct sequence. For example, the initial step, 'breaking denial', is designed to increase motivation in the same way as moving from pre-contemplation to contemplation by developing a greater awareness of the problems caused by drug use.

Assessment

Having established a working relationship, the most important task is to find out how urgent the client feels their problems are and if they need immediate help. Only after the client's own understanding of their problem has been clarified is it appropriate to start the structured assessment to establish the categories of the client's problems and consequent needs. The factor most likely to cause failure of drug treatment is the inadequacy of assessments prior to clients making demanding life changes. The amount of support and help required is often underestimated as a consequence of incomplete assessments.

There are many specialist tools for carrying out assessments; these change over time, the most useful and up-to-date are available on the National Treatment Agency website (www.nta.gov.uk.) The following section will outline the basic process of making an assessment, in order to give an understanding of what should be assessed and why.

Purposes of assessment

The overall purpose of assessment is simply to determine what help and which interventions are appropriate at which stages in the helping process.

The motivation stage of the helping process can include a motivational interviewing assessment which enables the professional to determine whether or not the client wants to change and is ready for change.

- An initial assessment of client problems, needs and resources (skills and social support) allows the professional to identify whether or not a client has drug-related problems and if so, whether there is a need for support
- An assessment of type or category of drug use enables the professional to determine what is needed in terms of information, harm minimization and/or treatment
- Assessment for after-care informs the professional whether the client is capable of maintaining change, in terms of motivation, ability and social support networks and if so, what support they will need to do so
- Ongoing assessment enables the professional to monitor client progress and intervene rapidly if necessary
- Assessment as a whole also serves to inform the client of their needs, functioning as a feedback mechanism about the extent and nature of problems, necessity for change and progress

Assessment can be a long and complex procedure. Each type of assessment should be limited to what is both necessary and appropriate to the demands of each stage of the helping process. Assessment should follow client motivation and choices. If clients choose help, then they should first be assessed for basic health care maintenance and minimization of harm. Following this minimal initial assessment, they can be assessed for drug dependence. If they are assessed as dependent and they choose to change, only then should they be assessed for treatment and aftercare support.

Assessment can therefore be seen as a continual process, particularly in drug treatment where clients are working towards changes in behaviour and lifestyle. If a client is changing behaviour or working towards practical short-term goals, monitoring of progress on a regular basis allows for the identification of client readiness for decisions and action and also the renegotiation of short-term goals on the basis of progress made or failure to achieve these goals. Finally, assessment can also be used for 'therapeutic' purposes, to encourage the client to recognize that drug use is problematic and to monitor progress.

Deciding which drug use type or category provides the best 'fit'

In order for both professional and client to gain greater understanding of the client's problems it is necessary first to clarify the actual types and patterns of drug use and to explain the situations and circumstances that lead to this use and its consequences. It should be remembered that physical dependence is only one of a range of different problems that drug users may have. It is a serious mistake to focus only on signs of dependence for identification purposes and assessment procedures.

While all problems associated with drugs can be categorized conveniently as 'problematic' drug use, this definition is of little practical use to the professional as it gives no information about the particular problems and needs associated with different types of drug use. Assessment is concerned with identifying different categories of drug use and drug user, in order to distinguish the problems and so clarify the needs associated with each category. There is a need to have a clear cut idea of the risks and problems associated with each form of drug use. This will lead logically to an understanding of the needs, which can then be assessed within the context of the individual and agency resources available.

As has been discussed throughout the book, there are many difficulties in determining which category is most useful for defining different types of drug use, whether risky and harmful or dependent. It is also important to stress that the majority of drug users may not fit either category, being neither risky or dependent users, but simply using occasionally on a recreational basis.

In practical terms it is important to emphasize that these categories are not mutually exclusive. It is quite possible that any one client's drug use will fall into more than one category, both risky and dependent. It is then necessary to consider the problems and needs associated with both categories. In effect, a client can be several types of drug user at the same time; in the same way that a person can be both a schizophrenic and a depressive, a drug user can be both a risky user and a dependent user.

Recreational or risky?

The difficulty here is to determine when drug use becomes a health hazard or causes psychological problems. If there are few or no risks being taken there is no rationale for intervention which can be less than helpful, stigmatizing clients unnecessarily or even where substitute drugs are provided, increasing levels of dependence. It also wastes professional time and resources.

There is some guidance on safe and unsafe use in the alcohol field, where health authorities set (variable) safe and unsafe limits of alcohol consumption where it becomes statistically more likely that health will suffer. As it is unlikely that any government would have the knowledge or inclination to define the 'safe health limits' for illicit substances, there is little guidance for determining criteria for safer forms of drug use, in terms of either health, or psychological and social risks. The obvious difficulty with assessing illicit substance use is the lack of available, accurate information on the short and long-term effects of a range of different drugs.

In the absence of consistent research and formal guidelines, as for alcohol and cigarettes, professionals are thrown back on their own resources to a large extent and there is a need to carry out a detailed assessment of the long- and short-term risks taken by each individual.

Risky or dependent (or both)?

Similar difficulties apply in distinguishing between risky and dependent drug use. We cannot say simply that drug users' risky behaviour is illogical and therefore must be a consequence of dependence. It is clear from the earlier research data that many drug users think it only natural to take risks. It is necessary to draw a distinction between these two types of use as the interventions for each are different.

Dependent or self-medicating (or both)?

It is useful to identify causal direction in the development of any problem as this too will often determine the type of intervention. A recurring question in the drugs field is: which comes first, the drug or the problem? For each of the drug use categories (recreational, risky and dependent), drug use can be functional, providing a solution to certain needs or problems and/or be the cause of additional problems. Problems are often dealt with by using drugs as a remedy and drugs can cause problems. It is necessary to discover if the client is self-medicating for serious underlying psychological problems such as clinical depression because this will need to be dealt with separately from the drug use. This situation can call for two distinct assessments and two different interventions. This area of 'dual diagnosis' is a source of some controversy, particularly in the USA, where the abstinence aims of drug treatment may conflict with the necessary prescription of drugs for underlying problems (see Chapter 3).

Whilst it is necessary to determine the existence of underlying problems, it is often less than constructive to spend time consistently trying to disentangle cause and effect. Drugs initially used to solve one set of difficulties can cause others, which remain long after the initial problem has been resolved. In contrast, problems arising from drug use, such as unemployment, can remain long after the drug use has been controlled.

The question of cause and effect is often a source of controversy between clients and helpers. Clients may see their drug use as a solution or remedy for various matters ranging from boredom and depression to social deprivation, whereas professionals tend to see drug use as the cause of these problems. This argument can become a serious block to communication and in actuality may be as unimportant as the proverbial chicken and egg; the phenomenon is perhaps most usefully understood as a circular self-perpetuating process.

Changes in category over time

It is clear that clients may fall into the two categories simultaneously, it should also be stressed that that they are more than likely to fall into different categories at different periods in their lives. This is an extremely important concept as it emphasizes that drug problems change over time. In the long term this may mean that a small proportion of drug users move along a continuum from recreational to risky and eventually to dependent use. However, this is unusual and it is much more common for different categories of drug use to be temporary phenomena and to change at various times in a person's life.

In the short term, these variations in patterns of drug use mean that one person will use drugs in chaotic, risky ways for short periods of time only, gaining and losing control in response to different circumstances. For example, a young mother may respond to the stress of a broken relationship by using drugs in a chaotic way but will quickly get her drug use back under control if she receives support and help at the right time. Whilst it is clear that drug problems get worse as more drugs are used in a more uncontrolled manner, it is probably more accurate to say that individuals will have short periods of problematic use at different times in their lives.

Carrying out an assessment

A useful assessment attempts to understand the patterns of individual drug use over time within the social context of other life events. This helps clarify what type of problems the user has now, what precipitated these problems and what might lead to relapse after they have been dealt with.

The following areas are important:

- The client's own view of their drug use, definition of problem, pros and cons of use, resources and possible solutions.
- History of drug use and age at first use. Previous drug-using behaviour; types, amount, frequency and patterns of use; changing patterns of use over time, including periods of abstinence. This enables determination of which categories best fit the client's present drug use patterns.
- The functions of use or problems leading to use. This can include social and individual reasons why drugs are used; availability and group culture/norms, physiological effects and psychological reasons. This information helps determine whether drug use is recreational, risky, dependent or self-medicating.
- The problems arising from drug use.
- Medical history.
- Mental health history, including psychological problems, such as anxiety and depression.
- Social environment, problems and resources. Present social situation, relationships, dependants, accommodation, employment, legal status.
- Relationships; amount of emotional support available, including the level of family support and involvement and support from partner or spouse.
- Inter-relationships between drug use patterns and life circumstances and events in life history (particularly focusing on periods of abstinence and relapse).
- Present inter-relationships between daily and weekly patterns of drug use and other social/emotional life patterns (that is, when do they use and why?).
- History of help seeking, interventions used and outcomes.
- History of previous withdrawal episodes (if applicable).

By using this information the client's present problems can be placed in one or more categories. This will then provide a structure for clarifying problems, risks, needs, client resources and possible solutions. The types of drugs being used and pattern of use can be verified by knowing the effects and withdrawal characteristics of a range of drugs and the problems associated with different drugs, including the interactive effects of drugs. But the most important aspect of assessment is the understanding of the inter-relationships between the events associated with drug use, as it is the antecedents and consequences of drug use that need to be understood in assessing and modifying problematic use.

Assessment of the dependency syndrome

Whilst it is important to assess the full range of problems associated with drug use, it is equally important to determine if a user is, or is not, physically dependent on a particular type of drug. The concept of the dependency syndrome was developed to enable clinicians to identify this. This clinically useful concept was developed by Griffith Edwards (Edwards and Gross, 1976) and has since been adapted for drug use as a whole (Drummond, 1991). The following seven criteria are used to identify dependence: the first three are established medical criteria for physical dependence, the last four give an indication of the complexity of social and psychological factors associated with it:

- increased tolerance to the drug
- repeated withdrawal symptoms
- subjective awareness of compulsion to take the drug (craving)
- salience of drug-seeking behaviour
- relief or avoidance of withdrawal symptoms
- narrowing of the repertoire of drug taking
- re-instatement following a period of abstinence

Salience of drug-seeking behaviour describes the growing priority of drug use over other areas in an individual's life, the narrowing of drug repertoire indicates the increasingly regular and rigid patterns of drug use and reinstatement of drug-using behaviour highlights the speed with which drug use escalates when an individual relapses after a period of abstinence. This syndrome is very useful for identification and assessment of dependence on physically addictive drugs, particularly depressants such as opiates and benzodiazepines.

Assessment of problems leading to and arising from drug use

As explained earlier, drug use is often a solution to particular underlying problems. It is therefore useful, where possible, to distinguish between problems that lead to and problems that arise from drug use.

Problems contributing to drug use

Significant here are social factors such as stress, unemployment, poverty and housing and psychological factors such as depression and anxiety. If drugs are used as a solution to these problems, then clearly alternative solutions are needed if the drugs are removed.

Problems arising from drug use

Physical problems include the risks of chaotic, unplanned drug use, HIV, hepatitis and other health problems. Social problems include the

Table 8.1 Assessment grid

Signs and symptoms	Recreational	Risky	Dependent
Physical			
Psychological			
Social			

risk to dependants and others and drug-related crime. Psychological problems include depression and paranoia and, finally, drug dependence itself.

It is important to identify the functions of drug use to a client. The main functions can be seen as negative reinforcement (to escape unpleasant feelings) and positive reinforcement, ranging from mood alteration to social facilitation and enhancement of perceived control.

Assessment of physical, psychological and social problems

A basic assessment grid

The grid in Table 8.1 gives a structure for assessing the different types of categories and problems. It can also be useful for identifying signs and symptoms of drug use initially.

Earlier chapters have illustrated how physical, psychological and social factors affect both the continued use of drugs and the likelihood of relapse. Different drugs can have different short- and long-term effects. It is therefore necessary to be able to distinguish between them. The short-term effects of intoxication and the effects of prolonged drug use can influence mood, perception, memory and psychomotor ability. The effects of the drug leaving the bloodstream may likewise cause changes in normal physical and psychological states (whether withdrawals or simply 'comedowns'). It becomes difficult for professionals and for many drug users themselves to distinguish between the effects of a drug, the effects of withdrawal and associated problems. It is more than likely that the actual variation in levels of drug in the bloodstream is far more problematic than any effects of a constant supply.

This is complicated by the particular health problems associated with the effects of different drugs. For example, general signs of illness may be misinterpreted as side-effects of drug use or withdrawal or vice versa. General health problems are related to infections such as HIV and hepatitis (particularly hepatitis C), to problems arising from injection such as skin infections and damage to arteries and veins, and problems such as respiratory difficulty, vitamin deficiency and anaemia.

Care plans

A care plan should utilize the assessment to categorize the client's problems and determine appropriate solutions (see Table 8.2). It can include a review of the client's health, psychological and social needs and personal resources, together with other resources available to the practitioner. These might include, for example, the practitioner's counselling skills, health-care facilities and welfare-rights information, together with more specialist input from other agencies where necessary.

Table 8.2 Completed care plan

	Physical resources	Psychological resources	Social resources
Safety net	Needles and syringes. First aid and health care equipment	N/A	Information and lists of available services
Harm minimization care plan	As above plus prescribed drugs	N/A With exception of cognitive behavioural skills for some chaotic clients only	Developing social support networks and crisis intervention strategies
Treatment change care plan	Prescribed drugs	Counselling, psychotherapy cognitive behavioural methods	Ensure social support during change period
Aftercare maintenance and maintenance of change care plans	Prescribing if necessary	Improving cognitive behavioural coping skills; relapse prevention, relaxation plus self-control techniques	Developing supportive social networks, new social activities plus constructive occupations

Note: It should be emphasized that similar interventions may be given for different reasons. This has caused much confusion in the drugs field. For example, as outlined at the start of the book, a prescription of substitute drugs may be given to reduce drug related harm or as part of a long- or short-term withdrawal strategy.

Any care plan should follow the sequential process, providing the necessary help at both the intervention and post-intervention stages and including a provisional plan of service provision in the event of a relapse or crisis. In order to do this, plans will require several distinct assessments in order to determine the ability of the client to change, obstacles to change and the client's own resources for change and maintenance of change. A care plan and after-care plan should identify what support the client will need in order to reduce harm or to change in the first instance and what they will need in order to prevent relapse. A plan should also prioritize needs and set practical goals within the resources available. It should include providing equipment to ensure that clients reduce sharing of needles and syringes (and use condoms) and may include prescribing drugs in order to cut down the amount of illicit drug use and subsequent involvement in crime and debt.

Care plans should include the following information:

- client's needs in the short term
- client's needs for after-care maintenance
- client's resources in the short term (personal coping strategies and skills)
- client's resources in the long term (skills and social support networks)
- agency resources for intervention and aftercare

When the care plan is drawn up and a service is offered to a client, the terms and conditions should be made clear, including the extent of support available and penalties for non-compliance. Professional agreements with clients should include the negotiation of short- and long-term goals. Whilst all practitioners have a responsibility to help clients make informed decisions, there are often situations where the client and professional may have different priorities: it is necessary to clarify this when agreeing and defining goals for treatment.

The relevance of specialist theory and practice for generic professionals

This chapter has emphasized that the initial phase of any intervention should be health and safety. The first priority is to ensure that any drug-using client has information about safer drug use and access to the means to achieve it.

Once these basic health and safety precautions have been taken, the professional can then consider how to work with other agencies.

Generic professionals are often experienced in using a similar range of methods to those of specialist drug workers to maintain and support clients and to help the client to change behaviours and lifestyle. (These methods and the relevant skills are part of the basic training of most social and health care professionals.) In contrast, there is no pressing need for generic professionals to adhere to any one specialist theory or interpretation of drug dependence. As can be seen from the earlier chapters, the controversy regarding abstinence is still unresolved and may be largely redundant, as it seems effective to offer help both before and after abstinence: either way, specialists often use the same methods to deal with similar problems. It may simply be necessary to be flexible and adapt the sequence of events (and possibly the theoretical model) to fit the client's own beliefs and choices in order to increase the likelihood of cooperation.

The status of a particular theory in clinical practice is, in effect, dependent on its usefulness. In this case several competing theories are all useful for therapeutic purposes. If clients believe they have an addictive disease it may be a useful belief in helping them give up drug use; if they believe they can control their dependence, it could be equally useful for some clients. It should be remembered that the most respectable of scientists will use untested theories when they help make sense of a situation and even maintain several contradictory theories at the same time if they are practically useful (for example, the wave and particle theories of light).

It is only when there is a need to refer a client to one or another type of agency that it becomes important to know about the theories and philosophies underlying specialist practice (such as, a harm minimization outpatient service or a Twelve Step residential service), in order to determine if they are appropriate to the needs of each particular client. The theories of particular agencies may conflict with the beliefs of particular professionals, but this conflict should be of little consequence if the agency beliefs are in accordance with the beliefs and values of the client. It is the match of client to agency that is important, not the match of professional to professional. If a particular theoretical interpretation is useful to a client, it can be counterproductive for professionals to limit their client's choices to their own theoretical orientation.

Once armed with a basic understanding of drug problems, the professional can use specialist drug agencies as a source of specialist expertise, advice and prescription drugs, rather than a place to refer all clients who use occasionally use drugs. Drug agencies can provide advice and support if the situation become problematic, together with the option of syringe exchange and health care. They will carry out initial assessments, offer detoxification facilities and long-term pre-scribing. It is up to both the generic professional and their client how many of these services will be taken up.

Monitoring and evaluation

Monitoring is an essential part of the sequential helping process. It is important to keep notes to monitor progress and re-assess where neces-sary. The clinical aim is to maintain regular assessments which will determine the type of intervention appropriate at each new stage.

Monitoring can involve:

- Self-monitoring and self-assessment by the client. Clients can be asked to complete diaries, record feelings and behaviours and iden-tify the antecedents and consequences of using drugs
- Professional monitoring of the client's progress can be used to mod-ify interventions, change goals and increase support where appropri-ate (this will include re-assessments for treatment and after-care maintenance where necessary)
- Monitoring of after-care maintenance is also necessary to enable identification of danger signs and to facilitate early intervention if the client's situation deteriorates
- Professional monitoring and evaluation of their own input (with individual clients, with the agency population and with the targeted population as a whole)

Evaluation

Professional monitoring and evaluation of work must take account of the aims and purposes of each intervention. For example, if the aim is maintenance or prevention, outcome studies are inappropriate, as the effects are often only visible in total populations over long periods of time.

- Epidemiological measures give an indication of outcome in terms of changes of prevalence and incidence of problems such as HIV and drug-related overdoses in total populations. If the aim is harm mini-mization, this may be the most appropriate method of evaluation as maintenance precautions can only be evaluated as an absence of harm over periods of time.
- Outcome measures will be appropriate if the aim is controlled drug use or abstinence, but it is also important to carry out follow-up

studies in the two or three years following treatment which are crucial indicators of 'success' or 'failure'.

- Longitudinal studies can demonstrate how drug use changes over time throughout the life course.
- Process measures give an indication of what has been done, if not what has been achieved.

It can be seen that it is important to clarify the aims and objectives of any intervention before deciding what to measure and how to measure it. The understanding of the problem and its solution will influence what is counted as success. Events such as short lapses can be seen as failures or as part of the process of change itself. Abstinence at treatment outcome can be seen as success or the long-term maintenance of treatment gains can be assessed in follow-up several years later.

Chapter 9

After-Care: Relapse Prevention and Social Inclusion

Introduction

After-care and relapse prevention are necessary after any change in drug use, whether the client is using illicit drugs more safely, using prescribed drugs or abstinent. Earlier chapters have highlighted the need for continuing support and help over long periods of time. The problem with both harm minimization and treatment interventions is that whilst either approach benefits the client whilst they are in contact, the interventions do not last forever. Research indicates that when the client stops attending the services they start to take risks again or they relapse (Moos, 2008; Laffaye *et al.*, 2008). One of the most important tasks for generic professionals is therefore to support and maintain clients after interventions.

This stage in the sequential helping process should be seen as distinct from the initial interventions; it requires a separate assessment, care plan and methods. After-care plans should be designed to maintain clients over long periods of time with the minimal necessary professional input and to enable the immediate re-establishment of more intensive contact if and when this is necessary.

Developing psychological skills and new social networks

The foundation of good after-care is a comprehensive assessment of the client's needs and resources and an understanding of the reasons why a client might not be able to maintain changes in lifestyle over prolonged periods of time. The essence of relapse prevention is to equip the client to recognize risky situations and cope without reverting to old behaviours (whether these be drug use itself or associated risk behaviours).

Initial preparation for after-care may involve modification of the social environment and development of personal skills. For example it may involve the client developing a less stressful or dangerous lifestyle, building alternative social support networks with non-users and learning the necessary relapse prevention and coping skills (Humphreys *et al.*, 1999; Moos 2008). After-care support itself involves the development of a programme of regular after-care contacts, and procedures to re-establish contact in the event of a lapse or relapse (Toumbourou *et al.*, 2007; North *et al.*, 2008).

Initial preparation for relapse prevention involves the client developing personal cognitive behaviour skills designed to help prevent relapse. As early as 1986, Rounsaville (1986) identified relapse prevention as the most important problem for clinicians and suggested that treatment should focus on the likelihood of lapses or relapse and consequently encourage clients to return to treatment soon after lapse or relapse for help. In order to facilitate this he proposed that specialist agencies should develop policies and programmes that explicitly encourage re-entry into treatment after relapse and that clients should be taught to anticipate and cope with feelings and conditions that are a high risk for relapse.

Many cognitive behavioural treatment programmes lack a cohesive after-care or relapse prevention component. In Britain, where professionals may be unlikely to agree with the disease model (as it is not evidence based), they nevertheless often refer clients to Narcotics Anonymous because it provides a long-term socially orientated, self-help network lacking in any of the more mainline statutory services. In North America the situation is reversed, here cognitive behavioural relapse prevention programmes are less acceptable, but the majority of service provision, particularly the residential rehabilitation of Minnesota, links directly and cost-effectively into the self-help after-care provision of the Anonymous Fellowship. Therefore, in both Britain and America there are needs for the development of comprehensive after-care programmes which incorporate both social and psychological relapse prevention strategies and link with treatment programmes themselves.

Maintenance of harm minimization and treatment gains

Harm minimization: continuing care and relapse prevention

After-care maintenance following harm minimization simply means maintaining a support structure to ensure that clients do not take unnecessary risks in the future and do not relapse back into old unsafe habits (see Chapter 5). This can consist of the establishment of regular access to needles and syringes and the provision of crisis health-care support if necessary. It may also involve teaching cognitive behavioural methods to control chaotic drug use or to help prevent relapse to old patterns of behaviour.

Post-treatment: after-care and relapse prevention

Post-treatment after-care involves a structured approach to the maintenance of treatment change or treatment gains. Research indicates that social support networks and individual coping skills can be critical in preventing treatment relapse (see Chapter 3). Cognitive behavioural methods have been designed to prevent relapse. These methods can be used irrespective of the treatment theory itself, either to maintain abstinence or control drug use.

Pre-assessment of client ability to maintain change

Assessment of ability to maintain change and the availability of post-treatment resources should really be a part of initial assessment because if a client does not have the ability or resources to maintain treatment gains, it may be inappropriate for them to go through treatment. This is because there may be extra risks involved when clients reduce their drug use but cannot then maintain these changes over time. Becoming abstinent or reducing the amount of drugs used can lead to more problems in the short term, rather than less, such as short-term withdrawals, mood swings and depression. In the long term, if clients start to use drugs again, reductions in dose or abstinence will result in lowered tolerance levels and so the risks of overdose increase as clients try to give up, then start again and give up in turn. In effect, varying the amount of drug used is likely to be more dangerous than maintaining a steady level of use. The professional may therefore need actively to dissuade a client from engaging in drug treatment, reducing or stopping drug use until they are sure that the client has the necessary skills and support to cope in the long term.

Assessment for after-care maintenance provides the information to develop essential after-care plans. Only when the future ground has been thoroughly prepared for changes in drug use should changes take place. If no account is taken of conditions, such as psychological problems or drug using social networks, contributing to drug use in the client's everyday life then relapse is more likely.

It has already been emphasized that motivation is an essential precursor to work with drug users. It is ineffective to try to make clients change their behaviour before they are ready. However, it may well be effective for professionals to suggest that clients postpone making drastic reductions in their drug use until they are fully prepared. Having helped motivate the client, the professional's responsibility is then to help the client prepare for change. Part of making any change is preparing the ground; assessment and after-care plans are therefore an integral part of drug treatment itself.

After-care assessment

Despite the utility of pre-treatment assessments of potential after-care needs, these assessments are seldom completed during the treatment process. It is therefore important to carry out this type of assessment as soon as possible after treatment completion. After-care assessment is in effect a secondary assessment to establish what the client's needs will be after the intervention, to determine whether the client is capable of maintaining changes in the future and, if so, what individual resources/ skills and professional support systems will be necessary. Assessment will need to be reviewed regularly for harm-minimization clients, and updated at the close of the treatment stage for treatment clients. This also includes assessing progress made in treatment to ensure that clients have resolved any underlying problems contributing to their drug use and have a clear understanding of their vulnerabilities to drug use in the future.

This assessment should involve:

- Identification of potentially dangerous situations for risky behaviour and/or relapse
- Assessment of social support and individual resources
- Examination of functional purposes of individual drug use

Following the assessment, the after-care plan should include both helping the client develop personal skills and preparing a supportive social environment. A strategy can be planned to develop the client's own skills and resources with minimal professional support. This plan should outline the extent of professional support and contact necessary and clarify a procedure for dealing with crisis situations, lapses and long-term relapses.

The after-care plan should be seen as a continuation of the care plan. It involves:

- Ongoing support on a regular basis
- The development of personal and life skills

- The development and maintenance of family, social and community support systems
- Alternative occupations, such as education, training, voluntary work or employment
- The use of self-help groups and other community support services
- Clear guidelines for intervention if the client lapses or relapses

The input during this stage involves simple maintenance care and a regular series of contacts and appointments to support and monitor the client's progress.

The psychological approach to after-care and relapse prevention

In Chapters 3 and 5 the reasons for loss of treatment gains or lapse from harm minimization programmes were identified as negative emotional states, interpersonal conflict and social pressure (Marlatt 1996 Moos *et al.*, 1988; Marlatt and Gordon, 1985; Marlatt, 1985; Wilson, 1992). The cognitions that are associated with these behavioural lapses can be placed in three categories; perceived inability to cope, decreased perception of control in high-risk situations and positive expectancies of outcome (Donovan and Marlatt, 1980). For example, if a client sees a situation as stressful and feels that they do not have the necessary skills to cope, there is a decrease in perceived control; if this is accompanied by the perception of drug use as an effective means of decreasing stress and increasing personal sense of control, then the client is likely to use drugs.

Marlatt and Gordon (1996, 1980) and Larimer *et al.* (1999) suggest that the emphasis of relapse prevention should therefore be on the situational demands and stresses placed on an individual and the beliefs individuals hold of their own ability to deal with these stresses. They propose a series of cognitive and behavioural exercises. The aims of these techniques are to increase the client's perceived and actual self-control, self-confidence and coping ability, by altering cognitions and teaching new behavioural skills and coping strategies.

These researchers carried out much of their work in the alcohol treatment field, but their conclusions are equally useful for both drug dependency treatment and for maintaining safer drug use. In other words, cognitive behavioural techniques can be used to prevent 'relapses' in dependent behaviour as a whole and also to prevent relapse to unsafe drug use practices.

The following harm minimization and drug treatment goals can all be maintained by using relapse prevention techniques:

- Giving up drugs completely
- Using less regularly to avoid dependence
- Using in a more controlled way and less chaotically
- Using only with certain people in certain places
- Using fewer drugs and/or less harmful drugs
- Stopping sharing needles and syringes
- Stopping injecting

In order to maintain any of these behaviours the client can learn cognitive and behavioural skills designed specifically to prevent relapse to old behaviour patterns.

Relapse prevention: methods

Self-monitoring

The aim of self-monitoring is for clients to gain insight into their drug use and learn to recognize patterns in their behaviour. Having done this, they can find ways of avoiding that behaviour in the future. Self-monitoring varies from the use of diaries to complex behavioural assessments.

Seemingly automatic, habitual behaviours can result in relapse because of a lack of self-awareness. The client simply falls back on old familiar patterns of behaviour without realizing that they have done so. Becoming self-aware is seen as an integral part of preventing relapse because habitual cognitions and behaviours can only be controlled through an increased understanding of the client's own particular arousal states and patterns of behaviour. Behavioural assessment allows the client to assess the relative risks of particular moods and situations (Larimer *et al.*, 1999; Marlatt and Gordon, 1985).

Descriptions of past relapses and rehearsals of possible future lapses

This information can be supplemented by learning from previous relapses and rehearsals of possible future relapses. Role play, desensitization and self-control methods are useful here.

Information about the immediate and delayed effects of substances

Basic practical information about the effects of short- and long-term drug use (including tolerance, withdrawals and craving) can help contradict less accurate and/or maladaptive beliefs. For example, information about length of time and the expected effects of withdrawals or the effects of decreased tolerance after periods of abstinence may help dispel inappropriate beliefs about personal pathologies and helplessness. Similarly, learning to estimate the period of time an intense feeling of craving may last can help clients to 'surf the urge'.

Teaching clients to assess risks

In the same way that clients can learn self-awareness, they can become more adept at assessing risks in any given situation and so withdraw before they lose control of their behaviour. For example, well-remembered cues may stimulate a lapse, but if an individual avoids places where these cues are likely to occur the danger of relapse is also avoided. Clients can learn to identify and respond to situational, interpersonal and intrapersonal cues as early warning signals.

Planning specific strategies for high-risk situations

It is possible to decrease the probability of relapse by helping clients to plan step-by-step coping strategies for particular high-risk situations involving negative emotional states, interpersonal conflicts and social pressure.

Coping skills

A functional analysis of the purposes that drugs serve for each individual in lessening the effects of social and psychological stress can help identify individual deficits in coping skills which may cause relapse if drugs are given up after treatment. Social skills training has been shown to be effective in preventing relapse and a wide range of self-control or self-management programmes are designed to include the development of new skills and coping strategies. (Marlatt 1996; Marlatt and Gordon, 1980).

Skills training and coping strategies can include a wide range of generic techniques such as relaxation training, stress management, anxiety management and efficacy-enhancing imagery. In effect, the client is taught skills to help them cope and this in turn leads to increased confidence and perception of self-control, so relapse is less likely. Skills training programmes include problem-solving skills such as orientation, definition of problems, generation of alternatives and decision making.

Teaching can be in the form of basic instruction, modelling or cognitive and behavioural rehearsal:

- Assertiveness training gives the ability to express aspects of covert resentment
- Anger control teaches the client to recognize anger and its source in the environment and then communicate the anger in a less threatening way
- Self-control skills lead to a decrease in levels of arousal and irritability and so reduce anger and prevent aggression
- Cognitive behavioural stress management programmes teach the client to gain control over emotional and arousal states
- Relaxation and meditation techniques teach the client how to relax

It is clear that not all clients need social or coping skills training. However, many who stop using drugs find that these skills provide alternative coping mechanisms.

Coping strategies

It is not enough to teach clients specific individual skills appropriate for personally defined high-risk situations. As Laffaye *et al.* (2008), Billings and Moos (1982) and Marlatt (1985) found, it is also necessary to develop the individual's ability to deal with a broader range of situations and to exercise general self-control strategies to reduce the likelihood of relapse in any situation.

The overall influence of negative affect (such as anger, frustration and depression) on relapse suggests that more general mood control strategies may also be effective: for example, learning self-management skills, increasing involvement in pleasant activities, learning to relax, becoming more socially skilful in interpersonal relationships, controlling negative or self-defeating thoughts, increasing positive self-reinforcing thoughts, providing appropriate coping self-statements and gaining constructive problem-solving skills.

Relapse intervention

Relapse **intervention**, as distinct from relapse **prevention**, refers to the techniques used by both client and professional helper to prevent lapses from becoming full-blown relapses.

Relapse intervention serves a purpose for those attempting to maintain safer drug use behaviours and those attempting to remain abstinent, its function is to prevent rapidly escalating loss of control among those who experience craving and compulsion (as well as those who have been drug dependent), when they lapse after a period of abstinence or controlled use.

It will probably be necessary to continue to work with clients through several periods of dangerous drug use and/or relapse. The old-fashioned idea of meeting clients, helping them get off drugs and then ending the connection is not useful and it is now generally accepted that the relationship will last a long time and have no immediate outcome. Instead, workers support clients through difficult or dangerous periods of their drug use. They help them to control their drug use and to use in safer ways to prevent relapse and to learn to cope after relapse. Drug use and drug problems vary during the client's life. There will be times when they use fewer drugs or use non-problematically and there will be occasions when they give up altogether for a varying length of time.

Professional after-care procedures in the event of relapse

When clients go through drug treatment and stop using, the professional will help them to develop new skills and perhaps a new lifestyle to prevent relapse. The worker should then monitor the client's post-treatment progress in order to offer ongoing support and be available quickly in case the client lapses or relapses back to old dangerous patterns of use.

After-care support should include a clear procedure to be followed in the event of a lapse and/or relapse. The immediate priority is to be available to the client and offer harm minimization services if necessary. This can then be followed by the opportunity to re-enter treatment. A lapse can mean anything from a single mistake to a complete return to old lifestyles and patterns of behaviour. It is therefore important to determine its extent before acting further. A re-assessment of behaviour and circumstances may be necessary.

If potential relapse is presented to clients not as failure but as an expected part of the change process, they will then be more likely to return if they need help. Monitoring of progress is essential at this stage, to enable prompt intervention in the event of a lapse to prevent full relapse.

Relapse intervention: client action after a single lapse

The process of moving from lapse to relapse forms a continuum. The events that cause the initial lapse may be different from those which maintain it and from those which contribute to the re-establishment of the social and behavioural routines associated with a full-blown relapse. The practical implications of this are that relapse intervention as distinct from relapse prevention should become an essential part of an after-care programme.

Different strategies are needed at different stages of relapse, in the same way as different methods are tailored to different stages earlier in the sequential helping process. These strategies are designed to deal with temporary loss of control. The situation where many men and women feel most helpless is after the first lapse back into drug use. The concept of an 'AVE' or 'abstinence violation effect' is helpful here as a way of understanding the intense craving that dependent drug users can feel after a lapse. Whilst there is undoubtedly a physiological component to this effect for physically dependent users, the cognitive interpretation of this craving may also influence the feeling of loss of control.

It can be helpful for the initial lapse to be seen as controllable. A relapse can be defined in many ways. If it is seen as a 'slip' or 'lapse' but not as a complete remission, it may make it easier to deal with. Marlatt and Gordon (1980) suggest that the interpretation placed on a single lapse may determine whether or not it develops into a full relapse. So if a client expects the lapse to precipitate a serious relapse this may actually become more likely. This argument is often used as a criticism of the disease model and other abstinence-orientated approaches. (Although, by the same token, the client may be less likely to try a drug initially if they expect a full relapse.) Marlatt and Gordon suggest behavioural interventions to reduce the likelihood of transition from lapse to relapse. This involves developing a set of rules or guide-lines that govern behaviour after the initial drink or drug use. Clients may be given cards to remind them what to do if they lapse in order to prevent a full relapse.

Inability to cope in high-risk situations and personal beliefs about the usefulness of drugs in helping to cope are likely to precipitate relapse. Once potential relapse situations have been identified, client and professional can determine coping or avoidance strategies. This can involve skills such as learning to recognize and avoid high-risk situations, increasing confidence and developing coping skills, together with changes in the environment, from improving stressful relation-ships to developing new supportive networks.

Coping and avoidance strategies:

- Provide clients with a cognitive behavioural framework, in which they can understand their drug use behaviour patterns
- Help clients to identify high-risk situations (including the situational, relationship, cognitive, behavioural and emotional antecedents of drug use)

- Help clients to modify their own cognitions and behaviours that may lead them closer to relapse
- Teach clients about relapse and relapse management
- Teach new cognitions and behaviours to develop new confidence, coping skills and self-control
- Teach clients to modify their own environmental antecedents, to improve relationships and make work and social environments less stressful

The social approach to after-care

Developing new relationships and safer supportive environments

An additional or alternative approach to changing individual behaviour directly is to change relationships and the social environment itself. In Chapter 6, it became clear that drug users themselves believed that social relationships greatly influence relapse. In Chapter 3 it became clear that maintenance of treatment gains was associated with social factors rather than treatment variables themselves (Moos, 2008; Moos *et al.*, 1990; Lindstrom, 1992). In effect, the concept of 'treatment' focuses attention on the individual rather than more general social factors that may precipitate relapse. For relapse prevention, it may make more sense to reduce environmental stress, by helping clients change social relationships and adopt a less stressful lifestyle. Marlatt and Gordon (1980) argue that a 'lifestyle' balance is an essential part of a relapse prevention programme.

So a relapse prevention programme might look like any public health prevention initiative such as those preventing obesity, smoking or mental health problems. Although research is undeveloped in this area for drug users, it is possible that a more rewarding and less stressful lifestyle may provide a solution for certain types of vulnerable people. This can involve changes to reduce negative effects from stress in relationships and the environment and on a permanent basis. Clients can withdraw from old social networks and relationships, start new activities and build new (non-drug using) social support networks. Professional support can range from providing housing and occupational training to setting up support groups and working with families.

Do social factors cause relapse?

Moos *et al.* (1990) have demonstrated that individual variables interact with environmental factors to cause relapse. They suggest that support from family and friends and the existence of a relatively stable social and economic situation are important factors in the maintenance of behavioural change. Work with drinkers indicates that stress at work leads to heavy drinking, especially if this is a socially acceptable means of releasing tension (Humphreys *et al.*, 1999; Roman and Trice, 1970). North *et al.* (2008) and Kaufman and Kaufman (1979) identify both positive and negative implications of family relationships for drug and alcohol users and Steinglass (1979) applies a family systems theory to drinking, in order to highlight the influence of family dynamic on an individual, interpreting excessive drinking as a means of reducing stress in the system itself. There are gender differences in the effects of different kinds of social stress on drinking (Lemke *et al.*, 2008). Family-orientated techniques are not common in the drug field, though they have been developed in the alcohol field (Orford, 2008). The reactions of significant others to lapses and previous relapses can be influential, suggesting that it is important that relatives and family be involved in any relapse prevention strategies and that conjoint counselling to reduce more generalized stresses within a relationship may be useful (Lemke *et al.*, 2008).

Most of the research on social issues has focused on alcohol and drinking, however, it can be seen from the drug users' comments in Chapter 6 that many of these issues are likely to be exacerbated for drug users, where the stigma of illicit drug use and relationships with drug-using partners and friends may very well entail exclusion from non-using groups and conventional society and magnify the difficulties of finding new non-using social support networks and occupations (Gaitley and Seed, 1989).

Importance of social factors in treatment

The significance of social factors in treatment outcome was emphasized in Chapter 3. Of the wide range of interventions, the socially based seem most successful (Hodgson, 1994), particularly those approaches which are directed towards improving social and marital relationships or community reinforcement (Holder *et al.*, 1991). Lindstrom (1992: 30) suggests that rehabilitation of the highly dependent drinker 'seems to require a more fundamental psychological shift including a reappraisal of self and others' for this reason he suggests that Al Anon (self-help support for families of alcoholics), may be useful. Work in this area is extremely sparse but Longabaugh and Beattie (1985) have carried out a preliminary study which indicates that the greater a person's social investment, the more influential the social environment will be. Feigelman and Jaquith (1992) stressed the need for clients to change their relationships and therefore the importance of working with the families of drug users during treatment. Galanter (1993) also emphasized the necessity of change within the family as a whole if treatment was to be effective.

Importance of social factors in relapse

Humphreys *et al.* (1999) have shown that improved friendship networks are an important part of relapse prevention in self-help groups. Rhodes and Quirk (2003) and Friedman *et al.* (1999) highlighted the significance of social networks in prevention of drug related harm and HIV/AIDS. However, it became clear in Chapter 6 that many drug users lack any contact with everyday conventional social networks and as an additional handicap, users may be unaccustomed to social intercourse when sober and lack the necessary skills. The Anonymous Fellowship apparently best grasps the enormity of this task for some people and provides a self-help subculture which functions as an interim support group or even as a bridge back into non-drug-using society. Whilst it is not proposed that other treatment perspectives should replicate the Anonymous Fellowship, it is suggested that that they might consider the advantages of providing alternative forms of social after-care support.

Whilst investigations of those factors which predict relapse and recovery suggest that family stability, cohesion and social support are among the most important (Orford and Edwards, 1979; Billings and Moos, 1983), there is little research in this area, partly because it is difficult to control for social and relationship variables (Gaitley and Seed, 1989). However, there is some fragmentary evidence of the importance of relationships, for example Ravndal and Vaglum (1994) found a correlation in women patients between 'destructive relationships' and failure in treatment and Birke *et al.* (1990) found that interpersonal conflict was a predictor of relapse.

The most influential research on environmental stressors and social supports is that of Rudolph Moos and his colleagues; see Moos (2008) Finney (2009), Moos *et al.* (1990), Cronkite and Moos (1980), Moos *et al.* (1981) and Billings and Moos (1983). Moos and his colleagues found that drinkers who relapsed had more negative experiences and fewer positive life events that those who had not relapsed. They also found that those who did not relapse seemed to have created benign conditions for themselves, developed social support networks, experienced less conflict in family relationships and less pressure in work settings (North *et al.*, 2008, Humphreys *et al.*, 1999).

It seems clear that social relationships and social environment are likely to affect relapse and yet very little work has been carried out on the significance of the social in the drug field. As Brown (1990/91) points out:

> The ideology and tradition of drug user treatments, borrowed from the fields of psychiatry and psychology, emphasizes a development of the individual's coping skills ... to allow the individual to change his/her way of functioning in the community. The emphasis is on changing the individual, so that he/she can change their environment ... it has not included the service provider working to change the individual's environment beyond the limited effort of contracting community agencies for services on the client's behalf. (p. 1082)

Brown suggests that it would be useful to change role demands and expectations placed on the client by the family, school or employer and make efforts to develop new and pro-social networks. He points out that activity in these areas has been practically non-existent.

The importance of community

Researchers have argued that there should be a focus on communities rather than individual clients as part of the harm minimization response to prevention of HIV (Rhodes and Stimson, 1994). It has been proposed that harm minimization policies should focus on community change rather than individual care (Rhodes *et al.*, 1991), however, it has been difficult to identify what changes need to be made. (Rhodes and Humfleet, 1993; Stimson, 1995).

The importance of community and community projects in maintaining treatment gains has also been identified (Fitzpatrick and Gerard, 1993). Early projects for those who were dependent on alcohol were established in order to try and demonstrate the effectiveness of community programmes. The earliest example of a supportive communities project designed to support drinkers and prevent relapse was that of Hunt and Azrin (1973). These researchers designed and implemented a community-orientated programme to increase the quality of life. To do this they built reinforcement schedules into areas of social, family and vocational activities by employing 'social reinforcers', such as marital and family counselling, social clubs, telephone services and newspapers. They found that those who remained abstinent spent more time gainfully employed and with their families and more time on socially accepted recreational activities.

Evidence from similar early projects for drinkers suggested that it might be very effective (Hunt and Azrin, 1973; Azrin *et al.*, 1982; Mallams *et al.*, 1982; Sisson and Azrin, 1986). The community reinforcement approach involves the modification of the client's social environment; in effect, making an assessment of social resources, or 'reinforcement contingencies', available and using them, rather than taking the individual out of their environment to treat them (Azrin *et al.*, 1982). Azrin evaluated his project and followed up treatment and comparison groups at six months and two years. Drinkers in the community reinforcement group continued to abstain from drinking at least 90 per cent of the time, whereas drinkers in the matched comparison group drank at least 50 per cent of the time (in a three-month period following treatment). Azrin's initial success in developing and evaluating this type of programme indicates that long-term gains can be maintained if significant people in the alcoholic's natural environment remain in a position to influence their behaviour after treatment. Azrin's work suggests that the problem is the client's inability to deal with the problem on their own and that they need social support to learn to control themselves.

Other authors have also focused on the need for 'governance of self'; Lindstrom cites the work of Mack (1981) and Khantzian and Mack (1989) to show that it was recognized than that social treatment approaches offered a possible way forward in the alcohol field. Catalano and Hawkins (1985) describe one of the first projects 'Project Skills' which involved cognitive behavioural skills training and social network development using volunteer partners for each client to act as a bridge to the conventional world. They found the programme was effective if it succeeded in providing informal social supports in the community; involvement in productive roles in the community (whether in work, school or in the home); active recreational and leisure activities and skills training.

The Community Reinforcement Approach (CRA)

Perhaps the most well-researched example of community approaches is that of the Community Reinforcement Approach (CRA). Overall evaluations indicate that this type of programme is effective, but findings are mixed (Boulogne *et al.*, 2004). The CRA was developed for those with alcohol problems (Miller *et al.*, 1999; Leukefeld *et al.*, 1992; Sisson and Azrin, 1989). It was later developed for use with drug users (Budney and Higgins, 1994) and a specialized social approach built based on CRA was developed by Meyers and Smith in 1995 (Meyers *et al.*, 1998) this included social skills, relationship counselling, job club support and recreational activities. De Jong *et al.* (2007) found CRA was effective with heroin users. Secades-Villa *et al.* (2008) found that CRA was effective for cocaine users in achieving abstinence and in treatment retention.

Higgins *et al.* (2000) found that this was only effective if vouchers were given. Garner *et al.* (2009) found that CRA was effective in improving retention of treatment gains at follow-up. Fernandez *et al.* (2006) and Leukefeld *et al.* (1992) reviewed a range of community approaches and found that almost all appeared effective but that there was in there was a lack of good evidence or effective evaluations of projects. Meyers *et al.* (2002, 1998) found that the community reinforcement and family training programme (CRAFT) was very effective in actually engaging drug users in treatment and Waldron *et al.* (2007) found that this programme increased treatment gains.

Boulogne *et al.* (2004) reviewed the community reinforcement approach when used for cocaine, opiates and alcohol treatment. They found evidence that CRA is effective in reducing the amount of drinking, but not necessarily in maintaining abstinence. Similarly, they found that it was more effective in a Methadone maintenance programme and less effective in opioid detoxification programmes. However, there is evidence that CRA with 'incentives' (such as voucher schemes) was more effective in achieving cocaine abstinence than with alcohol or heroin abstinence.

Much of the work on CRA has been carried out in America, two studies have evaluated its impact in other countries, Secades-Villa *et al.* (2008) found it was effective for cocaine users in Spain and Ryan *et al.* (1999) that it could be effective for drug and alcohol users in the UK.

It should be remembered that the Anonymous Fellowship and the Twelve Step programme offer a type of social programme, as they are in effect utilizing the social environment to change relationships and maintain change over time (Moos, 2008). It can be seen that there are similarities between community reinforcement programmes and the Twelve Step programmes discussed in Chapter 3. It is perhaps therefore not surprising that Kirby *et al.* (1999) found that community reinforcement programmes were no more effective than a Twelve Step (disease model) self-help group, though community reinforcement interventions were more likely to retain clients and introduce them to formal treatment.

The future

The future of community programmes is uncertain. Despite the apparent usefulness of some of these interventions, they have not been widely developed outside the US. It is clear from research cited in Chapter 7 and the comments of users themselves in Chapter 6, that whilst new friendships can be developed and new social cultures conformed to, the obstacles to social re-integration may also include structural barriers in a society where social stigma and poverty are not so easily overcome (Fitzpatrick and Gerard, 1993).

In conclusion, if drug users are to stop using it is likely that they will need to move out of drug-using social networks and corresponding occupations and develop a complete change in lifestyle. It follows that old social networks will need to be discarded and new ones developed just at the time when the individual is most vulnerable and least able to cope on their own. It is during this period of transition that individuals will have to change their own behaviour and develop new skills. It is at this most crucial time that treatment ends and the help stops.

It is clear that after-care provision needs to be designed to cope, not only with the abstinence effects of craving and compulsion, but also with the loneliness which is the consequence of breaking old relationships and the poverty and stigma which are the effects of a previous illegal status within conventional society.

References

Advisory Council on the Misuse of Drugs (ACMD) (1988/1989) *AIDS and Drug Misuse*, Parts 1 and 2 (London: HMSO).

Alcoholics Anonymous (1981) *Survey of AA in Great Britain* (General Service Board of Alcoholics Anonymous Ltd).

Anderson, D. (1981) *The Minnesota Experience* (Minnesota: Hazelden Foundation).

Anderson, S. and Berridge, V. (2000) 'Opium in Twentieth-Century Britain: pharmacists, regulation and the people', *Addiction*, 95 (1) 23–36.

Anglin, M. D., Hser, Y., Huang, D. and Teruya, C. (2003) 'Gender comparisons of drug abuse treatment outcomes and predictors', *Drug and alcohol dependence*, 72 (3) 255–64.

Anonymous (1994) 'Position statement on the need for improved training for treatment of patients with combined substance use and other psychiatric disorders', *American Journal of Psychiatry*, 151 (5) 795–6.

Anonymous (1976) *Alcoholics Anonymous*, rev. edn (Minnesota: Watson & Witney).

Anonymous (1970) *The Little Red Book* (Minnesota: Hazelden Foundation).

Antze, P. (1979) 'The role of ideologies in peer psychotherapy groups', in M.A. Lieberman, L.D. Borman and P. Antze (eds), *Self Help Groups for Coping with Crisis* (San Francisco: Jossey-Bass).

Arbor, S. and Khlat, M. (2002) 'Introduction to social and economic patterning of women's health in a changing world', *Social Science and Medicine*, 54 (5), 643–7.

Ashton M. (2008) 'The new abstentionists', *Druglink*, March–April.

Azrin, N.H., Sisson, R.W., Meyers, R.W. and Godley, M. (1982) 'Alcoholism treatment by Disulfiram and community reinforcement therapy', *Journal of Behaviour Therapy and Experimental Psychiatry*, 13 (2), 105–12.

Babor, T.F., Ritson, E. and Hodgson, R. (1986) 'Alcohol related problems in the primary health care setting: a review of early intervention strategies', *British Journal of Addiction*, 81 (1), 23–46.

Babor, T.F., Aguirre-Molina, M., Marlatt, G.A. and Clayton, R. (1999) 'Managing alcohol problems and risky drinking', *American Journal of Health Promotion*, 14 (2) 98–103.

Babor, T.F., Dolinsky, Z., Rounsaville, B. and Jaffe, J. (1988) 'Unitary versus multidimensional models of alcoholism treatment outcome: an empirical study', *Journal of Studies on Alcohol*, 49 (2), 167–77.

Baekland, F., Lundwall, L. and Kissen, B. (1975) Methods for the treatment of chronic alcoholism: a critical appraisal, in R.J. Gibbens, Y. Israel, H. Kalant, R.E. Popham, W. Schmidt and R.G. Smart (eds) *Research Advances in Alcohol and Drug Problems*, 2, (New York: Wiley) 247–327.

Baer, J.S. and Carney, M.M. (1993) 'Biases in perceptions of the consequences of alcohol use among college students', *Journal of Studies on Alcohol*, 54 (1), 54–60.

Baer, M., Marlatt, G.A. and McMahon, M. (1981) *Addictive Behaviours across the Lifespan: Prevention, Treatment and Policy Issues* (California: Sage).

Bailey, S.L. (1992) 'Adolescents' multi-substance use patterns: the role of heavy alcohol and cigarette use', *American Journal of Public Health*, 82 (9) 1220–4.

Baldock, J. (1997) 'Social care in old age: more than a funding problem', *Social Policy and Administration*, 31 (1) 73–89.

Balfour, D.J.K. (1990) *Psychotropic Drugs of Abuse* (New York: Pergamon).

Balfour, D.J.K. (1994) 'Neural mechanisms underlying nicotine dependence', *Addiction*, 89 (11) 1419–23.

Bandura, A. (1977) *Social Learning Theory* (Englewood Cliffs: Prentice-Hall).

Banks, A. and Waller, T. (1988) *Drug Use, A Practical Handbook for GPs* (Oxford: Blackwell Scientific Publications).

Baron, S. W., and Kennedy, L. W. (1998) 'Deterrence and homeless male street youths', *Canadian Journal of Criminology*, 40 (1) 27–60.

Battjes, R. J., Gordon, M. S., and Kinlock, T. W. (2004) 'Factors associated with criminal severity among adolescents entering substance abuse treatment', *Journal of Drug Issues*, 34 (2), 293–318.

Battjes, R.J., Pickens, R. and Amsel, Z. (1991) *Trends in HIV Infection and AIDS Risk Behaviours among Intravenous Drug Users in Selected US Cities.* Seventh International Conference on AIDS, Florence, Abstract THC46.

Bean, P. and Wilkinson, C. (1988) 'Drug taking, crime and the illicit supply system', *British Journal of Addiction*, 83 (5), 533–9.

Bean, P. and Winterburn, D. (1997) *Persistent Drug-Using Offenders*, Home Office Research Findings. No. 50 (London: Home Office).

Bechara, A., Damasio, H., Tranel, D. and Anderson, S.W. (1998) 'Dissociation of Working Memory from Decision-Making within the Human Prefrontal Cortex', *Journal of Neuroscience*, 18 (1), 428–37.

Beck, A.T. (1989) *Cognitive Therapy and the Emotional Disorders* (New York: International Universities Press, Inc.).

Becker, H.S. (1964) *The Other Side* (New York: Free Press).

Becker, M.H. and Maiman, L.A. (1975) 'Sociobehavioural determinants of compliance with health and medical care recommendations', *Medical Care*, 13, 10–24.

Bell, D.S. (1990) 'The irrelevance of governmental policies on drugs', *Drug and Alcohol Dependence*, 25 (2), 221–4.

Bell, J., Digiusto, E. and Byth, K. (1992) 'Who should receive Methadone maintenance?' *British Journal of Addiction*, 87 (5) 689–94.

Bellack, A.S. and Gearon, J.S. (1998) 'Substance abuse treatment for people with Schizophrenia', *Addictive Behaviours*, 23 (6) 749–66.

Benda, B. B., Corwyn, R. F. and Toombs, N. J. (2001) 'Recidivism among adolescent serious offenders: Prediction of entry into the correctional system for adults', *Criminal Justice and Behaviour*, 28 (5) 588–613.

Bennett, T. (1998a), *Drug Testing Arrestees,* Home Office Research Findings, no. 70, (London: Home Office).

Bennett, T. (1998b), *Drugs and Crime: The results of research on drug testing and interviewing arrestees,* Home Office, Research Study 183 (London: Home Office).

Berg, I.K. and Hopwood, L. (1991) 'Doing with very little: treatment of homeless substance abusers', *Journal of Independent Social Work,* 5 (3/4) 109–19.

Bergin, A. and Garfield, S. (eds) (1978) *Psychotherapy and Behaviour Change* (New York: Wiley).

Berridge, V. (1999) 'Histories of harm reduction: illicit drugs, tobacco, and nicotine', *Substance Use and Misuse,* 34 (1) 35–47.

Berridge, V. (1998) 'AIDS and drug policy; the 1970s or the 1990s?' *Drugs: Education, Prevention and Policy,* 5 (3) 319–21.

Berridge, V. and Edwards, G. (1981) *Opium and the People* (London: Allen Lane).

Berridge, V. and Stanton, J. (1999) Science and policy: historical insights', *Social Science and Medicine,* 49 (9) 1133–8.

Best, D., Loaring, J., Ghufran, S. and Day, E. (2008) 'Different Roads', *Drink and Drugs News* May, 61–2.

Billings, A.G. and Moos, R.H. (1983) 'Psychosocial processes of recovery among alcoholics and their families: implications for clinicians and programme evaluators', *Addictive Behaviours,* 8 (3) 205–18.

Billings, A.G. and Moos, R.H. (1982) 'Social support and functioning among community and clinical groups: a panel model', *Journal of Behavioural Medicine,* 5 (3) 295–311.

Birke, S.A., Edelmann, R.J. and Davis, P.E. (1990) 'An analysis of the abstinence violation effect in a sample of illicit drug users', *British Journal of Addiction,* 85 (10), 1299–307.

Blackpool Community Safety Partnership (2003) 'Tower Project. Community Safety Partnership', Blackpool (www.csp.blackpool.org.uk/Tower).

Bloor, M. (1995) *The Sociology of HIV Transmission* (London: Sage).

Bloor, M.J., McIntosh, J., McKeganey, N.P. and Robertson, M. (2008) 'Topping up Methadone: An analysis of patterns of heroin use among a treatment sample of Scottish drug-users', *Public Health,* 10, 1016.

Bloor, M., Neal, J. and McKeganey, N.P. (2006) 'Persisting local variations in prevalence of hepatitis C virus among Scottish problem drug users: results from an anonymous screening study', *Drugs: Education, Prevention and Policy,* 13, 189–91.

Bloor, M., Frischer, M. and Taylor, A. (1994) 'Tideline and turn: possible reasons for the continuing low HIV prevalence among Glasgow's injecting drug users', *Sociological Review,* 42 (4) 738–57.

Bodin, M.C. and Romelsjo, A. (2006) 'Predictors of Abstinence and Non-problem Drinking after 12-Step Treatment in Sweden', *Journal of Studies on Alcohol,* 67 (1) 139–146.

Bolles, R.C. (1979) *Learning Theory* (New York: Holt, Rinehart & Winston).

Bolton, K. and Sellick, S. (1991) 'Out on your own: making solo outreach work', *Druglink,* 6, 9–10.

Boulogne, J.J., De Jong, C.A. J., Kerkhof, A.J. F. M., Roozen, H,G., van den Brink, W. and van Tulder, M.W. (2004) 'A systematic review of the effectiveness of the community reinforcement approach in alcohol, cocaine and opioid addiction', *Drug and Alcohol Dependence*, 74 (9) 1–13.

Brach, C., Falik, M., Law, C., Robinson, G., Trentadames, S., Ulmer, C. and Wright, A. (1995) 'Mental health services – critical component of integrated primary care and substance abuse treatment', *Journal of Health Care for the Poor and Undeserved*, 6 (3) 322–41.

Bratt, I. (1953) *Alcoholism, a Disease?* (Stockholm: Bonniers).

Brown, B.S. (1993) 'Observations on the recent history of drug user counselling', (review). *International Journal of Addictions*, 28 (12) 1243–55.

Brown, B. (1990/91) Introduction to special edition of *International Journal of Addictions*, 25 (9A and 10A) 1081–2.

Brown, B.S. (1979) *Addicts and Aftercare: Community Integration of the Former Drug User* (California: Sage).

Brown, B.S. and Ashery, R.S. (1979) 'Aftercare in drug abuse programming', in R.I. DuPont, A. Goldstein and J. O'Donnell (eds), *Handbook on Drug Abuse* (Washington, DC: National Institute of Drug Abuse).

Brown, L.S., Mitchel, J.L., DeVorre, S.L. and Primm, B.J. (1989) 'Female intravenous drug users and perinatal HIV transmission', *New England Journal of Medicine*, 320 (22), 1493–4.

Brown, S.A., Goldman, M.S. and Christiansen, B.A. (1985) 'Do alcohol expectancies mediate drinking patterns of adults?' *Journal of Consulting and Clinical Psychology*, 53 (4) 419–26.

Budney A. and Higgins S.T. (1994) *A Community Reinforcement Approach: treating cocaine addiction*, NIDA Publication n.98–4309 (Rockville, Maryland: National Institute of Drug Abuse).

Buning, E. (1991) 'The role of harm reduction programmes in curbing the spread of HIV by drug injectors', in J. Strang and G.V. Stimson (eds), *AIDS and Drug Use* (London: Routledge).

Burke, A.C. (1992) 'Between entitlement and control: dimensions of U.S. drug policy', *Social Service Review*, 66 (4) 571–81.

Burt, J. and Stimson, G.V (1990) *Strategies for Protection: Drug Injecting and the Prevention of HIV Infection* (Monitoring Research Group, Centre for Research on Drugs and Health Behaviour, Charing Cross and Westminster Medical School, London).

Caddy, G.R. and Block, T. (1985) 'Individual differences in response to treatment', in M. Galizio and S.A. Maisto (eds) *Determinants of Substance Abuse: Biological, Psychological and Environmental Determinants* (New York: Plenum Press).

Caldwell, C. (1976) 'Physiological aspects of cocaine usage', in S.J. Mule (ed.) *Cocaine; Chemical, Biological, Clinical, Social and Treatment Aspects* (Cleveland, Ohio: CRC Press).

Callaghan, J.; Pace, F.; Young, B., Vostanis, P. (2003) 'Primary Mental Health Workers within Youth Offending Teams: a new Service Model', *Journal of Adolescence*, 26 (2) 185–99.

Caplehorn, J.R.M., Bell, J., Kleinbaum, D.G. and Gebski, V. J. (1993) 'Methadone dose and heroin use during maintenance treatment', *Addiction*, 88 (1) 119–24.

Carroll, K.M., Rounsaville, B.J. and Bryant, K.J. (1993) 'Alcoholism in treatment-seeking cocaine abusers: clinical and prognostic significance', *Journal of Studies on Alcohol*, 54 (2) 1993–2208.

Carter, A. and Hall, W. (2007) 'The social implications of neurobiological explanations of resistible compulsions', *American Journal of Bioethics*, 7 (1) 15–17.

Casey, T., McFadden, M., Mwesigye, S. and Smithson, M. (2004) 'The impact of illicit drug supply reduction on health and social outcomes: The heroin shortage in the Australian Capital Territory', *Addiction*, 99 (3) 340–8.

Catalano, R.F. and Hawkins, J.D. (1985) 'Project skills: preliminary results from a theoretically based aftercare experiment', in R.S. Ashery (ed.), *Progress in the Development of Cost-Effective Treatment for Drug Abuse* (Rockville, MD: National Institute on Drug Abuse.

Catalano, R.F., Hawkins, J.D., Krenz, C. and Gilmore, M. (1993) 'Special populations: using research to guide culturally appropriate drug abuse prevention', *Journal of Consulting and Clinical Psychology*, 61 (5) 804–11.

Catalano, R.F., Hawkins, J.D., Wells, E.A. and Miller, J. (1990/91) 'Evaluation of effectiveness of adolescent drug abuse treatment, assessment of risks for relapse and promising approaches for relapse prevention', *International Journal of Addictions*, 25 (9A and 10A) 1085–140.

Catania, C., and Hamad, S. (eds) (1988) *The Selection of Behaviour* (Cambridge: CUP).

Chalder, M., Elgar, F.J. and Bennett, P. (2006) 'Drinking and motivations to drink among adolescent children of parents with alcohol problems', *Alcohol and Alcoholism*, 41 (1) 107–13.

Chalmers, J.W.T. (1990) 'Edinburgh's community drug problem service, pilot evaluation of Methadone substitution', *Health Bulletin*, 48, 62–72.

Cochrane Collaboration, The, www.cochrane.org/reviews (John Wiley & Sons and WileyInterScience).

Collison, M. (1994), 'Drugs and delinquency; a non-treatment paradigm', *Probation Journal*, Dec, 203–7.

Copello, A., Templeton, L., Orford, J., Velleman, R., Patel, A., Moore, L., MacLeod, J. and Godfrey, C. (2009) 'The relative efficacy of two levels of a primary care intervention for family members affected by the addiction problem of a close relative: a randomized trial', *Addiction*, 104 (1) 49–58.

Cook, C. (1988) 'The Minnesota Model in the management of drug and alcohol dependency: Part I, philosophy and programme; Part II, guidance and conclusions', *British Journal of Addiction*, 83, 626–34 and 735–43.

Craig, R.J. and Olson, R.E. (1990) 'MCMI comparisons of cocaine abusers and heroin addicts', *Journal of Clinical Psychology*, 46 (2) 230–7.

Crawford, V., Crome, I. and Clancy, C. (2003) 'Co-existing problems of mental health and substance misuse (dual diagnosis): a literature review', *Drugs: Education, Prevention and Policy*, 10 May Supplement, S.1–S.74.

Cronkite, R.C. and Moos, R.H. (1980) 'Determinants of post treatment functioning of alcoholic patients: a conceptual framework', *Journal of Consulting and Clinical Psychology,* 48 (1), 35–16.

Curren, H.V., Kleckham, J. Bearn, J., Strang, J. and Wanigaratne, S. (2001) 'Effects of Methadone on cognition, mood and cravings in detoxifying opiate addicts: a dose response study', *Psychopharmacology* 152 (2) 153–60.

Dackis, C.A. and Marks, S.G. (1983) 'Opiate addiction and depression: cause or effect', *Drug and Alcohol Dependence,* 11 (1), 105–9.

Dai, B. (1973) *Opium Addiction in Chicago* (Shanghai: Commercial Press).

Darke, S., Swift, W., Hall, W. and Ross, M. (1994) 'Predictors of injecting and injecting risk taking behaviour among Methadone maintenance clients', *Addiction,* 89 (3) 311–16.

Davey-Rothwell, M.A.; Kuramoto, S.J. and Latkin, C.A. (2008) 'Social Networks, Norms, and 12-Step Group Participation', *American Journal of Drug and Alcohol Abuse,* 34 (2) 185–93.

Davidson, R., Rollnick, S. and MacEwan, I. (eds) (1991) *Counselling Problem Drinkers* (Routledge: London).

Davies, J.B. (1993) *The Myth of Addiction* (Switzerland: Harwood Academic Publishers).

Davies, J.B. and Coggans, N. (1991) *The Facts about Adolescent Drug Use* (London: Cassel).

Davies, M. (1985) *The Essential Social Worker: A Guide to Positive Practice* (Ashgate, Hants: Community Care Practice Handbooks).

Day, C., Topp, L., Rouen, D., Darke, S., Hall, W. and Dolan, K. (2003) 'Decreased heroin availability in Sydney in early 2001', *Addiction, 98* (1) 93–5.

Deakin, E.Y., Levy, J.C. and Wells, V W. (1987) 'Adolescent depression, alcohol and drug abuse', *American Journal of Public Health,* 77 (2), 178–82.

De Jong, C.A.J., Roozen, H.G., van Rossum, L.G.M., Krabbe, P.F.M. and Kerkhof, A.J.F.M. (2007) 'High Abstinence Rates in Heroin Addicts by a New Comprehensive Treatment Approach', *American Journal on Addictions,* 16 (2) 124–30.

De Li, S., Priu, H. D. and MacKenzie, D. L. (2000) 'Drug involvement, lifestyles, and criminal activities among probationers', *Journal of Drug Issues, 30* (3) 593–619.

Decorte, T. (2001) 'Quality control by cocaine users: underdeveloped harm reduction strategies', *European Addiction Research* 7 (4), 161–75.

Denzin, N.K. (1987a) *Treating Alcoholism: An Alcoholics Anonymous Approach* (California: Sage).

Denzin, N.K. (1987b) *The Alcoholic Self* (California: Sage).

Denzin, N.K. (1986) *The Recovering Alcoholic* (California: Sage).

Department of Health (2004) *Draft Mental Health Bill* (London: Department of Health, Cm 6305–1).

Department of Health (2002) *Mental Health Policy Implementation Guide: dual diagnosis good practice guide* (London: Department of Health).

Department of Health (1999) *Drug Misuse and Dependence: Clinical Guidelines on Clinical Management* (London: HMSO).

Dermott, F. and Pyett, P. (1994) 'Co-existent psychiatric illness and drug abuse: a community study', *Psychiatric and Psychological Evidence,* 22, 45–52.

Des Jarlais, D.C. (1990) 'Stages in the response of the drug abuse treatment system to the AIDS epidemic in New York City', *Journal of Drug Issues,* 20, 335–47.

Des Jarlais, D. and Friedman, S.R. (1988) 'HIV and intravenous drug use', *AIDS,* 2 (suppl. 1), S65–S69.

Des Jarlais, D.C., Arasteh, K., Semaan, S. and Wood, E. (2009) 'HIV among injecting drug users: current epidemiology, biologic markers, respondent-driven sampling, and supervised-injection facilities', *Current Opinion on HIV AIDS.* 4 (4) 308–13.

Des Jarlais, D.C., Friedman, S.R. and Casriel, C. (1990) 'Target groups for preventing AIDS among intravenous drug users: 2 The 'hard' data studies', *Journal of Consulting and Clinical Psychology,* 58 (1) 50–6.

Deykin, E.Y., Buka, S.L. and Zeena, T.H. (1992) 'Depressive illness among chemically dependent adolescents', *American Journal of Psychiatry,* 149 (10) 1341–7.

DiClemente, C.C. and Prochaska, J.O. (1985) Processes and stages of change: coping and competence in smoking behaviour change, in S. Shipman and W. Wills (eds) *Coping and Substance Abuse* (New York: Academic Press).

Dolan, K.A., Donoghoe, M.C., Jones, S. and Stimson, G.V. (1991) *A Cohort Study at Four Syringe Exchange Schemes and Comparison Groups of Drug Injectors,* Report to the Department of Health (The Centre for Research on Drugs and Health Behaviour, London).

Dole, V.P. and Nyswander, M.E. (1968) 'The use of Methadone for Narcotic Blockade', *British Journal of Addiction,* 63 (1), 55–7.

Donoghoe, M.C., Dolan, K.A. and Stimson, G.V. (1991) *The 1989–1990 National Syringe Exchange Monitoring Study* (Monitoring Research Group, Centre for Research on Drugs and Health Behaviour, Charing Cross and Westminster Medical School, London).

Donoghoe, M.C., Stimson, G.V and Dolan, K. (1989) 'Sexual behaviour of injecting drug users and associated risks of HIV infection for non-injecting sexual partners', *AIDS Care,* 1, 51–8.

Donovan, D.M. and Marlatt, G.A. (1980) 'Assessment of expectancies and behaviours associated with alcohol consumption: a cognitive behavioural approach', *Journal of Studies on Alcohol,* 41, 1156–85.

Downs, W.R. and Morrison, L. (1998), 'Childhood maltreatment and the risk of substance problems in later life', *Health and Social Care in the Community,* 6 (1) 35–46.

Drake, R.E., Mercer-McFadden, C., Mueser, K.T., McHugo, G.J. and Bond, G.R. (1998) 'Review of integrated mental health and substance abuse treatment for patients with dual disorders', *Schizophrenia Bulletin,* 24 (4) 589–608.

Drummond, C. (1991) 'Dependence on psychoactive drugs: finding a common language', in L.B. Glass (ed.) *Addiction Behaviour* (London: Routledge).

Drummond, D.C., Cooper, T. and Glautier, S.P. (1990) 'Conditioned learning in alcohol dependence: implications for cue exposure treatment', *British Journal of Addiction,* 85 (6) 725–43.

Duffe, D.E. and Carlson, B.E. (1996) 'Competing value premises for the provision of drug treatment to probationers', *Crime and Delinquency,* 42 (4) 574–92.

Dunn, C., Deroo, L., Rivara, F.P., Rollnick, S., Miller, W. R., Heather, N. and Longabaugh, R. (2001) 'The use of brief interventions adapted from motivational interviewing across behavioral domains: a systematic review', *Addiction,* 96 (12) 1725–42.

Edmunds, M., Hough, M., Turnbull, P.J. and May, T. (1999) *Doing justice to Treatment. Referring offenders to drug services.* Briefing paper 2. Drugs Prevention Advisory Services (PDAS) London (www.homeoffice.gov.uk/dpas/ dpas.htm).

Edmunds, M., Hough, M. and Urquia, N. (1996) *'Tackling Local Drug Markets',* Police Research Group, Crime Detection and Prevention Series, paper 80 (London: Home Office).

Edwards, G. (1989a) 'As the years go rolling by: drinking problems in the time dimension', *British Journal of Psychiatry,* 154, 18–26.

Edwards, G. (1989b) 'What drives British drug policies?' *British Journal of Addiction,* 84 (2) 219–26.

Edwards, G. (1988) 'Long term outcome for patients with drinking problems: the search for predictors', *British Journal of Addiction,* 83 (8) 917–27.

Edwards, G. (1986) 'The alcohol dependence syndrome', *British Journal of Addiction,* 81(2) 171.

Edwards, G. and Davies, D.L. (1994) 'Normal drinking in recovered alcohol addicts: the genesis of a paper', *Drug and Alcohol Dependence,* 35 (3) 249–59.

Edwards, G. and Taylor, C. (1994a) 'Drinking problems, the matching hypothesis and a conclusion revised', *Addiction,* 89 (5) 609–11.

Edwards, G. and Taylor, C. (1994b) 'A test of the matching hypothesis: alcohol dependence, intensity of treatment, and 12-month outcome', *Addiction,* 89 (5) 553–61.

Edwards, G. and Orford, J. (1977) 'Alcoholism: a controlled trial of treatment and advice, *Journal of Studies on Alcohol,* 38 (5), 1004–31.

Edwards, G. and Grant, M. (eds) (1977) *Alcoholism* (Oxford: Oxford University Press).

Edwards, G. and Grant, M. (eds) (1976) *Alcoholism: New Knowledge and Responses* (London: Croom Helm).

Edwards, G. and Gross, M.M. (1976) 'Alcohol dependence: provisional description of a clinical syndrome', *British Medical Journal,* 1 (1), 1058–61.

Edwards, G., Meyer, R. E., Miller, W. R., Hall, W., Poikolainen, K., Crome, I.B., Fischer, G. and Winters, K. (2000) 'Addiction treatment and the making of large claims', *Addiction,* 95 (12) 1755–7.

Edwards, G., Parry, C.D.H., Seivewright, N., Giesbrecht, N., Raistrick, D., Romelsjo, A. and San, L. (1999) 'Comments on Drug Misuse and the Environment: a recent British report', *Addiction,* 94 (9) 1299–309.

Edwards, G., Holder, S., West, R. and Babor, T. F. (1997) 'Addiction journals: amazing happenings, landmark meeting, historic consensus, evolving process', *Addiction,* 92 (12) 1613–18.

Edwards, G., Brown, D., Duckitt, A., Oppenheimer, E., Sheehan, M. and Taylor, C. (1987) 'Outcome of alcoholism: the structure of patient attributions as to what causes change', *British Journal of Addiction*, 82 (5) 533–45.

Egan, G. (1990) *The Skilled Helper: A Systematic Approach to Effective Helping* (California: Brooks Cole).

Eiser, C., Eiser, J.R. and Pritchard, M. (1988) 'Reactions to drug education: a comparison of two videos', *British Journal of Addiction*, 83 (8) 955–63.

Eiser, J.R. (1982) Addiction as attribution, cognitive processes in giving up smoking', in *Social Psychology and Behavioural Medicine*, ed. J.R. Eiser (Chichester: Wiley).

Eiser, J.R. and Gossop, M. (1979) 'Hooked or sick: addicts' perceptions of their addiction', *Addictive Behaviours*, 4 (2), 185–91.

Eiser, J.R. and Sutton, S.R. (1977) 'Smoking as a subjectively rational choice', *Addictive Behaviours*, 2 (2–3), 129–34.

Elliott, L., Jackson, A., Orr, L. and Watson, L. (2005a) 'Secondary prevention interventions for young drug users: a systematic review of the evidence', *Adolescence*; 40 (157) 1–22.

Elliott, L, Jackson, A, Orr, L, Watson, L. (2005b) 'How effective are secondary prevention interventions for young drug users?' *Family Therapy*, 2 (1) 15–30.

Ellis, A. (1987) 'The evolution of rationale-emotive therapy (RET) and cognitive-behaviour therapy (CBT)', in *The Evolution of Psychotherapy*, ed. J. Zeig (New York: Brunner/Mazel).

Ellis, A. (1962) *Reason and Emotion in Psychotherapy* (New York: Lyle Stuart).

Ellis, R. and Stephens, R.C. (1976) 'The arrest history of narcotic addicts prior to admission. A methodological note', *Drug Forum*, 5, 211–24.

Erikson, L., Bjornstad, S. and Gotestam, K.G. (1986) 'Social skills training in groups for alcoholics: one year treatment outcome for groups and individuals', *Addictive Behaviours*, 11 (3), 309–29.

Erickson, P.G. (1990) 'A public health approach to demand reduction', *Journal of Drug Issues*, 20, 563–75.

Evandrou, M. and Glaser, K. (2004) 'Family, work and quality of life: changing economic and social roles through the lifecourse', *Ageing and Society*, 24 (1) 1–21.

Everson, M. (2002) 'The Crisis of Indeterminacy: A Reasoned and Reasoning European Market Administration', in *Collected Courses of the Academy of European Law 2000* (Oxford: Oxford University Press) pp. 231–52.

Fairhead, S. (1981) *Persistent Petty Offenders*, Home Office Research Findings No. 66 (London: Home Office).

Farrell, M. (1990) 'Beyond platitudes: problem drug use, a review of training', *British Journal of Addiction*, 85 (12) 1559–62.

Farrell, M., Howes, S., Taylor, C. *et al.* (1998) *National Psychiatric Co-morbidity Study* (London: OPCS).

Farrell, M., Battersby, M. and Strang, J. (1990) 'Screening for Hepatitis B and Vaccination of Injecting Drug Users in NHS Drug Treatment Services', *British Journal of Addiction*, 85 (12), 1657–9.

Feigelman, B. and Jaquith, P. (1992) 'Adolescent drug treatment, a family affair: a community day centre approach, *Social Work in Health Care*, 16 (3) 39–52.

Fernandez, A.C., Marlatt, G.A. and Begley, E.A. (2006) 'Family and Peer Interventions for Adults: Past Approaches and Future', *Psychology of Addictive Behaviors*, 20 (2) 207–13.

Fine, J. and Miller, N.S. (1993) 'Evaluation and acute management of psychotic symptomatology in alcohol and drug addictions', *Journal of Addictive Diseases*, 12 (3) 59–72.

Fingarette, H. (1988) *Heavy Drinking: The Myth of Alcoholism as a Disease* (Berkeley: University of California Press).

Finney, J.W. (2009) 'Meta-analyses and the search for specific and common mediators of substance misuse intervention effects', *Addiction*, 104 (5) 716–7.

Finney, J.W., Moos, R.H. and Mewborn, C.R. (1980) 'Post treatment experiences and treatment outcome of alcoholic patients six months and two years after hospitalisation', *Journal of Consulting and Clinical Psychology*, 48, 17–29.

Fishbein, M. and Ajzen, I. (1985) *Belief, Attitude, Intention and Behaviour: An Introduction to Theory and Research* (Reading, Mass: Addison-Wesley).

Fitzpatrick, J.L. and Gerard, K. (1993) 'Community attitudes towards drug use: the need to assess community norms', *International Journal of the Addictions*, 28 (10) 947–57.

Ford, G., Ecob, R., Hunt, K, *et al.* (1994) 'Patterns of class inequality in health through the lifecourse', *Social Science and Medicine*, 39, 94–9.

Foster, J. (2000). 'Social exclusion, crime and drugs', *Drugs: Education, Prevention and Policy*, 7 (4) 317–30.

Frank, J. (1981) 'Therapeutic Components Shared by All Psychotherapies', *Master Lecture Series*, 1 (London: Psychological Association).

Frank, J. (1974) *Persuasion and Healing: A Comparative Study of Psychotherapy* (Baltimore: Johns Hopkins University Press).

Frank, J., Marel, R. and Schmeidler, J. (1984) 'An overview of substance use among New York State's upper income householders', *Advances in Alcohol and Substance Use*, 4, 14–26.

Friedman, S.R., Curtis, R., Neaigus, A., Jose, B. and Des Jarlais, D.C. (1999) *Social Networks, Drug Injectors Lives and HIV /AIDS* (New York: Springer).

Frischer, M. and Akram, G. (2000) 'Prevalence of co-morbid mental illness and drug use recorded in General Practice', *Drugs: Education, Prevention and Policy*, 8 (3) 275–80.

Frischer, M., Hickman, M., Kraus, L., Mariani, F. and Wiessing, L. (2002) 'A comparison of different methods for estimating the prevalence of problematic drug misuse in Great Britain', *Addiction*, 97 (3) 359–60.

Frischer, M., Shaw, S., Bloor, M. and Goldberg, D. (1993) 'Modeling the behaviour and attributes of injecting drug users: a new approach to identifying HIV risk practices', *International Journal of Addictions*, 28 (2) 129–52.

Gaitley, R. and Seed, P. (1989) *A Social Network Approach* (London: Jessica Kingsley).

Galanter, M. (1993) 'Network therapy for addiction: a model for office practice', *American Journal of Psychiatry,* 150 (12) 28–36.

Galanter, M., Kaufman, E., Taintor, Z., Robinowitz, C.B., Meyer, R.E. and Halikas, J. (1989) 'The current status of psychiatric education in alcoholism and drug abuse', *American Journal of Psychiatry,* 146 (l) 35–9.

Galizio, M. and Maisto, S.A. (1985) 'Towards a biopsychosocial theory of substance abuse', in M.Galizio and S.A. Maisto (eds) *Determinants of Substance Abuse: Biological, Psychological and Environmental* (New York: Plenum).

Garner, B.R., Godley, S.H., Funk, R.R., Dennis, M.L., Smith, J.E. and Godley, M.D. (2009) 'Exposure to Adolescent Community Reinforcement Approach treatment procedures as a mediator of the relationship between adolescent substance abuse treatment retention and outcome', *Journal of Substance Abuse Treatment,* 36 (3) 252–64.

Garrard, J. (1990) 'Evaluation in drug education: some issues and options', *Drug Education Journal of Australia,* 4 (l) 1–15.

Gawin, E.H. and Kleber, H.D. (1984) 'Cocaine abuse treatment: an open pilot trial with lithium and desipramine', *Archives of General Psychiatry,* 41, 903–9.

Gibson, G.S. and Manley, S. (1991) 'Alternative approaches to urinalysis in the detection of drugs', *Social Behavior and Personality,* 19 (3) 195–204.

Gibson, D.R., Sorensen, J.L., Wermuth, L. and Bernal, G. (1992) 'Families are helped by drug treatment', *International Journal of the Addictions,* 27 (8) 961–78.

Gilman, M. (1992) *Outreach,* ISDD Drugs Work 2 (London: Institute for the Study of Drug Dependence).

Gilman, M. (1991) 'Beyond opiates ... and into the 90s', *Druglink,* 6, 16–18.

Ginzburg, H.I.M. (1989) 'Syringe exchange programmes: a medical or policy dilemma?' *American Journal of Public Health,* 79 (10) 1350–1.

Glaser, B.G. and Strauss, A. (1992) *Grounded Theory* (New York:Aldine Press).

Glaser, B.G. and Strauss, A. (1970) *The Discovery of Grounded Theory* (New York: Aldine Press).

Glaser, F. (1980) 'Anybody got a match? Treatment research and the matching hypothesis', in *Alcoholism Treatment in Transition,* ed. G. Edwards and M. Grant (Baltimore: Baltimore University Press).

Glatt, M. (1972) *The Alcoholic and the Help He Needs* (London: Priory Press).

Godden, S. and Pollock, A.M. (1998) 'How to profile the population's use of health care and social care in one district', *Journal of Public Health Medicine,* 20 (2) 175–9.

Godden, S., Pollock, A. and Pheby, D. (2002) 'Editorial', *British Medical Journal,* 320, 265.

Godfrey, C., Stewart, D., Gossop, M. (2004) 'Economic analysis of costs and consequences of the treatment of drug misuse: 2-year outcome data from the National Treatment Outcome Research Study (NTORS)', *Addiction,* 99 (6) 697–707.

Goldfried, S.L. and Bergin, A.E. (eds) (1986) *Handbook of Psychotherapy and Behaviour Change* (New York: Wiley).

Gossop, M. (1998) 'The National Treatment Outcome Research Study (NTORS.)' Quoted in *Tackling Drugs To Build A Better Britain: The Government's 10-Year Strategy For Tackling Drug Misuse*, 1998, HMSO Cm 3945. (London: Home Office).

Gossop, M. (1996) 'The National Treatment Outcome Research Study (NTORS.)' in *Tackling Drugs To Build A Better Britain: The Government's 10-Year Strategy For Tackling Drug Misuse*, 1998, HMSO Cm 3945. (London: Home Office).

Gossop, M. (1992) 'Severity of dependence and route of administration of heroin, cocaine and amphetamines', *British Journal of Addiction*, 87 (11) 1527–36.

Gossop, M., Healey, A., Knapp, M., Marsden, J. and Stewart, D. (2003) 'Criminal outcomes and costs of treatment services for injecting and non-injecting heroin users: Evidence from a national prospective cohort survey', *Journal of Health Services Research and Policy*, 8 (3) 134–41.

Gossop, M., Marsden, J., Stewart, D. and Kidd, T. (2002) 'Changes in use of crack cocaine after drug misuse treatment: 4–5 year follow-up results from the National Treatment Outcome Research Study (NTORS)', *Drug and Alcohol Dependence*. 66 (1) 21–8.

Gossop, M., Marsden, J., Stewart, D. and Treacy, S. (2001) 'Outcomes after methadone reduction treatments: two-year follow-up results from the National Treatment Outcome Research Study', *Drug and Alcohol Dependence*, 62 (3), 255–64.

Gossop, M., Marsden, J., Stewart, D., and Rolfe, A. R. (2000a) 'Reductions in acquisitive crime and drug use after treatment of addiction problems: 1-year follow-up outcomes', *Drug Alcohol Dependence*, 58 (1–2) 165–72.

Gossop, M., Marsden, J., Stewart, D. and Rolfe, A. (2000b) 'Patterns of improvement after Methadone treatment. One year follow-up results from the National Treatment Outcome Research Study (NTORS)', *Drug and Alcohol Dependence*, 60 (3) 275–86.

Gould, A. (1993) 'Opposition to syringe exchange schemes in the UK and Sweden', *Journal of European Social Policy*, 3 (2) 107–18.

Gould, L.C., Walker, A.C., Crane, L.E. and Lidz, C.W. (1974) *Connections: Notes from the Heroin World* (New Haven: Yale University Press).

Grady, K. E. O., Hanlon, T. E. and Kinlock, T. W. (2003) 'Prediction of the criminal activity of incarcerated drug-abusing offenders', *Journal of Drug Issues*, 33 (4) 897–920.

Granfield, R. and Cloud, W. (1996) 'The elephant that no one sees: natural recovery among middleclass addicts', *Journal of Drug Issues*, 26 (1) 45–61.

Green, J. and Sinclair, J. (2005) 'Understanding resolution of deliberate self harm: qualitative interview study of patients' experiences', *British Medical Journal*, 330, 112–13.

Griffiths, P, Gossop, M., Powis, B. and Strang, J. (1994) 'Transitions in patterns of heroin administration: a study of heroin chasers and heroin injectors', *Addiction*, 89 (3) 301–9.

Griffiths, P., Gossop, M., Powis, B. and Strang, J. (1992) 'Extent and nature of transitions of route among heroin addicts in treatment – preliminary data from the Drug Transitions Study', *British Journal of Addiction*, 87 (3), 485–91.

Groh, D.R., Jason, L.A., Ferrari, J.R. and Davis, M.I. (2009) 'Oxford House and Alcoholics Anonymous: The Impact of Two Mutual-Help Models on Abstinence', *Journal of Groups in Addiction and Recovery*, 4 (1) 23–31.

Gross, J. and McCaul, M.E. (1992) 'An evaluation of a psychoeducational and substance abuse risk reduction intervention for children of substance abusers', *Journal of Community Psychology*, special issue, 75–87.

Grunberg, N. (1994) 'Overview: biological processes relevant to drugs of dependence', *Addiction*, 89 (11) 1443–6.

Grundy, E. (2006) 'Ageing and vulnerable elderly people: European perspectives', *Ageing and Society*, 26, 105–34.

Gyarmathy, V.A. and Latkin, C.A. (2008) 'Individual and Social Factors Associated With Participation in Treatment Programs for Drug Users', *Substance Use & Misuse*, 43 (12) 1865–81.

Hall, S.M., Havassy, B.E. and Wasserman, D.A. (1990) 'Commitment to abstinence and acute stress in relapse to alcohol, opiates and nicotine', *Journal of Consulting and Clinical Psychology*, 58 (2) 175–81.

Hall, W. and Farrell, M. (1997) 'Co-morbidity of mental disorder with substance abuse', *British Journal of Psychiatry*, 171, 4–5.

Hammer, T. and Vaglum, P. (1990) 'Use of alcohol and drugs in the transition from adolescence to young adulthood', *Journal of Adolescence*, 13 (2), 129–42.

Hammersley, R., Lavelle, T.L. and Forsyth, A.J.M. (1992) 'Adolescent drug use, health and personalty', *Drug and Alcohol Dependence*, 31 (1) 91–9.

Hammersley, R., Forsyth, A. and Lavelle, T. (1990) 'The criminality of drug users in Glasgow', *British Journal of Addiction*, 85 (12) 1583–94.

Hanslope, J. (1994) 'Healthy women', *Druglink*, 9 (2) 16–17.

Harding, G. (1988) *Opiate Addiction, Morality and Medicine* (London: Macmillan).

Harding-Price, D. (1993) 'A sensitive response without discrimination. Drug use in children and adolescents', *Professional Nurse*, 8 (7) 419–22.

Havassy, B.E., Alvidrez, J. and Owen, K.K. (2004) 'Comparisons of patients with comorbid psychiatric and substance use disorders: implications for treatment and service delivery', *American Journal of Psychiatry*, 161 (1) 139–45.

Hawkins, J.D. and Catalano, R. (1985) 'Aftercare in drug abuse treatment', *International Journal of the Addictions*, 20 (6–7) 917–45.

Hawkins, J.D., Catalano, R.F. and Miller, J.Y. (1992) 'Risk and protective factors for alcohol and other drug problems: implications for substance abuse prevention', *Psychological Bulletin*, 112 (1) 64–105.

Haynes, P. (1998) 'Drug using offenders in south London. Trends and outcomes', *Journal of Substance Abuse Treatment*, 15 (5) 449–56.

Heather, N. (1991) Foreword, in *Counselling Problem Drinkers*, ed. R. Davidson, S. Rollnick and I. MacEwan (London: Tavistock/Routledge).

Heather, N. (1989) 'Psychology and brief interventions', *British Journal of Addiction*, 84 (4) 357–70.

Heather, N. and Robertson, I. (1986) *Problem Drinking, The New Approach* (Harmondworth: Penguin Books).

Heather, N. and Robertson, I. (1981) *Controlled Drinking* (New York: Methuen).

Heather, N., Sterling, R.C., Buhringer, G. and Drummond, C. (2002) 'Commentaries', *Addiction*, 97 (3) 293–9.

Higgins, S.T., Wong, C. J., Badger, G. J., Ogden, D.E.H., Dantona, R. L. (2000) 'Contingent reinforcement increases cocaine abstinence during outpatient treatment and 1 year of follow-up', *Journal of Consulting Clinical Psychology*, 68, 64–72.

Hilton, B.A., Thompson, R., Moore-Dempsey, L. and Janzen, R.G. 'Review of Harm reduction theories and strategies for control of human immunodeficiency virus: a review of the literature', *Journal Advanced Nursing*, 33 (3) 357–70.

Hodgson, R. (1994) 'Treatment of alcohol problems; section 5, Treatment', *Addiction*, 89 (11) 1529–34.

Hodgson, R. J. (1980) 'The Alcohol Dependence Syndrome, a step in the wrong direction', *British Journal of Addiction*, 75 (3), 255–63.

Hodgson, R. (1976) 'Modification of compulsive behaviour', in *Case Histories in Behaviour Therapy*, ed. H. Eysenk (London: Routledge & Kegan Paul).

Hodgson, R.J. and Stockwell, T.R. (1977) 'Does alcohol reduce tension?' in G. Edwards (ed.), *Alcoholism* (Oxford: Oxford University Press).

Holder, H., Longabaugh, R., Miller, W.R. and Rubonis, A.V. (1991) 'The cost of effectiveness of treatment for alcohol problems: a first approximation', *Journal of Alcohol Studies*, 52 (6) 517–40.

Holland, M. (1999) 'How substance use affects people with mental illness', *Nursing Times*, 95 (24) 46–8.

Home Office (2004) *Drug Strategy Progress Report. Tackling Drugs. Changing Lives. Keeping Communities Safe from Drugs*. Ref TDMAD (London: Home Office (www.drugs.gov.uk/NationalStrategy/DrugInterventionsProgrammes).

Home Office (2002) *Updated Strategy* (London: Home Office).

Home Office (2001) *Drugs and Crime; the results of research on drug testing and interviewing arrestees* (London: Home Office).

Home Office (1998) *Tackling Drugs To Build A Better Britain: The Government's 10-Year Strategy For Tackling Drug Misuse*, London, HMSO Cm 3945. Updated Drug Strategy (03/12/2002) (Home Office: London).

Hope, V.D., Judd, A., Hickman, M., Sutton, A., Stimson, G.V., Parry, J.V. and Gill, O.N. (2005) 'HIV prevalence among injecting drug users in England and Wales 1990 to 2003: evidence for increased transmission in recent years', *AIDS,*. 19 (11) 1207–14.

Hopkins, T. (1991) 'Safe from harm?' *Nursing Times*, 87, 42–3.

Huebert, K. and James, D. (1992) 'High-risk behaviours for transmission of HIV among clients in treatment for substance use', *Journal of Drug Issues*, 22 (4) 885–901.

Humphreys, K., Mankowski, E.S., Moos, R.H and Finney, J.W. (1999) 'Do enhanced friendship networks and active coping mediate the effect of self-help groups on substance abuse?' *Annals of Behavioural Medicine*, 21 (1) 54–60.

Hunt, G.H. and Azrin, N.H. (1973) 'A community-reinforcement approach to alcoholism', *Behaviour Research and Therapy*, 11 (1), 91–104.

Iguchi, M.Y., Handelsman, L., Bickel, W.K. and Griffiths, R.R. (1993) 'Benzo-diazepine and sedative use/abuse by Methadone maintenance clients', *Drug and Alcohol Dependence*, 32 (3) 257–66.

Ilgen, M.A,, Hu, K.U., Moos, R.H. and McKellar, J. (2008) 'Continuing care after inpatient psychiatric treatment for patients with psychiatric and substance use disorders', *Psychiatric Services*, 9, 982–8.

Institute for the Study of Drug Dependence (1995) *Annual National Audit of Drug Use* (London: ISDD).

Institute for the Study of Drug Dependence (1995) *Drugs, Pregnancy and Childcare: a Guide for Professionals* (London: ISDD).

Jarvis, G. and Parker, H. (1989) 'Young heroin users and crime. How do the new users finance their habits?' *British Journal of Criminology*, 29 (2) 175–89.

Jellinek, E.M. (1960) *The Disease Concept of Alcoholism* (New Haven: Hillhouse Press).

Jellinek, E.M. and Bowman, G. (1946) 'Alcohol addiction and its treatment', *Quarterly Journal of Studies on Alcohol*, 2, 98–176.

Jensen, E.L., Gerber, J. and Babcock, G.M. (1991) 'The new war on drugs: grass roots movement or political construction?' *Journal of Drug Issues*, 21, 651–67.

Joint Committee on the Draft Mental Health Bill (2004) 'Transcript of oral evidence taken on behalf of the Joint Committee Wed 27 October 2004' (House of Commons, uncorrected minutes of evidence).

Judd, A., Hickman, M., Jones, S., McDonald, T., Parry, J.V., Stimson, G.V. and Hall, A.J. (2005) 'Incidence of Hepatitis C virus and HIV among new injecting drug users in London: prospective cohort study', *British Medical Journal*, 330 (7481) 24–5.

Kail, B.L. and Litwak, E. (1989) 'Family, friends and neighbours: the role of primary groups in preventing the use of drugs', *Journal of Drug Issues*, 19, 261–81.

Kandel, D.B. (1982) 'Epidemiological and psychosocial perspectives on adolescent drug use', *Journal of the American Academy of Child Psychology*, 4, 328–47.

Kandel, D. and Yamaguchi, K. (1993) 'From beer to crack: developmental patterns of drug involvement', *American Journal of Public Health*, 83 (6) 851–5.

Kanfer, F. and Goldstein, A. (eds) (1986) *Helping People Change: A Textbook of Methods* (Oxford: Pergamon Press).

Kaufman, E. and Kaufman, P.N. (eds) (1979) *Family Therapy and Drug and Alcohol Abuse* (New York: Gardner Press).

Keene, J. (2005a) 'A case linkage study of the relationship between drug misuse, crime and psychosocial problems in a total criminal justice population', *Addiction Research and Theory*, 13 (5) 489–502.

Keene J. (2005b) 'A Case Linkage study of co-morbidity in mental health and substance misuse care populations', *Journal of Drug Education, Policy and Practice*, 12 (4) 291–303.

Keene, J. (2001a) *Clients with Complex Needs: Inter-professional Practice*, (Oxford: Blackwell Science).

Keene, J. (2001b) 'A Social Work Perspective on Drug Misuse: Implications for Practice' *Journal of Social Work*, 1 (2) 187–99.

Keene, J. (2000) 'Do therapeutic models limit comprehensive assessment, interventions and evaluation? A qualitative study of substance misuse agencies', *International Journal of Drug Policy*. 11, 337–349.

Keene, J. (1997a) 'Drug use among prisoners before, during and after prison', *Addiction Research*, 4 (4) 343–53.

Keene, J. (1997b) 'Drug use in prison: views from inside', *The Howard Journal of Criminal Justice*, 36 (1) 27–41.

Keene, J. (1994) 'Drug Use and HIV: High Risk Groups in Prison', *International Journal of Drug Policy*, 5 (3) 142–6.

Keene, J. and Raynor, P. (1993) 'Addiction as Soul Sickness: The Influence of Client and Therapist Beliefs' *Addiction Research*, 1 (1), 77–87.

Keene, J. and Rodriguez, J. (2005) 'Mentally Disordered Offenders: A Case Linkage Study of Criminal Justice and Mental Health Populations in the UK', *Journal of Forensic Psychiatry and Psychology*, 16 (1) 167–91.

Keene, J. and Stimson, G.V. (1997) 'Professional ideologies and the development of syringe exchange: Wales a case study', *Medical Anthropology*, special issue, 18, 1–21.

Keene, J. and Trinder, H. (1995) ' Evaluation and comparison of different treatment approaches for drug and alcohol problems in Wales' (Cardiff: Welsh Office).

Keene, J., Rodriguez ,J. and Badger, G. (2005) 'Mental Health and Criminal Justice partnerships: a case study from the substance misuse field', Editorial, *Journal of Forensic Psychiatry and Psychology*, 16 (1) 1–10.

Keene, J., Howell, D. and Janacek, G. (2003) 'Mental Health in Criminal Justice Populations: needs, treatment and criminal behaviour', *Criminal Behaviour and Mental Health*, 13 (3) 20–3.

Keene, J., Willner, P. and Love, A. (1999) 'The relevance of problems and models to treatment outcome: a comparative study of two agencie's, *Substance Use and Misuse*, 34 (10) 1347–69.

Keene, J., James, D. and Willner, P. (1998) 'Social influences on individual drug misuse: three distinct sub-cultures among agency non-attenders', *Addiction Research*, 6 (1) 43–62.

Keene, J., Willner, P. and James, D. (1996) *A Study of Drug Use and Drug Related Problems in the Neath and Afan Valleys* (Swansea, University of Wales: Centre for Substance Abuse Research).

Keene, J., Stenner, K., Connor, M. and Fenley, S. (2007) 'A case-study of Substitute Opiate Prescribing for Drug Using Offenders', *Drugs: Education, Prevention and Policy*, 14 (5) 443–56.

Keene, J., Ahmed, S., Fenley, S. and Walker, M. (2004) 'A qualitative study of a successful shared care project for heroin Users: the Berkshire Four Way Agreement'. *International Journal of Drug policy*, 15 (3) 196–201.

Keene, J., Stimson, G.V, Jones, S. and Parry-Langdon, N. (1993) 'Evaluation of syringe exchange for HIV prevention among injecting drug users in rural and urban areas of Wales', *Addiction*, 88 (8) 1063–70.

Keene, J., Parry-Langdon, N. and Stimson, G.V. (1991) 'HIV Prevention amongst Drug Users: Specialist and Community Based Provision', *International Journal on Drug Policy*, 2 (6) 282–8.

Kerr, G. (1894) *Inebriety or Narcomania: Its Etiology, Pathology, Treatment and Jurisprudence*, 3rd edn (London: H.K. Leis).

Khantzian, E.J. (1985) 'The self medication hypothesis of addictive disorders; focus on heroin and cocaine dependence', *American Journal of Psychiatry*, 142 (11), 1259–64.

Khantzian, E.J. and Mack, J.E. (1989) 'Alcoholics Anonymous and contemporary psycho dynamic theory', in *Recent Developments in Alcoholism* 7 ed. M. Galanter (New York: Plenum Press, pp. 67–89).

Kidorf, M. and Stitzer, M.L. (1993) 'Descriptive analysis of cocaine use of Methadone patients', *Drug and Alcohol Dependence*, 32 (3) 267–75.

Killias, M. and Ribeaud, D. (1999) 'Drug use and crime among juveniles. an international perspective', *Studies on Crime and Crime Prevention*, 8 (2) 189–209.

Kirby, K.C., Marlowe, D.B., Festinger, D.S., Garvey, K.A. and LaMonaca, V. (1999) 'Community reinforcement training for family and significant others of drug abusers: a unilateral intervention to increase treatment entry of drug users', *Drug and Alcohol Dependence*, 56 (1) 85–96.

Kofoed, L. (1993) 'Outpatient vs. inpatient treatment for the chronically mentally ill with substance use disorders', *Journal of Addictive Diseases*, 12 (3) 123–37.

Kostyk, D., Fuchs, D., Tabisz, E. and Jacyk, W.R. (1993) 'Combining professional and self help group intervention: collaboration in co-leadership', *Social Work with Groups*, 16 (3) 111–23.

Kranzler, H.R. and Rosenthal, R.N. (2003) 'Dual diagnosis: alcoholism and co-morbid psychiatric disorders', *American Journal of Addiction*, 12 Suppl 1: S26–40.

Krause, N. (2005) 'Negative interaction and heart disease in late life: exploring variations by socioeconomic status', *Journal of Ageing and Health*, 17 (1) 28–55.

Kurtz, E. (n.d.) '*Not God*': A History of Alcoholics Anonymous (Minnesota: Hazelden Foundation).

Ladwig, G.B. and Anderson, M.D. (1989) 'Substance Abuse in Women: The Relationship Between Chemical Dependency of Women and Past Reports of Physical and/or Sexual Abuse', *International Journal of the Addictions*, 24 (8) 739–54.

Laffaye, C., McKellar, J.D., Ilgen, M.A. and Moos, R.H. (2008) 'Predictors of 4-year outcome of community residential treatment for patients with substance use disorders', *Addiction*, 103 (4) 671–80.

Landry, M.J., Smith, D.E., McDuff, D.R. and Baughman, O.L. (1991) 'Anxiety and substance use disorders: the treatment of high-risk patients', *Journal of the American Board of Family Practice*, 4 (6) 447–56.

Larimer, M.E., Palmer, R.S. and Marlatt, G.A. (1999) Relapse prevention. An overview of Marlatt's cognitive-behavioral model, *Alcohol Research and Health*, 23 (2) 151–60.

Leason, K. (2002). 'GPs oppose prescribing more heroin to addicts as a form of treatment', *Community Care*, 24, 20.

Lefevre, R. (n.d.) *How to Combat Alcoholism and Addictions* (London: Promis Publishing).

Lehman, W.E.K., Barrett, M.E. and Simpson, D.D. (1990) 'Alcohol use by heroin addicts 12 years after drug abuse treatment', *Journal of Studies on Alcohol, 51*, 233–44.

Lemke, S., Schutte, K.K., Brennan, P.L. and Moos, R.H. (2008) 'Gender differences in social influences and stressors linked to increased drinking', *Journal of Studies in Alcohol Drugs*, 69 (5):695–702.

Leukefeld, C.G. and Tims, F.M. (1989) 'Relapse and recovery in drug abuse: research and practice', *International Journal of the Addictions*, 24 (3) 189–201.

Leukefeld, C., Pickens, R.W. and Schuster, C. R. (1992) 'Recommendations for improving drug treatment', *International Journal of the Addictions*, 27 (10) 1223–39.

Leventhal, H. and Cameron, L. (1987) 'Behavioural theories and the problem of compliance', *Patient Education and Counselling, 10*, 117–38.

Leventhal, H. and Nerenz, D. (1985) 'The assessment of illness cognition', in *Measurement Strategies in Health Psychology,* ed. P. Karoly (New York: Wiley, pp. 517–54).

Lindstrom, L. (1992) *Managing Alcoholism. Matching Clients to Treatments* (Oxford: Oxford University Press).

Littleton, J. and Little, H. (1994) 'Current concepts of ethanol dependence', *Addiction*, 89 (11) 1397–412.

Lofland, J. (1971) *Analysing Social Settings; A Guide to Qualitative Observation and Analysis* (California: Wadsworth).

Longabaugh, R. and Beattie, M. (1985) 'Optimising the cost effectiveness of treatment for alcohol abusers', Research monograph no. 15, in *Future Directions in Alcohol Abuse Treatment Research,* (eds) B.S. McCrady, N.E. Noel and T.D. Nirenberg Rockville: National Institute on Alcohol Abuse and Alcoholics, pp. 104–36).

Longshore, D., Hsieh, S., Danila, B. and Anglin, M.D. (1993) 'Methadone maintenance and needle/syringe sharing', *International Journal of the Addictions*, 28 (10) 983–96.

Lopez, J.M.O., Miron Redondo, L. and Leungo Martin, A. (1989) 'Influence of family and peer group on the use of drugs by adolescents', *International Journal of the Addictions*, 24 (11) 1065–82.

Ludwig, A.M. (1972) 'On and off the wagon: reasons for drinking and abstaining by alcoholics', *Quarterly Journal of Studies on Alcohol, 33* (1), 91–6.

Luke, D.A., Mowbray, C.T., Klump, K., Herman, S.E. and Boots-Miller, B. (1996) 'Exploring the diversity of dual diagnosis; utility of cluster analysis for program planning', *Journal of Mental Health Administration*, 23 (3) 298–316.

Lungley, S. (1988) *Intravenous Drug Use in New Zealand: A Baseline Study of Intravenous Drug Users and Their Risk of AIDS* (Wellington: Wellington Health Services Research and Development Unit).

Lyvers, M. and Yakimoff, M. (2003) 'Neuropsychological correlates of opiate dependence and withdrawal', *Addictive Behaviours*, 28 (3) 605–11.

MacDonald, R. (2005) 'Prioritising neglected diseases related to poverty', *British Medical Journal*, 331, 12 (2 July).

Mack, J.E. (1981) 'Alcoholism, AA and the governance of self', in M.H. Bean and N.E. Zinberg (eds) *Dynamic Approaches to the Understanding and Treatment of Alcoholism* (New York: The Free Press, pp. 128–62).

Madden, A., Swinton, M. and Gunn, J. (1992) 'A survey of pre-arrest drug use in sentenced prisoners', *British Journal of Addiction*, 87, 27–33.

Magruder-Habib, K., Hubbard, R.L. and Ginzburg, H.M. (1992) 'Effects of drug use treatment on symptoms of depression and suicide', *International Journal of the Addictions*, 27 (9) 1035–65.

Maisto, S.A. and Carey, K.B. (1987) 'Treatment of alcohol abuse', in T.D. Nirenberg and S.A. Maiston (eds), *Developments in the Assessment and Treatment of Addictive Behaviours* (Norwood, New Jersey: Abllex, pp. 173–211).

Makala, P., Gmel, G., Grittner, U., Kuendig, H., Kuntsche, S., Bloomfield, K. and Room, R. (2006) 'Drinking patterns and their gender differences in Europe', *Alcohol and Alcoholism*, 41 (Supplement) 8–18.

Makkai, T., Moore, R. and McAllister, I. (1991) 'Health education campaigns and drug use', *Health Education Research*, 6 (1) 65–76.

Mallams, J.H., Godley, M., Hall, G.M. and Meyers, R. (1982) 'A social systems approach to re-socialising alcoholics in the community', *Journal of Studies on Alcohol*, 43 (11), 1115–23.

Malpas, D. (1990) 'The addicted mother's conflict', *Community Care*, March, 18–29.

Maltzman, I. and Schweiger, A. (1991) 'Individual and family characteristics of middle class adolescents hospitalised for alcohol and other drug use', *British Journal of Addiction*, 86 (11) 1435–7.

Maremmani, I., Hardini, R., Zolesi, O. and Castrogiovanni, P. (1994) 'Methadone dosages and therapeutic compliance during a Methadone maintenance programme', *Drug and Alcohol Dependence*, 34 (2) 163–6.

Marlatt, G.A. (1996) 'Taxonomy of high-risk situations for alcohol relapse: evolution and development of a cognitive-behavioural model', *Addiction*, 91 Suppl: S37–49.

Marlatt, G.A. (1988) 'Matching clients to treatment: treatment models and stages of change', in D.M. Donovan and G.A. Marlatt (eds), *Assessment of Addictive Behaviours* (New York: Guilford Press).

Marlatt, G.A. (1985) Cognitive assessment and intervention procedures for relapse prevention, in G.A. Marlatt and J.R. Gordon (eds), *Relapse Prevention: Maintenance Strategies in the Treatment of Addictive Behaviours* (New York: Guilford Press).

Marlatt, G.A. and George, W.H. (1984) 'Relapse prevention: introduction and overview of the model', *British Journal of Addiction,* 79 (3) 261–73.

Marlatt, G.A. and Gordon, J.R. (1996) 'Determinants of relapse: Implications for the maintenance of behavior change', *Addiction,* 91, supplement 1, (12) 37–50 (14).

Marlatt, G.A. and Gordon, J.R. (eds) (1985) *Relapse Prevention: Maintenance Strategies in the Treatment of Addictive Behaviours* (New York: Guilford Press).

Marlatt, G.A. and Gordon, J.R. (1980) 'Determinants of relapse: implications for the maintenance of behaviour change', in P. Davidson and S. Davidson (eds) *Behavioural Medicine: Changing Health Lifestyles* (New York: Plenum, pp. 410–57).

Marlatt, G.A., Demming, B. and Reid, J. (1997) '*Loss* of control drinking in alcoholics: an experimental analogue', *Journal of Abnormal Psychology,* 812, 233–41.

Marsden, J., Gossop, M., and Stewart, D. (2000) 'Psychiatric symptoms among clients seeking treatment for drug dependence. Intake data from the National Treatment Outcome Research Study', *British Journal of Psychiatry,* 176, 285–9.

Marston, A.R., Jacobs, D.F., Singer, R.D., Wideman, K.F.E. and Little, T.D. (1988) 'Adolescents who apparently are invulnerable to drug, alcohol and nicotine use', *Adolescence,* 23, 593–8.

Martin, S. E., Maxwell, C. O., White, H. R. and Zhang, Y. (2004). 'Trends in alcohol use, cocaine use, and crime 1989–1998', *Journal of Drug Issues,* 34 (2) 333–60.

Mash, E.J. and Terdal, L.G. (eds) (1976) *Behaviour Therapy Assessment: Diagnosis, Design and Evaluation* (New York: Springer).

Mason, D.T., Lusk, M.W. and Gintzler, M. (1992) 'Beyond ideology in drug policy: the primary prevention model', *Journal of Drug Issues,* 22 (4) 959–76.

Mason, P. and Marsden, J. (1994) 'The State of the market', *Druglink,* 9 (2) 8–11.

Mayer, E. and Timms, N. (1970) *The Client Speaks: Working Class Impressions Of Case Work.* (London: Routledge & Kegan Paul).

McCarty, D., Argerious, M., Huebner, R.B. and Lubran, B. (1991) 'Alcoholism, drug abuse and the homeless.', *American Psychologist,* 46 (11) 1139–48.

McCaughrin, W.C. and Price, R.H. (1992) 'Effective outpatient drug treatment organisations: program features and selection effects', *International Journal of the Addictions,* 27 (11) 1335–58.

McCoy, C.B., Rivers, J.E. and Khoury, E.L. (1993) 'An emerging public health model for reducing AIDS related risk behaviour among injecting drug users and their sexual partners', *Drugs and Society,* 7 (3/4) 143–59.

McCrady, B.S. and Sher, K.J. (1983) 'Alcoholism treatment approaches: patient variables, treatment variables', in B. Tabakoff, P .B. Sutker and C.L. Randell (eds) *Medical and Social Aspects of Alcohol Abuse* (New York: Plenum Press).

McDermont, P. (2003) 'Crack harm reduction doesn't wash', *Druglink* July/ August 8, 11–12.

McDermott, P. and McBride, W. (1993) 'Crew 2000: peer coalition in action', *Druglink*, 8 (6) 13–15.

McDermott, P., Matthews, A. and Bennett, A. (1992) 'Responding to recreational drug use', *Druglink*, 7, 12–13.

McKeganey, N.P. (2007) 'The challenge to UK drug policy', *Drugs: Education, Prevention and Policy*, 14 (6) 559–71.

McKeganey, N.P. (2006) 'The lure and the loss of harm reduction in UK drug policy and practice', *Addiction Research and Theory*, 14 (6) 557–88.

McKeganey, M. and Barnard, M. (1992) *AIDS, Drugs and Sexual Risk: Lives in the Balance* (Buckingham: Open University Press).

McKeganey, N.P., Bloor, M.J. , Robertson, M., Neale, J. and MacDougall, J. (2006) 'Abstinence and Drug Abuse Treatment: Results from the Drug Outcome Research in Scotland Study', *Drugs: Education, Prevention and Policy*, 13 (6) 537–550.

McKeganey, N.P., Morris, Z., Neale, J. and Robertson, M. (2004) 'What are Drug Users Looking for When They Contact Drug Services: abstinence or harm reduction?', *Drugs: Education, Prevention and Policy*, 11 (5) 423–35.

McKellar, J.D., Harris, A.H. and Moos, R.H. (2006) 'Predictors of Outcome for Patients with Substance-Use Disorders Five Years after Treatment Dropout', *Journal of Studies on Alcohol*, 67 (5) 685–93.

McLachlan, C., Crofts, N., Wodak, A. and Crowe, S. (1993) 'The effects of Methadone on immune function among injecting drug users: a review', *Addiction*, 88 (2) 257–63.

McMurran, M., Hollin, C. and Bowen, A. (1990) 'Consistency of alcohol self report measures in a male young offender population', *British Journal of Addiction*, 85, 205–8.

Measham, F. C. (2006) 'The new policy mix: alcohol, harm minimization and determined drunkenness in contemporary society', *International Journal on Drug Policy*, 17 (4) 258–68.

Measham, F., Newcombe, R. and Parker, H. (1993) *An Investigation into the Relationship between Drinking and Deviant Behaviour amongst Young People* (London: Alcohol Education and Research Council).

Menezes, P.R., Johnson, S., Thornicroft, G., Marshall, J. and De Crespigny, P.K. (1996). 'Drug and alcohol problems among individuals with severe mental illnesses in South London', *British Journal of Psychiatry*, 168 (5) 612–19.

Mensch, B.S. and Kandel, D.B. (1988) 'Dropping out of high school and drug involvement', *Sociology of Education*, 61, 95–113.

Meyers, C. and Moss, I. (1992) 'Residential treatments: linkage with community drug treatment programs', *Child Welfare*, 71 (6) 537–45.

Meyers, R. J., Miller, W.R., Smith, J.E., Tonigan, J.S. (2002) 'A randomized trial of two methods for engaging treatment-refusing drug users through concerned significant others', *Journal of Consulting and Clinical Psychology*, 70 (5) 1182–5.

Meyers, R.J, Miller, W.R., Hill, D.E, and Tonigan, J.S. (1998) 'Community reinforcement and family training (CRAFT): engaging unmotivated drug users in treatment', *Journal of Substance Abuse*, 10 (3) 291–308.

Miller, W.R. (1983) 'Motivational interviewing with problem drinkers', *Behavioural Psychotherapy*, 11 (2) 147–72.

Miller, W.R. and Hester, R.K. (1986a) 'The effectiveness of alcoholism treatment: what research reveals', in W .R. Miller and N. Heather (eds), *Treating Addictive Behaviours: Processes of Change* (New York: Plenum).

Miller, W.R. and Hester, R.K. (1986b) 'Matching problem drinkers with optimal treatments', in W.R. Miller and N. Heather (eds) *Treating Addictive Behaviours: Processes of Change* (New York: Plenum).

Miller, W.R., Meyers, R.J. and Hiller-Sturmhofel, S. (1999) The Community-Reinforcement Approach, *Alcohol Research and Health*, 23 (92) 116–21.

Miller, W.R., Sovereign, R.G. and Krege, B. (1988) 'Motivational interviewing with problem drinkers: The drinkers check-up as a preventive intervention', *Behavioural Psychotherapy*, 16 (4) 251–68.

Millman, R.B. (1988) 'Evaluation and clinical management of cocaine abusers', *Journal of Clinical Psychiatry*, 49, 27–33.

Mishara, B.L. and McKim, W. (1993) 'Methodological issues in surveying older persons concerning drug use', *International Journal of the Addictions*, 28 (4) 305–26.

Moggi, F. Ouimette, P.C., Finney, J.W. and Moos, R.H. (1999) 'Effectiveness if treatment for substance misuse and dependence for dual diagnosis patients'. *Journal of Studies on Alcohol*, 60 (6) 856–66.

Moos, R.H. (2008) 'How and why twelve-step self-help groups are effective', *Recent Developments in Alcohol*, 8, 393–412.

Moos, R.H. (2007) 'Theory-based active ingredients of effective treatments for substance use disorders', *Drug and Alcohol Dependence*, 88 (2–3) 109–21.

Moos, R.H., Finney, J.W. and Cronkite, R.C. (1990) *Alcoholism Treatment. Context, Process and Outcome* (Oxford: Oxford University Press).

Moos R.H., Fenn C.B. and Billings A.G. (1988) 'Life stressors and social resources: an integrated assessment approach', *Social Science and Medicine*, 27 (9) 999–1002.

Moos, R.H., Finney, J.W and Chan, D.A. (1981) 'The recovery process from alcoholism: comparing alcoholic patients and matched community controls', *Journal of Studies on Alcohol*, 42 (5), 383–402.

Moos R.H., Fenn, C.B., Billings, A.G. and Moos, B.S. (1989) 'Assessing life stressors and social resources: applications to alcoholic patients', *Journal of Substance Abuse*, 1 (2) 135–52.

Morgenstern, J. and McKay, J.R. (2007) 'Rethinking the paradigms that inform behavioral treatment research for substance use disorders', *Addiction*, 102 (9) 1377–389.

Mowbray, C.T., Jordan, L.C., Ribisl, K.M., Kewalramani, A., Luke, D., Herman, S. and Bybee, D. (1999) 'Analysis of post-discharge change in a dual diagnosis population'. *Health and Social Work*, 24 (2) 91–101.

Mueser, K.T., Drake, R.E. and Wallach, M.A. (1998) 'Dual diagnosis: a review of etiological theories', *Addictive Behaviours*, 23 (6) 717–34.

Mumme, D. (1991) 'Aftercare: its role in primary and secondary recovery of women from alcohol and other drug dependence', *International Journal of the Addictions*, 26 (5) 549–64.

Mundal, L.D., Van der Weele, T., Berger, C. and Fitsimmons, J. (1991) 'Maternal-infant separation at birth among substance using pregnant women: implications for attachment', *Social Work in Health Care*, 16 (1) 133–43.

Murphy, R.N. and Bentall, R.P. (1992) 'Motivation to withdraw from heroin: a factor analysis study', *British Journal of Addiction*, 87 (2) 245–50.

Murray, J.B. (1986) 'An overview of cocaine use and abuse', *Psychological Reports*, 59, 243–64.

National Campaign Against Drug Abuse (1988) *Task Force Evaluation*, (Australia: NCADA).

National Treatment Agency (NTA) (2002) *Models of Care for the Treatment of Drug Users. Part II. Full reference report* (London: National Treatment Agency for Substance Misuse).

Neale, J., Bloor, M.J. and McKeganey, N.P. (2007) ' How do heroin users spend their spare time?', *Drugs: Education, Prevention and Policy*, 14, 231–46.

Newburn, T. and Elliot, J. (1999), *Risks and Responses: drug prevention and Youth Justice*, DPAS paper 3 (London: Home Office).

Newcomb, M. D., Galaif, E. R. and Carmona, J. V. (2001) 'The drug-crime nexus in a community sample of adults', *Psychology of Addictive Behaviors*, 15 (3) 185–93.

Newcombe, R. (1992) 'A researcher report from the rave', *Druglink*, 7, 14–16.

Newcombe, R. (1991) *Raving and Dance Drugs: House Music Clubs and Parties in North-West England* (Liverpool: Rave Research Bureau).

Nordstrom, G. and Burgland, M. (1986) 'Successful adjustment in alcoholism; relationships between causes of improvement, personality and social factors', *Journal of Nervous and Mental Disease*, 174 (11), 664–8.

North, R.J., Holahan, C.J., Moos, R.H. and Cronkite, R.C. (2008) 'Family support, family income, and happiness: a 10-year perspective', *Journal of Family Psychology*, 22 (3) 475–83.

Novick, D.M., Richman, B.L., Friedman, J.M. and Friedman, J.E. (1993) 'The medical status of Methadone maintenance patients in treatment for 11–18 years', *Drug and Alcohol Dependence*, 33 (3) 235–45.

Nurco, D.M., Wegner, N., Stephenson, P., Makofsky, A. and Shaffer, J.W. (1983) *Ex-Addicts Self-Help Groups* (New York: Praeger).

Nutbeam, D. (1988) Planning for a Smokefree Generation. *Smoke free Europe 6* (Copenhagen: World Health Organization).

O'Brien, C. and McLellan, A.T. (1996) 'Myths about the treatment of addiction', *Lancet* 347 (8996), 237–40.

O'Callaghan, R.V. and Caalan, V.J. (1992) 'Young adult drinking behaviour: a comparison of diary and quantity-frequency measures', *British Journal of Addiction,* 87 (5) 723–32.

O'Malley, P. (1991) 'The demand for intoxicating commodities: implications for the war on drugs', *Social Justice, 18,* 49–75.

OPCS (1969) *General Household Survey* (London: OPCS).

Orford, J. (2008) 'Asking the right questions in the right way: the need for a shift in research on psychological treatments for addiction', *Addiction,* 103 (6) 875–85.

Orford, J. (1985) *Excessive Appetites, A Psychological View of the Addictions* (London: Wiley).

Orford, J. (1977) 'Alcoholism and what psychology offers', in *Alcoholism,* ed. G. Edwards and J. Grant (Oxford: Oxford University Press).

Orford, J. and Edwards, G. (1979) *Alcoholism: A Comparison of Treatment and Advice,* Maudsley Monograph No. 26 (London: London University Press).

Orford, J. and Velleman, R. (1990) 'Offspring of parents with drinking problems: drinking and drug taking as young adults', *British Journal of Addiction,* 856, 779–94.

Orford, J., Oppenheimer, E. and Edwards, G. (1979) 'Abstinence or control: the outcome for excessive drinkers two years after consultation', *Behaviour, Research and Therapy,* 14, 409–18.

Orford, J., Hodgson, R., Copello, A., Wilton, S. and Slegg, G. (2009a) 'To what factors do clients attribute change? Content analysis of follow-up interviews with clients of the UK Alcohol Treatment Trial', *Journal of Substance Abuse Treatment,* 36 (1) 49–58.

Orford, J., Rolfe A., Dalton, S., Painter, C. and Webb, H. (2009b) 'Pub and community: The views of Birmingham untreated heavy drinkers', *Journal of Community and Applied Social Psychology,* 19, (1) 68–82.

Parker, H. (1993) *Pick and Mix: Alcohol, Drugs and the 1990s adolescent,* (British Criminology Conference, Cardiff, Wales).

Parker, H., Baker, K. and Newcombe, R. (1988) *Living with Heroin* (Buckingham: Open University Press).

Parole Release Scheme (1989) *The Parole Release Scheme Report 1987–89* (London: HMSO).

Parssinen, P. (1983) *Secret Passions, Secret Remedies* (Manchester: Manchester University Press).

Paton, S.M., Kessler, R. and Kandel, D. (1977) 'Depressive mood and adolescent illegal drug use: a longitudinal analysis', *Journal of Genetic Psychology,* 31, 267–89.

Pattison, E.M., Sobell, M.B. and Sobell, L.C. (eds) (1977) *Merging Concepts of Alcohol Dependence* (New York: Springer Publishing Company).

Pearson, G., Ditton, J., Newcombe, R. and Gilman, M. (1991) 'Everything starts with an "E"', *Druglink,* 6, 10–11.

Petursson, H. and Lader, M. (1984) *Dependence on Tranquillisers* (Oxford: Oxford University Press).

Phillips, P. and Johnson, S. (2003) 'Drug and alcohol misuse among in-patients with psychotic illnesses in three inner-London psychiatric units', *Psychiatric Bulletin*, 27, 217–20.

Pilling, S., Strang, J. and Gerada, C. (2007) 'Psychosocial interventions and opioid detoxification for drug misuse: summary of NICE guidance', *British Medical Journal* 335 (7612) 203–5.

Poland, M.L., Combrowski, M.P., Ager, J.W. and Sokol, R.J. (1993) 'Punishing pregnant drug users: enhance flight from care', *Drug and Alcohol Dependence*, 31 (3) 199–203.

Pottieger, A.E. (1981) 'Sample Bias in drugs/crime research', in James Incardi (ed.) *The Drugs Crime Connection: Annual Review of Drug and Alcohol Abuse*, vol. 5 (London: Sage).

Powell, J.E. and Taylor, D. (1992) 'Anger, depression, and anxiety following heroin withdrawal', *International Journal of the Addictions, 27 (1)* 25–35.

Power, K., Markova, I., Rowlands, A. *et al.* (1992) 'Intravenous drug use and HIV transmission amongst inmates in Scottish prisons', *British Journal of Addiction*, 87 (1), 35–45.

Preble, E. and Casey, J. J. (1998) 'Taking care of business', *Druglink*, 3 (4), 10–11.

Preston, A. (1993) *The Methadone Handbook* (London: ISDD).

Preston, A. (1992) 'Pointing out the risk', *Nursing Times*, 88, 24–6.

Prochaska, J.O. (1979) *Systems of Psychotherapy: A Transtheoretical Perspective* (Homewood, Ill.: Dorsey Press).

Prochaska, J.O. and DiClemente, C.C. (1994) *The Transtheoretical Approach: Crossing Traditional Boundaries of Therapy* (New York: Dow-Jones, Irwin).

Prochaska, J.O. and DiClemente, C.C. (1986) 'Towards a comprehensive model of change', in *Treating Addictive Behaviours: Processes of Change*, ed. W.R. Miller and N. Heather (New York: Plenum).

Prochaska, J.O. and DiClemente, C.C. (1983) 'Stages and processes of self change of smoking: towards a more integrative model of change', *Journal of Consulting and Clinical Psychology*, 51, 390–5.

Prochaska, J.O. and DiClemente, C.C. (1982) 'Transtheoretical therapy: towards a more integrative model of change', *Psychotherapy Theory, Research and Practice*, 19 (3) 276–88.

Project MATCH Research Group (1997) 'Matching alcoholism treatments to client heterogeneity: Project MATCH post-treatment drinking outcomes', *Journal of Studies on Alcohol*, 58 (1), 7–29.

Project MATCH Research Group (1993) 'Project MATCH: rationale and methods for a multisite clinical trial matching patients to alcoholism treatment', *Alcoholism: Clinical and Experimental Research*, 17 (6) 120–43.

Raffoul, P.R. and Haney, C.A. (1989). 'Interdisciplinary treatment for drug use among older people of color: ethnic considerations for social work practice', *Journal of Drug Issues*, 19, 297–313.

Raine, A (1993) 'The Psychopathology of Crime', *Criminal Behavior and Mental Disorder* (California: Academic Press).

Raistrick, D. (1994) 'Report of the Advisory Council on the Use of Drugs; AIDS and drug use update', *Addiction,* 89 (10) 1211–13.

Raistrick, D. and Davidson, R. (1985) *Alcoholism and Drug Addiction* (Edinburgh: Churchill Livingstone).

Raveis, V .H. and Kandel, D.B. (1987) 'Changes in drug behaviour from the middle to the late twenties: initiation, persistence, and cessation of use', *American Journal of Public Health,* 77 (5) 607–11.

Ravndal, E. and Vaglum, P. (1994) 'Treatment of female addicts: the importance of relationships to parents, partners, and peers for the outcome', *International Journal of the Addictions,* 29 (l) 115–25.

Raymond, C.A. (1988) 'Study of IV drug users and AIDS finds differing infection rate, risk behaviours', *Journal of the American Medical Association,* 260 (21) 3105.

Regier, D.A., Farner, M. E. and Rae, D. S., *et al.* (1990) 'Co-morbidity of mental disorders with alcohol and other drugs of abuse: results from the epidemiological catchment area (ECA) study', *Journal of the American Medical Association,* 264, 2511–18.

Regier, D.A., Narrow, W.E. and Rae, D.S. (1990) 'The epidemiology of anxiety disorders – the epidemiologic catchment area (ECA) experience', *Journal of Psychiatric Research,* 24 (Suppl.2), 3–14.

Reijneveld, S.A. and Plomp, H.N. (1993) 'Methadone maintenance clients in Amsterdam after five years', *International Journal of the Addictions,* 28 (1) 63–72.

Rhodes, F. and Humfleet, G.L. (1993) 'Using goal-orientated counselling and peer support to reduce HIV/AIDS risk amongst drug users not in treatment', *Drugs and Society,* 7 (3/4) 189–204.

Rhodes, T. and Quirk, A. (2003) 'Heroin, Risk and Sexual Safety' in T. Rhodes and R. Hartnoll (eds), *AIDs Drug Prevention: Perspectives on Individual and Community Action* (London: Routledge).

Rhodes, T. and Stimson, G.V. (1994) 'Sex, drugs intervention and research: from the individual to the social', *International Journal of the Addictions,* 29 (4) 1203–9.

Rhodes, T., Hartnoll, R. and Johnson, A. (1991) *Out of the Agency and onto the Streets: A Review of HIV Outreach Health Education in Europe and the US,* ISDD Research Monograph 2 (London: Institute for the Study of Drug Dependence).

Rieder, B.A. (1990) 'Perinantal substance abuse and public health nursing intervention', *Children Today,* 19, 33–5.

Ries, R.K., Russo, J. and Wingerston, D. (2000) 'Shorter hospital stays and more rapid improvement among patients with schizophrenia and substance misuse disorders', *Psychiatric Services,* 51, 210–15.

Riley, D.M., Sobell, L.C., Leo, G.I., Sobell, M.B. and Klajner, F. (1987) 'Behavioural treatment of alcohol problems: a review and a comparison of behavioural and non-behavioural studies', in W.M. Cox (ed.), *Treatment and Prevention of Alcohol Problems: A Resource Manual* (Orlando: Academic Press, pp. 73–115).

Ringwalt, C., Ennett, S.T. and Holt, K.D. (1991) 'An outcome evaluation of project DARE', *Health Education Research*, 6 (3) 327–37.

Robertson, I. and Heather, N. (1986) *Let's Drink to Your Health: A Self Help Guide to Sensible Drinking* (London: British Psychological Society).

Robertson, J.R. (1989) 'Treatment of drug use in the general practice setting', *British Journal of Addiction*, 84 (4) 377–80.

Robertson, M.J. (1991) 'Homeless women with children: the role of alcohol and other drug abuse', *American Psychologist*, 46 (11) 1198–204.

Robinson, D. (1979) *Talking Out of Alcoholism: The Self Help Process of AA* (London: Croom-Helm).

Roche, A.M. and Richards, G.P. (1991) 'Doctors' willingness to intervene in patients' drug and alcohol problems', *Social Science and Medicine, 33* (9), 1053–61.

Rodriguez, J., Keene, J. and Li, X. (2006) 'A pilot study of the assessed needs and service use of mental health patients who are frequent offenders,' *Journal of Mental Health*, 15 (4), 411–21.

Rogers, C. (1951) *Client-Centered Counselling* (Boston: Houghton Mifflin).

Rollnick, S., Heather, N., Gold, R. and Hall, W. (1992) 'Developments of a short "readiness to change" questionnaire for use in brief, opportunistic interventions with excessive drinkers', *British Journal of Addiction*, 87 (5) 743–54.

Roman, P.M. and Trice, H.M. (1970) 'The development of deviant drinking behaviour: occupational risk factors', *Archives of Environmental Health, 20*, 424–35.

Rosenbaum, D., Flewelling, R., Bailet, S., Ringwalt, C. and Wilkinson, D. (1994) 'Cops in the classroom: a longitudinal study of drug abuse resistance education', *Journal of Research in Crime and Delinquency,* 1 (31) 3–31.

Rosenstock, L.M. (1966) 'Why people use health services', *Millbank Memorial Fund Quarterly,* 44, 94.

Rosenthal, D., Moore, S. and Buzwell, S. (1994) 'Homeless youths: sexual and drug related behaviour, sexual beliefs and HIV/AIDS risk', *AIDS Care*, 6 (l) – 3394.

Rounsaville, B.J. (1986) *Clinical Implications of Relapse Research,* National Institute of Drug Abuse Research Monograph, Series 72 (Rockville, MD).

Royal College of Physicians (1992) *Smoking and the Young* (London: RCP).

Rush, B., Simmons, M., Timney, C.B., Evans, J. and Finlay, R. (1987) 'A comparison of psychotropic drug use between the general population and clients of health and social service agencies', *International Journal of the Addictions*, 22 (9), 843–59.

Ryan, T., Smith, I., Hancock, J., Dovaston, G. and Smith, M. (1999) 'Applying aspects of the community reinforcement approach to alcohol and drug services', *Journal of Substance Use*, 4 (2) 70–5.

Sainsbury, E., Nixon, S. and Phillips, D. (1982) *Social Work in Focus: Client's and Social Worker's Perceptions in Long term Social Work* (London: Routledge & Kegan Paul).

San, L., Tato, J., Torrens, M. and Castillo, C. (1993a) 'Flunietrazepam consumption among heroin addicts admitted for TH – patient detoxification', *Drug and Alcohol Dependence,* 32 (3) 281–6.

San, L., Torrens, M., Castillo, C. and Porta, M. (1993b) 'Consumption of Buprenorphine and other drugs among heroin addicts under ambulatory treatment: results from crosssectional studies in 1988 and 1990', *Addiction,* 88 (10) 1341–9.

Sanchez-Craig, M. (1990) 'Brief didactic treatment for alcohol and drug related problems: an approach based on client choice', *British Journal of Addiction,* 85 (2) 169–77.

Sarvela, P.D. and McClendon, E.J. (1988) 'Indicators of rural drug use', *Journal of Youth and Adolescence,* 17, 335–47.

Saunders, J.B. and Aasland, O.G. (1987) *WHO Collaborative Project on the Identification and Treatment of Persons with Harmful Alcohol Consumption,* Report on Phase 1 Development of a Screening Instrument (Geneva: WHO).

Saunders, W.M. and Kershaw, P.W. (1979) 'Spontaneous remission from alcoholism: a community study', *British Journal of Addiction,* 74, 251–65.

Saxon, A.J. and Calsyn, D.A. (1995) 'Effects of psychiatric care for dual diagnosis patients treated in a drug dependence clinic', *American Journal of Drug and Alcohol Abuse,* 21 (3) 303–13.

Saxon, A.J., Calsyn, D.A. and Jackson, T.R. (1994) 'Longitudinal changes in injection behaviour in a cohort of injecting drug users', *Addiction,* 89 (2) 191–202.

Schapps, E., Dibartolo, R., Moskowitz, J., Palley, C.S. and Churgin, S. (1981) 'A review of 127 drug abuse prevention program evaluations', *Journal of Drug Issues,* 11, 17–23.

Scheider, L.M., Newcombe, M.D. and Skager, R. (1994) 'Risk, protection, and vulnerability to adolescent drug use: latent variable models of three age groups', *Journal of Drug Education,* 24 (1) 48–82.

Schoenbaum, E.E., Hartel, D. and Selwyn, P.A. (1989) 'Risk factors for human immunodeficiency virus infection in intravenous drug users', *New England Journal of Medicine,* 321, 874–9.

Schröder-Butterfill, E. and Marianti, R. (2006) 'A framework for understanding old-age vulnerabilities', *Ageing and Society,* 26 (1) 9–36.

Schukit, M.A., Tipp, J.E. and Bucholz, K.K. (1997) 'The life-time rates of three mood disorders and four major anxiety disorders in alcoholics and controls', *Addiction,* 92, 1289–304.

Schwartz, G.E. (1982) 'Testing the biopsychosocial model: the ultimate challenge facing behavioural medicine', *Journal of Clinical Psychology,* 50, 1040–53.

Secades-Villa, R., Garcia-Rodriguez, O., Higgins, S.T., Fernandez-Hermida, J.R. and Carballo, J.L. (2008) 'Community reinforcement approach plus vouchers for cocaine dependence in a community setting in Spain: Six-month outcomes', *Journal of Substance Abuse Treatment,* 34 (2) 202–7.

Seivewright, N. and Iqbal, M.Z. (2003) 'Prescribing to drug misusers in practice—often effective, but rarely straightforward', *Addiction Biology,* 8 (2) 251–2; author reply p.253.

Selwyn, P.A. (1991) 'Injection drug use, mortality, and the AIDS epidemic', *American Journal of Public Health*, 81 (10) 1247–9.

Serpelloni, G., Carrieri, M.P., Rezza, G. and Morganti, S. (1994) 'Methadone treatment as a determinant of HIV risk reduction among injecting drug users: a nested case-control study', *AIDS Care*, 6 (2) 215–20.

Shearer, S.L. (1990) 'Frequency and correlates of childhood sexual and physical abuse in adult female borderline patients', *American Journal of Psychiatry*, 147 (2) 214–16.

Shewan, D., Gemmel, M. and Davies, J.B. (1994) 'Drug Use and Scottish Prisons', *Occasional Paper* 6 (Edinburgh: Scottish Prisons Service).

Siegal, H., Baumgartner, K. and Carlson, R. (1991) *HIV Infection and Risk Behaviours among Injectable Drug Users in Low Seroprevalence Areas in the Mid-west* (Seventh International Conference on AIDS, Florence, Abstract MC3213).

Silver, R.L. and Wortman, C.B. (1980) 'Coping with undesirable life events', in J. Garber and M. Seligman (eds), *Human Helplessness* (New York: Academic Press, pp. 271–341).

Simpson, D.D. (2004) 'A conceptual framework for drug treatment process and outcomes', *Journal of Drug Abuse Treatment*, 27 (2) 99–121.

Simpson, D.D. (2003) 'The relationship between drug use and crime: a puzzle inside an enigma', *International Journal of Drug Policy*, 14 (4) 307–19.

Simpson, D.D. and Marsh, K.L. (1986) 'Relapse and recovery among opoid addicts 12 years after treatment', in *Relapse and Recovery*, ed. F. Tims and C. Leukefeld, National Institute of Drug Abuse Research Monograph 72, DHHA publication No. (ADM) 86–1473 (US Department of Health and Human Services, Rockville, MD).

Simpson, D.D. and Sells, S.B. (1982) *Effectiveness of Treatment for Drug Abuse, Institute of Behavioural Research*, Report 81–1 (Fort Worth: Texas Christian University).

Single, E, Kandel, D. and Johnson, B.D. (1975) 'The reliability and validity of drug use responses in a large scale longitudinal survey', *Journal of Drug Issues*, 5, 426–43.

Sisson, R.W. and Azrin, N.H. (1989) The Community Reinforcement approach, in R. Hester and W.R. Miller (eds), *Handbook of Alcoholism Treatment Approaches* (New York: Pergamon Press).

Sisson, R.W. and Azrin, N.H. (1986) 'Family-member involvement, to initiate and promote treatment of problem drinkers', *Journal of Behaviour Therapy and Experimental Psychiatry*, 17 (l) 15–21.

Sloan, K.L. and Rowe, G. (1995) 'Substance abuse and psychiatric illness: psychosocial correlates', *American Journal on Addictions*, 4 (1) 60–69.

Smith, D.G. (1990) 'Thailand: AIDS Crisis Looms', *Lancet*, 335, 781–2.

Smith, J.P. (1991) 'Research, public policy and drug abuse: current approaches and new directions', *International Journal of the Addictions*, 25 (2A) 181–99.

Solivetti, L.M. (1994) 'Drug diffusion and social change: the illusion about a formal social control', *Howard Journal of Criminal justice*, 33 (1) 41–61.

Solomon, L., Frank, R., Vlahov, D. and Astemborski, J. (1991) 'Utilisation of health services in a cohort of intravenous drug users with known TV-1 serostatus', *American Journal of Public Health,* 81 (10) 1285–90.

Somers, N.M. and Marlatt, A. (1992) 'Alcohol problems', in P. Wilson (ed.), *Principles and Practice of Relapse Prevention* (New York: Guilford Press).

Sondi, A., O'Shea, J. and Williams, T. (2002) 'Arrest referral: emerging findings from the national monitoring and evaluation programme', Briefing paper 18, Drugs Prevention Advisory Services (DPAS) http:/www.homeoffice.gov.uk/dpas/dpas.htm (London: Home Office).

Sorenson, J.L., Costantini, M.F., Wall, T.L. and Bison, D.R. (1993) 'Coupons attract highrisk untreated users into detoxification', *Drug and Alcohol Dependence,* 31 (3) 247–52.

Spear, S.F. and Mason, M. (1991) 'Impact of chemical dependency on family health status', *International Journal of the Addictions,* 26 (2) 179–87.

Spencer, L. and Dale, A. (1979) 'Integration and Regulation in organisations: a contextual approach', *Sociological Review,* 27, 679–702.

Spradely, J.P. (1980) *Participant Observation* (New York: Holt, Rinehart & Winston).

Stastny, D. and Potter, M. (1991) 'Alcohol abuse by patients undergoing Methadone treatment programmes', *British Journal of Addiction,* 86 (3) 307–10.

Steele, J., Darjee, R. and Thomson, L.D. (2003) 'Substance dependence and schizophrenia in patients with dangerous, violent and criminal propensities: a comparison of co-morbid and non-co-morbid patients in a high-security setting', *Journal of Forensic Psychiatry and Psychology,* 14 (3) 569–84.

Steinberg, L., Fletcher, A. and Darling, N. (1994) 'Parental monitoring and peer influences on adolescent substance use', *Paediatrics,* 93 (6) pt. 2, 1060–4.

Steinglass, P. (1979) 'Family therapy and alcoholics: a review', in E. Kaufman and P.N. Kaufman (eds), *Family Therapy and Drug and Alcohol Abuse* (New York: Gardner Press).

Stewart, D., Gossop, M., Marsden, J., Kidd, T. and Treacy, S. (2003) 'Similarities in outcomes for men and women after drug misuse treatment: results from the National Treatment Outcome Research Study (NTORS)', *Drug and Alcohol Review,* 22 (1) 35–41.

Stimson, G.V. (2007) '"Harm reduction – coming of age": a local movement with global impact', *International Journal of Drug Policy,* 18 (2) 67–9.

Stimson, G.V. (1995) 'AIDS and injecting drug use in the United Kingdom, 1988–1993: the policy response and the prevention of the epidemic', *Social Science and Medicine,* 41 (5) 699–716.

Stimson, G.V. (1990) 'AIDS and HIV: the challenge for British drug services', *British Journal of Addiction,* 85 (3), 329–39.

Stimson, G.V. (1989) 'AIDS and HIV: The Challenge for British Drug Services', The Fourth Thomas James Okey Memorial Lecture, reprinted in *AIDS and Drug Use: Understanding and Responding to the Drug User in the Wake of HIV,* ed. J. Strang and G.V. Stimson (London: Routledge).

Stimson, G.V. and Keene, J. (1991) *Development of Syringe Exchange Services in Wales* (Cardiff: Welsh Office).

Stimson, G.V., Dolan, K. and Donoghoe, M.C. (1990) 'The future of UK syringe exchange', *International Journal of Drug Policy,* 2 (2) 14–17.

Stimson, G., Keene, J., Parry-Langdon, N. and Jones, S. (1992) *Evaluation of the Syringe Exchange Programme in Wales* (Cardiff: Welsh Office Report).

Stimson, G.V., Alldritt, L.J. Doland, K.A., Donoghoe, M.C. and Lart, R.A. (1988) *Injecting Equipment Exchange Schemes: Final Report,* Monitoring Research Group (London: Goldsmiths College).

Stockwell, T. (2006) 'Alcohol Supply, Demand, and Harm Reductions: What Is the Strongest Cocktail?' *International Journal of Drug Policy,* 17 (4) 269–77.

Stockwell, T. (1994) 'Alcohol withdrawal: an adaption to heavy drinking of no practical significance?', *Addiction,* 89 (11) 1397–412.

Strain, E.C., Stitzer, M.L., Liebson, I.A. and Bigelow, G.E. (1993) 'Methadone dose and treatment outcome', *Drug and Alcohol Dependence,* 33(2) 105–17.

Strang, J. (1999) 'Updated guidance on drug misusers focuses on primary care'. *Guidelines in Practice,* 2 (London: Department of Health).

Strang, J. and Gossop, M. (1994) *Heroin Addiction and Drug Policy: the British System* (Oxford: Oxford University Press).

Strang, J. and Sheridan, J. (1998) 'National and regional characteristics of Methadone prescribing in England and Wales: local analysis of data from the 1995 national survey of community pharmacies', *Journal of Substance Misuse,* 3, 240–6.

Strang, J. and Stimson, G.V. (1990) *AIDS and Drug Use* (London: Routledge).

Strang, J, Griffiths, P. and Gossop, M. (1990) 'Crack and Cocaine use in South London drug addicts', *British Journal of Addiction,* 85 (2), 193–6.

Strang, J., Manning, V., Mayet, S., Ridge, G., Best, D. and Sheridan, J. (2007) 'Does prescribing for opiate addiction change after national guidelines? Methadone and buprenorphine prescribing to opiate addicts by general practitioners and hospital doctors in England, 1995–2005', *Addiction,* 102 (5) 761–70.

Strang, J., Kelleher, M., Best, D., Mayet, S. and Manning, V. (2006) 'Emergency naloxone for heroin overdose', *British Medical Journal,* 333 (7569) 614–15.

Summerhill, D. (1990) 'Some reflections on dynamics and dilemmas in a DDU', *British Journal of Addiction,* 85 (5) 589–92.

Sutton, S.R. (1992) 'Commentaries', *British Journal of Addiction,* 87, 24.

Swadi, H. and Zeitlin, H. (1988) 'Peer influence and adolescent substance abuse: a promising side?' *British Journal of Addiction,* 83 (2) 153–17.

Taylor, A. (1994) *Women Drug Users: An Ethnography of a Female Injecting Community* (New York: Clarendon Press).

Tilki, M. (2006) 'The social context of drinking among Irish men in London', *Drugs: Education, Prevention and Policy,* 13 (3) 247–61.

Timko, C. and Debenedetti, A. (2007) 'A randomized controlled trial of intensive referral to 12-step self-help groups: One-year outcomes', *Drug and Alcohol Dependence,* 90 (2–3) 270–9.

Thompson, R. (1988) 'Action research applied to drug education – the DAPPS Study', *Drug Education Journal of Australia,* 2 (1) 7–14.

Toombs, D.L. (2000) *Introduction to Addictive Behaviors,* 2nd edn (New York: Guilford Press).

Toumbourou, J.W., Stockwell, T., Neighbors, C., Marlatt, G.A., Sturge, J. and Rehm, J. (2007) 'Interventions to reduce harm associated with adolescent substance use, *Lancet,* 369 (9570) 1391–401.

Trower, P., Casey, A. and Dryden, W. (1991) *Cognitive-Behavioural Counselling in Action* (London: Sage).

Turnbull, P.J., Dolan, K.A. and Stimson, G.V. (1992) 'Prevalence of HIV infection among ex-prisoners in England', *British Medical Journal,* 304, 90–1.

Tumbull, P.J., Dolan, K. and Stimson, G.V. (1991) *Prisons, HIV and AIDS: Risks and Experiences in Custodial Care* (London: Centre for Research on Drugs and Health Behaviour).

Turnbull, P., Webster, R. and Stillwell, G. (1995) *Get It While You Can: An Evaluation of an Early Intervention Project for Arrestees with Alcohol and Drug problems,* Drugs Prevention Initiative paper 9 (London: Home Office Drugs Prevention Unit).

Ulrich, L.B. and Brott, P.E. (2005) 'Older workers and bridge employment: redefining retirement', *Journal of Employment Counseling,* 42, 159–70.

Ungerson C. (1994) *Becoming Consumers of Community Care* (York: Joseph Rowntree Foundation).

United States Department for Health and Human Services (1989) *Reducing Health Consequences of Smoking: Twenty-five Years of Progress,* A Report of the Surgeon General (Washington DC).

Valliant, G.E. (1983) *The Natural History of Alcoholism: Causes, Patterns and Paths to Recovery* (Harvard University Press).

Van den Hoek, J.A.R., Van Haastrecht, H.J.A. and Coutinho, R.A. (1989) 'Risk reduction among intravenous drug users in Amsterdam under the influence of AIDS', *American Journal of Public Health,* 79 (10) 1355–7.

Volkow, N.D. and Fowler, J.S. (2000) 'Addiction, a disease of compulsion and drive: involvement of the orbitofrontal cortex', *Cerebral Cortex,* 10 (3), 318–25.

Volkow, N.D. and Li, T.K. (2005) 'The neuroscience of addiction', *Nature Neuroscience,* 8 (11) 1429–30.

Volkow, N.D. and Li, T.K. (2004) 'Drug Addiction. The neurobiology of behaviour gone awry', *Nature Neuroscience,* 5 (12) 963–70.

Volkow, N.D. and Li, T.K. (2000) 'Addiction, a disease of compulsion and drive: involvement of the orbitofrontal cortex', *Cerebral Cortex,* 10 (3) 318–25.

Volkow, N.D., Fowler, J.S. and Wang, G.J. (2003) 'The addicted human brain: Insights from imaging studies', *Journal of Clinical Investigation,* 111 (10) 1444–51.

Waldron, H.B., Kern-Jones, S., Turner, C.W., Peterson, T.R., Ozechowski, T.J. (2007) 'Engaging resistant adolescents in drug abuse treatment', *Journal of Substance Abuse Treatment,* 32 (2) 133–42.

Waldron, S. (1969) *Statement to Select Committee on Crime* (House of Representatives, 91st Congress, July 29).

Walitzer, K. Dermen, K. and Barrick, C. (2009) 'Facilitating involvement in Alcoholics Anonymous during out-patient treatment: a randomized clinical trial', *Addiction*, 104, (3), 391–401.

Warner-Smith, M., Darke, S., Lynskey, M. and Hall, W. (2001) 'Heroin Overdose: causes and consequences', *Addiction*, 96 (8), 1113–25.

Watkins, K.E., Burnham, A., Kung, F.Y. and Paddock, S. (2001) 'A national survey of care for persons with co-occurring mental health and substance misuse disorders', *Psychiatric Services*, 52 (8) 1062–8.

Weaver, T., Renton, A., and Stimson, G. (1999) 'Severe mental illness and substance misuse', Editorial, *British Medical Journal*, 318: 137–8.

Weaver, T., Madden, P., Charles, V., Stimson, G., Renton, A., Tyrer, P., Barnes, T., Bench, C., Middleton, H., Wright, N. Patterson, S., Shananhan, W., Seivewright, N. and Ford, C. (2003) Comorbidity of Substance Misuse and Mental Illness Collaborative study team. 'Comorbidity of substance misuse and mental illness in community mental health and substance misuse services', *British Journal of Psychiatry*, 183, 304–13.

Weaver, T., Charles, V., Madden, P. and Renton, A. (2002) Co-morbidity of Substance Misuse and Mental Illness Collaborative Study (COSMIC). *A study of the Prevalence and Management of Co-Morbidity amongst Adult Substance Misuse & Mental Health Treatment Populations*. Research report submitted to the Department of Health (London: Centre for Research on Drugs and Health Behaviour, Imperial College of Science, Technology and Medicine).

Wechsberg, W.M., Dennis, M.L., Cavanagh, E. and Rachel, J.V. (1993) 'A comparison of injecting drug users reached through outreach and Methadone treatment', *Journal of Drug Issues*, 23 (4) 668–87.

Weisner, C. and Schmidt, L. (1993) 'Alcohol and drug problems among diverse health and social service populations', *American Journal of Public Health*, 83 (6) 824–9.

Welsh Office (1993) *Welsh Drug Use Database: Report 5* (Oct 92–Mar 93), Health Statistics and Analysis Unit (Cardiff: Welsh Office).

West, R. and Gossop, M. (1994) 'Overview: a comparison of withdrawal symptoms from different drug classes', *Addiction*, 89 (11) 1483–9.

Williams, A.B., McNelly, E.A., Williams, A.E. and D'Aquila, R.T. (1992) 'Methadone maintenance treatment and HIV type 1 seroconversion among injecting drug users', *AIDS Care*, 4 (1) 34–41.

Wilson, P. (1992) 'Relapse prevention: conceptual and methodological issues', in *Principles and Practice of Relapse Prevention*, ed. P. Wilson (New York: Guilford Press).

Witkiewitz, T. and Marlatt, A. (2006) 'Overview of Harm Reduction Treatments for Alcohol Problems', *International Journal of Drug Policy*, 17 (4) 285–94.

Wodak, A. (1994) 'How do communities achieve reductions in alcohol and drug-related harm?', *Addiction*, 89 (2) 147–50.

Wodak, A. and Cooney A. (2006) 'Review; Do needle syringe programs reduce HIV infection among injecting drug users: a comprehensive review of the international evidence', *Substance Use and Misuse*, 41 (6–7) 777–813.

Woogh, C.M. (1990) 'Patients with multiple admissions in psychiatric record linkage system', *Canadian Journal of Psychiatry*, 35 (5) 401–6.

World Health Organization Expert Committee on Drug Dependence (1994) *28th Report* (Geneva: WHO).

World Health Organization (1989) *International Classification of Diseases* (Geneva: WHO).

Wright, N., Smeeth, L. and Health, I. (2003). 'Moving beyond single and dual diagnosis', *British Medical Journal*, Editorial 326, 512–14.

Wright, S., Gournay, K. and Glorney, E. (2000) 'Dual diagnosis in the suburbs: prevalence, need and in-patient service use', *Social Psychiatry and Psychiatric Epidemiology*, 35, 297–304.

Yin, R.E. (1989) *Case Study Research, Design and Methods*, Applied Social Research Methods Series 5 (London: Sage).

Young, J. (1971) *The Drug Takers* (London: MacGibbon & Kee).

Yu, J. and Williford, W.R. (1992) 'Drug and alcohol use', *International Journal of the Addictions*, 27 (11) 1313–23.

Yucel, M. and Luban, D.I. (2007) 'Neurocognitive and neuroimaging evidence of behavioural dysregulation in human drug addiction: Implications for diagnosis , treatment and prevention', *Drug and Alcohol Review*, 26 (1) 33–9.

Zador, D., Lintzeris, N., van der Waal, R., Miller, P., Metrebian, N. and Strang, J. (2008) 'The fine line between harm reduction and harm production – development of a clinical policy on femoral (groin) injecting', *European Addiction Research*, 14 (4) 213–8.

Zemore, S. and Kaskutas, L.A . (2008) '12-Step Involvement and Peer Helping in Day Hospital and Residential Programs', *Substance Use and Misuse*, 43 (12–13) 1882–903.

Zinberg, N.E. (1984) *Drug, Set and Setting* (New Haven: Yale University Press).

Index

Key: **bold** = extended discussion or term highlighted in the text; f = figure; n = note; t = table.